WOMEN IN GEORGE WASHINGTON'S WORLD

WOMEN IN GEORGE WASHINGTON'S WORLD

Edited by
CHARLENE M. BOYER LEWIS
and GEORGE W. BOUDREAU

UNIVERSITY OF VIRGINIA PRESS
Charlottesville and London

University of Virginia Press
© 2022 by the Rector and Visitors of the University of Virginia
All rights reserved
Printed in the United States of America on acid-free paper

First published 2022

9 8 7 6 5 4 3 2

Library of Congress Cataloging-in-Publication Data

Names: Lewis, Charlene M. Boyer, editor. | Boudreau, George, editor.
Title: Women in George Washington's world / edited by Charlene M. Boyer
    Lewis, and George Boudreau.
Description: Charlottesville : University of Virginia Press, 2022. | Includes
    bibliographical references and index.
Identifiers: LCCN 2022007612 (print) | LCCN 2022007613 (ebook) |
    ISBN 9780813947440 (hardcover) | ISBN 9780813947457 (ebook)
Subjects: LCSH: Washington, George, 1732–1799—Relations with women. |
    Washington, George, 1732–1799—Family. | Washington, George,
    1732–1799—Friends and associates. | Washington, George, 1732–1799—
    Relations with slaves.
Classification: LCC E312.17 .W66 2022 (print) | LCC E312.17 (ebook) |
    DDC 973.4/10924—dc23/eng/20220304
LC record available at https://lccn.loc.gov/2022007612
LC ebook record available at https://lccn.loc.gov/2022007613

Cover art: Frances Bassett Washington, by Robert Edge Pine, ca. 1785 (Mount
Vernon Ladies' Association); Abigail Smith Adams, by Gilbert Stuart, ca.
1800–1815 (National Gallery of Art, gift of Mrs. Robert Homans, 1954.7.2);
Elizabeth Willing Powel, attrib. Joseph Wright, ca. 1793 (Mount Vernon
Ladies' Association); Martha Washington, by James Peale, ca. 1795 (Mount
Vernon Ladies' Association); Phillis Wheatley, frontispiece of *Poems on Various
Subjects, Religious and Moral,* London, 1773 (The Gilder Lehrman Institute of
American History, GLC06154)

For our grandmothers
and all the ancestors
who lived these stories
and taught us about our pasts

And in honor of Vice President Kamala Harris

CONTENTS

ACKNOWLEDGMENTS

"For most of history, 'Anonymous' was a woman," Virginia Woolf related more than a century ago. Too often in history, women's thoughts and contributions were shuffled to the periphery. In this book, they take center stage.

Like many of the most important experiences of women and men in the eighteenth century, this book began in a sociable fireside conversation. Gathered around the hearth one evening during Mount Vernon's 2018 symposium, the conversation turned to what presenters had related that day, and one editor of this volume said to the other "this is really a book." Several of the presenters at that event agreed; other scholars joined in later to explore the history of gender and society in America's critical founding era. We are deeply grateful to Stephen McLeod and Anthony King who organized "'A Sensible Woman Can Never Be Happy with a Fool': The Women of George Washington's World" in November of that year. These gentlemen, and the entire staff at Mount Vernon, allowed us to share ideas and provoke one another into new explorations about gender, family, race, material culture, mental worlds, and the lives of George and Martha Custis Washington and the women who they knew. The enthusiastic welcome from Doug Bradburn, Kevin Butterfield, Susan Schoelwer, and all of Mount Vernon's leadership, and the kind response from the audience, as well as the Mount Vernon Ladies' Association reminded us that these stories are vital.

Many institutions and their incredible staffs made this volume possible, both in relating details, documents, and the material worlds of these women, and in discussing the ways publics engage the story of the women in George Washington's world. At Mount Vernon, we especially thank Samantha Snyder and Mary V. Thompson.

Numerous scholars offered feedback as these essays formed into a book, and we are grateful to Karin Wulf, Erica Armstrong Dunbar, and Judith Van Buskirk for their insights.

We would also like to thank the unflagging Nadine Zimmerli of the University of Virginia Press for her encouragement and guidance.

And finally, we are individually and collectively thankful to James Lewis and Paul Alles for their love and support over the years.

INTRODUCTION

CYNTHIA A. KIERNER

George Washington must have had mixed feelings as he crossed the Assunpink Creek on a rainy spring day in 1789. As he arrived in the town of Trenton on horseback, this most famous man in America likely braced himself for yet another formal reception—like those he had already experienced in Alexandria, Baltimore, Wilmington, and Philadelphia—as he made another stop on his week-long journey from Mount Vernon to New York, where on Thursday, 30 April, he would be inaugurated as the first president of the American republic. Nevertheless, this riverside New Jersey town held special memories for Washington, who led his troops to a much-needed victory there on the day after Christmas in 1776. Now, years later, townspeople remembered and celebrated the exploits of their revered leader.

The ladies of Trenton especially claimed this American hero as their own. In Trenton, unlike in other towns where the president-elect was feted, women were the festivities' central actors. As he crossed the creek, Washington passed under a large decorative arch festooned with flowers and a banner that proclaimed, "The Defender of the Mothers will also Protect their Daughters." On the far side of the bridge, a group of matrons, young ladies, and small girls "all dressed in white, and decorated with wreaths and chaplets of flowers" greeted Washington with a "sonata" welcoming this "mighty chief" to their "grateful shore." After receiving a printed copy of the commemorative ode, the usually reserved honoree responded with an eloquent and heartfelt tribute, observing that he could not "leave this place without expressing his acknowledgments, to the Matrons and Young Ladies who received him in so novel &

grateful a manner at the Triumphal Arch . . . for the exquisite sensation he experienced in that affecting moment." Mindful of the "astonishing" contrast between the current jubilation and the town's perilous wartime state, Washington praised "The elegant taste with which it was adorned for the present occasion—and the innocent appearance of the *white-robed Choir* who met him with the gratulatory song, [which] have made such impressions on his remembrance, as, he assures them, will never be effaced."[1]

Washington may have found the production so moving and memorable in part because of the notable women it featured, at least some of whom he knew, either personally or indirectly. Many of those present had participated in the bold effort, spearheaded by Esther De Berdt Reed of Philadelphia, to collect money and supplies for the Continental Army in 1780, an effort that historians generally acknowledge as a watershed in the emergence of women's organized public activism. Mary Dagworthy of Trenton, who exchanged letters with Washington concerning the funds they raised and the 380 pairs of stockings that New Jersey women made for the soldiers, was now among the matrons in white who greeted him eight years later. So, too, was Ann Richmond, who, with her husband Jonathan, ran the nearby True American Inn, which had served briefly as Washington's wartime headquarters. Many of these Trenton "ladies" were wives of military men who knew Washington and who that day accompanied him across the Assunpink bridge. One, Mary McCrea Hanna, was the sister of Jane McCrea, whose death at the hands of Britain's Native American allies in 1777 became a cause célèbre in patriot circles, despite Jane's likely loyalism. While Washington protected Mary in New Jersey, a patriotic onlooker might surmise, her sister Jane fell victim to his barbarous foes on New York's northern frontier.[2]

The most familiar female face that greeted Washington that day was that of Annis Boudinot Stockton, who had hosted him at Morven, her Princeton estate, when he was on his way to Yorktown in 1781. Since then, Stockton and Washington had become regular correspondents, with her sending him laudatory patriotic verses and him responding with expressions of friendship and admiration for her literary talents. Stockton's most recent missive had included a poem that celebrated Washington's elevation to the presidency and captured the spirit of his reception in Trenton:

When lo himself the chief rever'd
In native elegance appear'd
And all things smil'd around
Adorn'd with evry pleasing art
Enthron'd the sovereign of each heart
I Saw the Heroe *crownd*

An accomplished poet and an avid patriot who had saved the papers of the local Whig Society from enemy troops who plundered her house, Stockton was a widow whose husband had died after a brutal wartime stint in a British prison in New York. As one of two war widows among the welcoming ladies, Stockton also had the right to vote. New Jersey's first state constitution granted suffrage to "all Inhabitants . . . of full Age, who are worth Fifty Pounds proclamation Money . . . & have resided within the County in which they claim a Vote for twelve Months." Married women, who could not control property under the common law rule of coverture, were disqualified, but the state's constitution enfranchised widows and single women, as well as free African Americans, until 1807, when the state restricted suffrage to tax-paying white men.[3]

The removal of women from New Jersey's voting rolls was part of a more general postrevolutionary backlash against women's public visibility and political activism, which also shaped how people remembered the ladies of Trenton and their reception of Washington in 1789. Although Stockton and her associates would have likely been pleased that later generations did not forget Washington's joyful visit to their community, nineteenth-century representations of the day's events sadly effaced the women's identities as competent and politically engaged members of the community and contributors to the success of America's revolutionary cause.

As the near-deification of Washington flourished in the decades after his death, the scene at Trenton became the subject of at least three prints that glorified him as an American hero, just as the welcoming ladies had done in 1789. The first of these prints, by Thomas Kelley, a Boston engraver, circa 1830, portrayed Washington emerging from the festive arch followed by a group of men on horseback, with at least thirty-five women and girls hailing his arrival. Then, in the 1840s, the popular New York printmakers Currier and Ives published two widely distributed

Produced sometime between 1823 and 1835, Kelley's engraving was the earliest visual representation of the ladies' reception of Washington. Note the nearly identical female faces. The festive arch bears the date of the Battle of Trenton and the women's hopeful message: "The Hero Who Defended the Mothers Will Protect the Daughters." (Library of Congress, Prints and Photographs Division, LC-DIG-ds-05571)

lithographs of the scene, based on Kelley's image, both of which bore the title "Washington's Reception by the Ladies." One of these prints, like Kelley's, was oriented horizontally and showed Washington and his male attendants leaving the arch, but included at most twenty females in the foreground. A second vertically oriented lithograph by Currier and Ives was available in both black-and-white and multicolored versions. In this image, Washington, his horse, and the arch, fill most of the space; only nine "ladies" and one small girl are shown welcoming him.

Clearly, Washington's female admirers were becoming increasingly less central to the Trenton story, both to the artists who recreated it and in the historical memory of the general public. The best estimate is that at least forty-one white-clad females—twenty-two "matrons," thirteen "young ladies," and six "little girls"—met Washington that day on the streets of Trenton, but their numbers diminished in each successive

In this 1845 lithograph, Currier relegated the ladies to the margins of the Trenton story and diminished their numbers significantly. The banner's inscription is slightly different but strikes a similarly heroic note: "The Defender of the Mothers Will Be the Protector of the Daughters." (Library of Congress, Prints and Photographs Division, LC-DIG-ppmsca-07649)

visual iteration.[4] Equally important, the artists' depiction of these women and girls was consistently generic. In all the prints, including Kelley's, the faces and attire of all the female figures are virtually identical to each other. The only significant difference among them is that the "little girls" are portrayed as being smaller than the fully-grown "matrons" and "young ladies."

Contemporary artistic renderings of other historical scenes featuring Washington did not typically include similarly generic depictions of the less famous (or even non-famous) men who surrounded him. John Trumbull's paintings of events such as the signing of the Declaration of Independence and Washington's resigning his military commission are known for their painstakingly accurate miniature portraits of each individual depicted—but, after all, the men Trumbull painted, however obscure some may be today, were all members of the Continental Congress. A better comparison is Emanuel Leutze's iconic 1851 painting of Washington crossing the Delaware, on his way to attack the Hessians at Trenton in December 1776. Leutze included true likenesses of the well-known military men General Nathanael Greene and Lieutenant James Monroe (the future president), though many of the others he depicted were unnamed figures that he dressed in different types of clothing to represent a cross-section of American manhood. Although they were not identifiable as specific real-life people, these figures signaled that Leutze (and those who viewed his popular painting) saw men not as an undifferentiated mass, but rather as members of groups that had varying identities, experiences, and interests.[5]

A cultural predisposition to view women generically, rather than as individuals or even as representatives of specific social groupings, antedated Kelley's print and, indeed, was evident from the first civic celebrations of the revolutionary era. Toasts at Independence Day dinners lauded noteworthy men by name and others by their membership in the militia or in other valued groups or institutions. Women, if they were mentioned at all, were usually the subject of a perfunctory collective final toast to the "American Fair." Likewise, the Grand Federal Procession that was held in New York City to celebrate the U.S. Constitution in 1788 included some 5,000 men marching in ten divisions, based on their occupations or institutional affiliations. The parade's planners assigned white men specific places in the procession based on their occupation-based public identities as "Foresters with axes," "artificial florists," "Horse doctors," and "various others." Women were excluded from the parade, except as spectators, as a result of the commonly embraced fiction that the "American Fair" had no public identity and the equally dubious belief that their work did not contribute to the nation's overall prosperity.[6]

This propensity to see men as particular and women—or at least "ladies"—as generic also helps to explain the common practice of using female forms to represent "liberty" and other abstract political ideals throughout the Atlantic world. American patriots were perhaps unrivaled as vocal devotees of liberty, which they identified with virtue and saw as acutely vulnerable to predatory power, both attributes that contemporaries associated with respectable white ladies. Law and custom rendered men the chief possessors of liberty and the rights it conferred, just as men legally possessed their wives and other dependents. At the same time, reimagining "liberty" as a man would have posed vexing political challenges. If a single male figure represented "liberty," what kind of man would he be? A country gentleman? A merchant? An urban artisan? A yeoman farmer? Any choice would be divisive. By contrast, making "liberty" a female figure—specifically a generically beautiful white lady—exploited the visual tropes of contemporary conventions of gender (and race) to express a political ideal in a way that united white male citizens of the republic.[7]

Generic representations of women in patriotic toasts and historical prints stand in stark contrast to the real history of the women who inhabited Washington's world. The ladies of Trenton were a politically engaged and accomplished group with compelling individual and collective stories. Neither identical nor interchangeable, they were more different still from the vast majority of non-elite women—middling wives, shopkeepers and artisans, free and enslaved workers—who were relegated to the sidelines during Washington's visit rather than included among the ranks of welcoming "ladies." The essays in this volume reconstruct a sampling of Washington's widely varied interactions with women—and women's experiences with Washington. Altogether, these chapters are forceful reminders that roughly half of the people who inhabited Washington's world were females who related to him as family, friends, acquaintances, admirers, and underlings over the course of his lifetime. It would have been very odd, indeed, if Washington's words and actions had not affected these women and, conversely, if these women did not have diverse and sometimes deep impacts on his own storied and eventful life.

Thoughtful historians lament the inherent selectivity of archives, which traditionally have been assembled and curated to bolster the authority of the nation-state and document the accomplishments of powerful men who engaged in politics, war, business, or other highly visible and valued activities. In the United States, influential men who collected and preserved the papers of Washington (and other male American founders) as repositories of national identity and public memory never seriously considered saving the papers of their wives or daughters to make them available to researchers or to the general public. Institutional collecting practices presupposed that no one would be interested in reading women's letters, especially those that focused mainly on the quotidian aspects of domestic and social life.[8]

Obviously, early archivists did not foresee the development of gender studies, African American history, or even social and cultural history more generally as thriving scholarly fields. In part for that reason, scholars who work in these areas, and who seek to recover the history of people who left no documents—or whose documents have not survived—pioneered the use of new methodologies to extract evidence from less conventional sources, including oral traditions and especially material culture. Reading artifacts as texts, historians analyze clothing, tools, furniture, needlework, images, and other objects to gain insight into the lives and work of women, enslaved people, and others who were often absent from the papers of great white men. Such non-documentary sources can tell stories about all sorts of people—as both space and place, Mount Vernon reveals much about the both the Washington family and the estate's enslaved work force—and they have proven especially enlightening for students of women's history.[9]

Still, it is worth noting that some early historians of women maintained that so-called traditional archival sources could also be useful to their research despite their obvious bias in favor of men's activities and perspectives. "Much of what traditional sources tell us about women has come to us refracted through the lens of men's observation," noted Gerda Lerner, who nonetheless believed that a critical reading of those sources—what historians now call "reading against the grain"—in conjunction with other texts that provide "women's points of view" could correct their "androcentric bias."[10] As it turns out, the papers of George Washington, including his voluminous and recently digitized financial papers, are a compelling case in point.[11] Women are ubiquitous in Washington's archive as family and friends, neighbors, enslaved and free laborers, buyers and sellers of goods and services, and soldiers' wives or widows seeking help.

The essays in this volume suggest both strengths and limitations of the Washington archive as a source for women's history. In terms of weaknesses, the most noteworthy absence is Martha, who destroyed her correspondence with George after his death in 1799.[12] Nor are the Washington papers particularly helpful as sources for understanding the lives of women whose relations with Washington were entirely face-to-face and neither affective nor social. For example, though Washington's letters and account books include certain types of information on members of his enslaved workforce, George W. Boudreau relies heavily on an imaginative reading of Philadelphia's demography and urban space to understand how the president's enslaved domestics, Ona Judge and Moll, experienced their move from rural Virginia to this bustling city with its highly visible and growing free African American community. On the other hand, many of the essays here effectively draw on Washington's papers to reconstruct women's stories and probe the social construction of gender in late eighteenth-century America. Like so many of the fine and thoughtful histories of women and gender that scholars have produced in recent decades, these essays make a powerful case for taking seriously not only women's contributions to the history we think we already know but also for using women's experiences to interrogate the past, question comfortably familiar narratives about the American Revolution and its significance, and, more generally, reimagine what it was like to live in Washington's world.

First and foremost, despite the puzzlingly enduring tendency to imagine men and women as inhabiting different "spheres," the Washington family story demonstrates that both sexes partook of, valued, and even cherished, domestic life. Both George and Martha Washington periodically ached to return to Mount Vernon. Like George's mastery on the plantation and in the workshops, Martha's work as the household's mistress had both economic and cultural value. Mary V. Thompson's essay details the responsibilities and varying managerial styles of Martha Washington and her three kinswomen who oversaw sewing, weaving, food production, and myriad other domestic tasks performed by enslaved workers or hired help when Martha herself was not at home. The war and its consequences—the disruption of trade, threats of assaults by enemy troops or freedom-seeking enslaved people—along with the postwar need to provide hospitality to legions of admirers posed new challenges. Although many ventured to the banks of the Potomac to see the celebrated George Washington and his Mount Vernon home, women's work made possible the charming domestic tableaux that became part of the Washington mystique, often remarked on by guests who praised the tranquility of the estate and the congenial reception they received there. Mount Vernon was "kept with great Neatness," one visitor mused, and "the good Order of the Masters Mind appears extended to everything around it."[13]

The fact that hospitality proffered at Mount Vernon was part of Washington's identity and public image reminds us that the putative boundaries between public and private, man's world and woman's place, were hopelessly blurry and permeable. Take, for instance, the cases of Martha Washington and Abigail Adams, the best-known women featured in these pages, who until relatively recently were mostly imagined only as supportive wifely types, complementary accessories to great men, because of the widely held conceit that women inhabited a domestic sphere that was somehow insulated from public life. Often portrayed as retiring and subservient (and, indeed, frumpy), Martha Washington was in fact an engaging, competent, and energetic woman who, as Lynn A. Price Robbins shows, played a consequential role in the revolutionary movement, serving not only as George's indispensable companion but also as a morale booster for his troops and a committed wartime fundraiser. Less of a celebrity than Martha Washington, Abigail Adams has long been justly famed for her wry admonition—in a private letter to her husband, John—that Congress "remember the Ladies," but, as Sara Georgini makes clear, she was also a shrewd observer of war and politics, and of the respective roles that George and Martha played during their precedent-setting presidential administration. The first two presidents also valued her opinions; Washington respected Abigail, and she was John's foremost political advisor, even after he became president, an office that came with a full complement of formally appointed male counselors. Both women wielded significant, though unofficial, public influence that went far beyond the weekly levees and teas that—despite their undeniably political purposes—were more readily reconciled with contemporary ideals of female virtue and respectability.

Probably the single most important insight to be gleaned from these essays is that women were pretty much everywhere in Washington's world, playing a range of both conventional and less expected roles. Washington spent his formative years in a house full of brothers and half-brothers, but he also had three sisters, only one of whom lived to adulthood. Although childhood experiences and family connections are clearly fundamental to identity formation, Washington's biographers typically ignore Betty Washington Lewis, despite the fact that she was an ongoing presence in the life of her brother.[14] Free and enslaved women labored at the various plantations where Washington lived and visited; ladies attended the balls he frequented as a colonial legislator in Williamsburg; he also encountered women in taverns and other establishments where he conducted business in Alexandria and elsewhere. Women served as nurses, cooks, and laundresses in Continental Army encampments, where officers' wives provided wintertime companionship for their war-weary husbands. Women across the social spectrum made political choices when they supported (or flouted) prerevolutionary boycotts of British goods and participated in postrevolutionary partisan debates. They wrote politically themed letters, poems, and newspaper essays. They orchestrated salons and other social gatherings that helped to grease the wheels of politics in the republic's early capitals.

Washington's encounters with those whose stories fill this volume suggest the breadth and diversity of women's public activism, as well as the various ways in which the personal could be political—and the political could be deeply personal—while also showing how Washington viewed women as potential public figures and political actors. James Basker argues persuasively that this Virginia planter who claimed ownership of more than one hundred people in 1776 appreciated the literary talent and impassioned patriotism of Phillis Wheatley, the remarkable enslaved poet, which helped inspire his eventual manumission of his own enslaved workforce. Samantha Snyder's revealing analysis of Washington's relationship with Elizabeth Willing Powel, the urbane Philadelphia salonnière, shows that he admired her social skills and political acumen, and, indeed, during his time in Philadelphia, almost became her student in such matters because he was astute enough to recognize that her experience and connections far outpaced his own.

Washington's ability to see women as distinct beings whose experiences, responsibilities, and talents extended beyond the standard domestic roles of wife, mother, and servant/slave was most evident in cases like these, when women observed contemporary gender conventions and expressed opinions that fit his own. Contrast, for instance, the respect he showed toward Wheatley, who modestly approached him as a heroic figure who might look with favor on the cause of antislavery, with his heartlessly dogged pursuit of Ona Judge, the Washingtons' enslaved domestic who defiantly claimed freedom as her own.[15] At the same time, Charlene Boyer Lewis suggests that Margaret Shippen Arnold's behavior on the fateful night when her husband's treason was revealed—and the political determination that gave rise to her extraordinary performance—left Washington utterly befuddled. The general could fathom Benedict Arnold's vile deception, and he acknowledged that women had political interests and allegiances; he may have even accepted the notion that a patriot wife might defy her loyalist husband. But he, Alexander Hamilton, and the rest were utterly incapable of imagining that a lady could or would, of her own volition, commit treason, a choice that ran counter to everything they believed about feminine virtue and sensibility.

His hyper-masculine martial bearing notwithstanding, Washington avidly embraced the ascendant values of the culture of sensibility. His enjoyment of women's company, his openness to female influence, and his appreciation for poetry and other forms of polite literature and conversation revealed him to be a man of feeling, a much-admired cultural ideal in the eighteenth-century Atlantic world, and one that represented a far more demanding and emotionally complex code of conduct than the largely formulaic "Rules of Civility" that he had famously studied as a youngster.[16]

Yet if women constituted an important part of Washington's world, their presence in the historical memory and early public commemorations of his life was sketchy at best. Kate Haulman chronicles the sad case of George's mother, Mary Ball Washington, a consequential woman who was first negatively caricatured by Mason Locke Weems—best known today for inventing the cherry tree myth—and then recast as a generically virtuous maternal figure, robbed of her personhood and made an empty cipher to serve the ends of reactionary white nationalism in the turbulent antebellum years. Ann Bay Goddin suggests that the temper of those times also inspired the strong-willed (and unmarried) Ann Pamela Cunningham and her associates to don the armor of domesticity and feminine weakness in spite of—or because of—their audaciously unladylike ambition to buy and preserve Mount Vernon as a monument to the heroic George. While it is not at all surprising that the elite white women of the Mount Vernon Ladies' Association neglected to commemorate the role of enslaved workers in creating, maintaining, and interpreting Mount Vernon, it is worth noting that they also mostly ignored Martha.

Mount Vernon without Martha, Benedict without Margaret, Federalist Philadelphia without its salons and levees—the essays in this collection add to an ever-growing body of scholarship that argues powerfully that omitting women from the historical narrative, or rendering them generic and monolithic, makes for bad history. Women were present at and active in wars, politics, and other historical events and milieus. They shared their domestic lives with men who valued home and family and who—if Washington was at all representative—did not see themselves as inhabiting a superior and separate public sphere. Uncovering women's experiences, including their relationships with famous (and comparatively well-documented) men, while intrinsically worthwhile and important, can also challenge deeply entrenched assumptions about the past and inform a more nuanced understanding of history.

Which brings us back to the ladies' reception of Washington in Trenton, yet another case in which taking gender (and women) seriously casts a historical event or episode in a stunningly different light. To be fair, those printmakers and pundits who later recounted the Trenton story got some things right. The date was correct, as were the texts of the women's tribute and Washington's response to it. Multiple accounts corroborate the size and style of the decorations and the general atmosphere of the occasion. Nevertheless, by ignoring women's distinctive experiences and perspectives, these chroniclers either overlooked or misunderstood the reason why women in Trenton—but not in the other cities Washington visited—orchestrated this particular celebration. They also missed the significance of the specific message that the ladies chose to inscribe on the banner that greeted Washington when he arrived in their community, and they thereby misinterpreted the true meaning of the ensuing celebration.

The war in New Jersey had been particularly violent, especially in 1776 and 1777, when Trenton and its environs had been the site of notorious rapes of local women by British soldiers. Washington knew of these rapes and, in response, he publicly ordered his own troops to show "humanity and tenderness to women and children," in contrast to those brutish enemy "ravagers." When Congress took the unprecedented step of investigating the New Jersey rapes—less to satisfy the women than to show that American soldiers were morally superior to their foes— Washington supplied crucial evidence documenting the atrocities. People in New Jersey certainly knew of his attention to the matter and his involvement in the official investigation. The resulting congressional report was widely publicized in American newspapers.[17]

When the ladies of Trenton honored Washington and expressed their gratitude for his protection, then, they were doing more than celebrating his military success and his elevation to the presidency. Their ceremony with its banner referenced women's uniquely gendered wartime travails and acknowledged what Washington's actions as their "defender" and "protector" meant to them on the most intimate level. In this case as in so many others, eliding women's experiences and perspectives obscures historical meaning, turning a performance of profound gratitude for physical and sexual protection into a mere celebration of battlefield triumphs. Like the essays in this collection, the story of the ladies of Trenton shows that eliding women vastly underestimates the complexity of the past and results in less truthful history.

Notes

1. For a contemporary account of the reception, see *Columbian Magazine: or, Monthly Miscellany*, 2 (May 1787): 289–90. For Washington's trip from Mount Vernon to New York, see Kenneth Silverman, *A Cultural History of the American Revolution* (New York: Crowell, 1976), 604–7. See also

George Washington, "From George Washington to the Ladies of Trenton," 21 April 1789, *Founders Online*, National Archives, https://founders.archives.gov/documents/Washington/05-02-02-0095.

2. A list of those who greeted Washington, based on mid-nineteenth-century interviews with surviving participants and "others who remember to have seen it," can be found in William S. Stryker, *Washington's Reception by the People in New Jersey in 1789* (Trenton: Naar, Day & Naar, 1882). For the overlap in membership between the 1780 fundraisers and the women who met Washington in 1789, see Catherine Hudak, "The Ladies of Trenton: Women's Political and Public Activism in Revolutionary New Jersey," *New Jersey Studies: An Interdisciplinary Journal* 1 (2015): 45. Correspondence between Washington and Mary Dagworthy (later Hunt) is in *Founders Online*. On Jane McCrea, see Robert G. Parkinson, *The Common Cause: Creating Race and Nation in the American Revolution* (Chapel Hill: University of North Carolina Press, 2016), 339–49.

3. Martha J. King, "'A Lady of New Jersey': Annis Boudinot Stockton, Patriot and Poet in an Age of Revolution," in *Women in the American Revolution: Gender, Politics, and the Domestic World*, ed. Barbara B. Oberg (Charlottesville: University of Virginia Press, 2019), 104, 108–15; Carla Mulford, ed., *Only for the Eye of a Friend: The Poems of Annis Boudinot Stockton* (Charlottesville: University of Virginia Press, 2012), 24–26; Elizabeth F. Ellet, *The Women of the American Revolution* (New York: Baker and Scribner, 1850), 3:13–34; Judith Apter Klinghoffer and Lois Elkis, "'The Petticoat Electors': Women's Suffrage in New Jersey, 1776–1807," *Journal of the Early Republic* 12 (1992): 159–93; Rosemarie Zagarri, *Revolutionary Backlash: Women and Politics in the Early America Republic* (Philadelphia: University of Pennsylvania Press, 2007), 30–37.

4. Stryker, *Washington's Reception*, 8–18.

5. Peter A. Harrington, "Artist: Father Figure," *Quarterly Journal of Military History* 31 (Winter 2019): 89–90. For keys identifying the specific men depicted in Trumbull's history paintings in the Capitol Rotunda, see "John Trumbull: American Painter, Diplomat and Architect," Architect of the Capitol, https://www.aoc.gov/capitol-hill/artists/john-trumbull.

6. Cynthia A. Kierner, *Beyond the Household: Women's Place in the Early South, 1700–1835* (Ithaca: Cornell University Press, 1998), 130–34; Paul A. Gilje, "The Common People and the Constitution: Popular Culture in New York City in the Late Eighteenth Century," in *New York in the Age of the Constitution, 1775–1800*, ed. Paul A. Gilje and William Pencak (Rutherford, NJ: Fairleigh Dickinson University Press, 1992), 53–56.

7. See the useful discussions in Marina Warner, *Monuments and Maidens: The Allegory of the Female Form* (Berkeley: University of California Press, 1985), 12–13, 16–17; Lynn Hunt, *The Family Romance of the French Revolution* (Berkeley: University of California Press, 1992), 82–84.

8. A classic statement is Michel-Rolph Trouillot, *Silencing the Past: Power and the Production of History* (1995; repr., Boston: Beacon Press, 2015), esp. 48–53, but see also Eva Mosely, "Women in the Archives: Documenting the History of Women in America," *American Archivist* 36 (1973): 215–22; Richard Harvey Brown and Beth Davis-Brown, "The Making of Memory: The Politics of Archives, Libraries, and Museums in the Construction of National Consciousness," *History of the Human Sciences* 11 (November 1998): 18–20.

9. Laurel Thatcher Ulrich, "Of Pens and Needles: Sources in Early American Women's History," *Journal of American History* 77 (1990): 200–207; Laurel Thatcher Ulrich, *The Age of Homespun: Objects and Stories in the Creation of an American Myth* (New York: Vintage Books, 2001); Susan Kern, "The Material World of the Jeffersons at Shadwell," *William and Mary Quarterly,* 3rd ser., 62 (2005): 213–42.

10. Gerda Lerner, "The Challenge of Women's History," in *The Majority Finds Its Past: Placing Women in History* (New York: Oxford University Press, 1979), 48–53. A powerful recent reformulation of this idea, with particular reference to the histories of enslaved women, is Marisa J. Fuentes, *Dispossessed Lives: Enslaved Women, Violence, and the Archive* (Philadelphia: University of Pennsylvania Press, 2016).

11. The latter collection encompasses business and household accounts. See Jennifer E. Stertzer et al., eds., *The George Washington Financial Papers Project* (Charlottesville: Washington Papers, 2017), at http://financial .gwpapers.org/.

12. A born-digital edition of her surviving papers is currently underway. See *The Martha Washington Papers Project,* at https://washingtonpapers.org /martha-washington-papers-project/.

13. Samuel Powel, quoted in Jean B. Lee, ed., *Experiencing Mount Vernon: Eyewitness Accounts, 1784–1865* (Charlottesville: University of Virginia Press, 2006), 52.

14. Ron Chernow's recent biography is the exception, but even he mentions Lewis only when she appears in the voluminous Washington archive, which was almost exclusively after her husband died in 1781. See Ron Chernow, *Washington: A Life* (New York: Penguin Books, 2010), 7, 98, 158, 422, 524–26, 588–90, 647, 775, 795.

15. Erica Armstrong Dunbar, *Never Caught: The Washingtons' Relentless Pursuit of Their Runaway Slave, Ona Judge* (New York: 37Ink/Atria Books, 2017), esp. chaps. 10–12.

16. See "The Rules of Civility," at https://www.mountvernon.org/george -washington/rules-of-civility/1/. On the man of feeling, see Janet Todd, *Sensibility: An Introduction* (London: Methuen, 1986), chap. 6; G. J. Barker-Benfield, *Culture of Sensibility: Sex and Society in Eighteenth-Century Britain* (Chicago: University of Chicago, 1992), 247–50.

17. Holger Hoock, *"Jus in Bello:* Rape and the British Army in the American Revolutionary War," *Journal of Military Ethics* 14 (2015): 84–87; Washington to William Livingston, 3 Mar. 1777, *Founders Online,* https://founders .archives.gov/documents/Washington/03-08-02-0524.

THE MOTHER OF THE FATHER

Memorializing Mary Washington in Antebellum Virginia

KATE HAULMAN

In the spring of 1833, President Andrew Jackson traveled to Fredericks-burg, Virginia, to attend a cornerstone-laying ceremony for a monument to Mary Ball Washington, mother of George. The event was the culmi-nation of years of effort, even struggle, to get such a memorial (literally) off the ground. The story of the monument's origins, creation, and fate reveals much about the nature and function of commemoration and the operation of gender within it during the antebellum period, in Virginia in particular.

Most obviously, perhaps, the late 1820s and early 1830s were a moment of remembering the American Revolution, as anniversaries cropped up and the "founding" generation passed on. The visit of the Marquis de La-fayette and his extensive tour of the eastern United States in 1824–1825 both coincided with and inspired scenes of public remembering. But that alone tells us little about the "how" of revolutionary commemoration — the cultural and political work such acts accomplished or attempted to — and how Mary Ball Washington figured into it. It is a truism that what and who is memorialized, and in what ways, says a great deal about the moment in which such acts occur and the people doing the memorial-izing.[1] Likewise, remembering in the form of public commemoration frequently depends also on forgetting, on silences and erasures.

In this light, as well as that of calls for national unity in the face of growing sectionalism, the monument to the Mother of Washington pro-vided an opportunity for the men of Fredericksburg and beyond to use the past in several ways: to tacitly admonish the newly public, political white women in their midst; to ignore the free Black men and women legally pushing to remain there; and to attempt to forget enslaved people resisting and revolting. They defended against these challenges in part by championing motherhood, embodied in a paragon of maternal virtue and relational status, that had quite literally given birth to the father of the country—and, by extension perhaps, the country itself. It did not hurt that this exemplar was dead, her absence offering productive possibilities. Another idealized figure, Mary's famous son George, loomed deity-like over the enterprise, and the monument had as much to do with him as with her.[2]

The story of the initial attempt to create a monument to Mary Washington shows that her remains threatened to become a site of family and sectarian conflict, one that stretched beyond northern Virginia into the newspapers of New York. At issue was who got to decide how and where to commemorate her and, not insignificantly, how such a project would be funded. But the monument's meaning extends further. The resolution of these matters and erection (or the beginnings, at least) of a monument demonstrates that at a time of local sectarian and increasing sectional struggle, the actors involved—elite white men all—were able to come together across denominations, regions, and parties on the ground of maternalism, in the name of honoring the most famous of dead American mothers. It was a cause that all could agree was in the highest national interest, and one which might promote unity within state and nation. The support and presence of President Andrew Jackson, who fashioned himself more inheritor of the mantle of Thomas Jefferson than the Federalist George Washington, lent this elite and establishment-feeling Virginia idyll a "democratic" cast. But when it came to the gender and racial politics the monument signified, Jackson likely had few qualms about connecting himself to the Virginia oligarchy. And so the fantasy of an orderly present and a statement against its own revolutionary potential took material form. Placing what was essentially a very large headstone, its creators conjured a "founding" past characterized by unity, one that featured the idealized mother of Washington and a monument to it built literally atop her bones.[3]

Given that Mary Washington was the Mother of the Father, her son's position as *pater patrie* secured during his life, why did more than three decades pass after her death before a monument arose? The answers may lie to some degree in her life, one revealed neither by a memorial nor by many "monuments" to her in print over the years. But it likely had something to do with her depiction in the first biography of her son, Mason Locke Weems's *The Life of George Washington*. With its publication in 1800, a portrait—a sketch, really, as Weems was far more concerned with George's father, Augustine—of a distant yet grasping mother figure began to emerge, establishing tropes that writers returned to again and again over the years. Of particular note is the story of young George wishing to join the British Navy at fourteen being thwarted by Mary, who "wept bitterly" and begged him piteously not to go. In Weems's telling, Mary is an emotionally manipulative wreck, and the bonds of filial love and duty trump George's desire for adventure. He puts her "happiness" before his own, ultimately to the good, for, Weems writes, "had George left his fond mother to a broken heart and gone off to sea 'tis next to certain that he would have never taken that active part in the French and Indian war which, by securing him in the hearts of his countryman, paved the way for all his future greatness." Mary's display, however unbefitting, inadvertently kept her son safe for another, higher purpose. Yet George gets the credit, and this account may mark the beginnings of her bad reputation.[4]

Yet Mary Ball Washington was neither the harridan nor clinging vine that many of George Washington's biographers (usually men) depicted, nor the sainted mother of a savior that nineteenth-century women writers and society doyennes championed. Rather, she was a white Virginia woman of her time, one who endured many losses during her life but occupied a position of privilege. She was born in 1707 into an established family, part of a ruling, slaveholding elite. She also came into the world female in the eighteenth century, with all the attendant restrictions in terms of public power, no matter how wellborn the lady. She was a pious person, yet uncompromising in her exercise of dominion (or attempted control) over enslaved people and belief in her right to wield it.[5]

As a child, Mary Ball suffered several losses, relocations, and reversals of fortune. When she was three years old her father, Joseph, died. Such a death, although mourned, was not particularly unusual in early eighteenth-century Virginia. But his bequest to Mary of four hundred acres of land and three enslaved people was unusual: as a toddler Mary became a slaveholder and landowner. Not long after, Mary's mother (also named Mary) remarried and they moved to a farm near the Potomac, about three hours away by horse. Her stepfather died just two years later. Young Mary had already learned about death and the resigned, restrained mourning typical of her Episcopalian denomination. Now she learned about tobacco farming and house management from her mother, as well as how to read and write. But her lessons in loss were not over, for in 1721 Mary's mother died, followed in short order by her half-brother. Still-young Mary was taken into yet another household by a half-sister from her mother's first marriage. In this period, her teens, she continued to practice housekeeping; she also learned to dance and to ride, becoming an excellent horsewoman, and, if her collection of devotional literature is suggestive, deepened her Christian piety.[6]

In 1731 she married the planter and widower Augustine "Gus" Washington. The couple came together through mutual relationships in the world of the Virginia oligarchy, in what was a "good match" for both given her landholdings, but a better one for Mary. They established themselves as a planter family, with land and enslaved people to work it, and Mary bore six children (the last of whom died very young). The Washingtons ultimately settled on the Rappahannock River at a place later called Ferry Farm, where Mary would spend nearly thirty years, but not without strife.

When Augustine died in 1746, Mary became a single mother at the age of thirty-five. Unusual for her time, she opted never to remarry, likely to protect her children's patrimony. On the one hand their inheritance was more secure than hers because she really had none other than the traditional widow's "use" of the property until George's age of majority; on the other, to wed again might have jeopardized their claims. Although benefiting from the labor of enslaved people, as mistress of what later became known as Ferry Farm she struggled financially and hoped to secure her offsprings', perhaps especially George's, place in the Virginia oligarchy.[7] Thus she did not want her son joining the British Navy at age fourteen. Both the past, in terms of the losses of loved ones she had sustained (her husband just three years earlier), and the future, in terms of her visions for George's life, dictated against it. Mary did not seem to desire grandly for herself, but she may have harbored aspirations for her eldest son, perhaps realizing that her security as a widow depended on his success.

Mary Washington had high expectations of herself and others, and some of this comes through in George's life. Although she possessed some of the trappings of eighteenth-century gentility, she may not have embraced and performed the more refined social graces expected of her class—habits that George himself set out to master. She was not one for eighteenth-century salon culture. By all accounts Mary was direct in expression and did not seem to care much about putting people at ease. George himself felt plagued by her expectations of him when it came to attention and material support late in her life, as she experienced life as an aging, single woman of diminished means.[8]

She lived a long life even by today's standards, dying in 1789 of breast cancer just as George was assuming the presidency. After her death many in her town of Fredericksburg observed a period of public mourning, as did members of Congress, who passed a resolution to erect a monument to her. But she soon faded from the collective imagination. In part this had to do with the age—commemorations were not much a thing in a still infant nation. George Washington's death in 1799, which spurred an outpouring of national mourning, might have prompted a revisiting of Mary's life, but it did not. It did, however, give quick rise to Weems's *Life of Washington*. But according to one early twentieth-century historian, "nothing but a little headstone marked the grave of Mary Washington when Lafayette visited this country."[9]

Enter George Washington Parke Custis, George Washington's adopted grandson and scion, and self-appointed preserver of Washingtoniana. Through him, Mary Washington became the subject of her own biography of sorts, one that contributes to the portrait of a stern and even fearsome figure, yet with the subtext that she must have done something right. His "Recollection," first published in 1826 in the *National Gazette*, was, perhaps predictably, as concerned with George as his mother, yet signaled her reemergence in the public consciousness, or at least the public prints.[10] He wrote toward the goal that she be memorialized, or at the very least her final resting place marked.[11] Custis concluded, "Thus lived and died this distinguished woman. Had she been of the olden time, statues would have been erected to her memory in the capitol and she would have been called the Mother of Romans." Not merely the creator of one person was Mary, but of a republican people through rearing one great man. But, he lamented, with an undertone of admonishment, "it will remain for another generation to appropriately recognize and commemorate this greatest of all Mothers." Perhaps then people would "repair to the now neglected grave of the Mother of Washington."[12]

"It is yet a neglected grave," begins the closing footnote to Custis's essay when it appeared in his *Recollections and Private Memoirs of the Life of Washington* decades later. Of the chapters that form the heart and majority of the tome, "The Mother of Washington" is the first, a verbatim reproduction of the *National Gazette* essay of thirty-four years earlier, but with notes. In them, Custis claimed that the original publication of his reminiscence "attracted a great deal of attention" and set in motion a project to reinter Mary's remains and erect a monument. "This movement," he insisted, was not confined to Virginia but "elicited the public sympathy throughout the Union." He continued, "the press, as usual, discussed the subject, and a New York paper proposed that the whole matter of raising the moderate sum of two thousand dollars for the erection of a monument be left in the hands of 'the American maids and matrons.'"[13]

As retrospectives often do, Custis's account of the monument campaign omitted as much as it included. First, the "New York paper" was the *Commercial Advertiser* and was the vehicle for publicizing the monument subscription plan but not its originator, as somewhat implied. Furthermore, "public sympathy" across the nation was a bit of a stretch. The local backstory that Custis left out was rife with family and sectarian tensions, but ended up getting a monument off the ground. He so desperately sought national commemoration of Mary that he was willing to see it supported and brought to fruition by anyone who would take on the project. Behind the piece in the *Advertiser* was an attempt by the Presbyterian Church of Fredericksburg to claim (and relocate) Mary's remains by tying the creation of a marker to their plans for a new building. This catalyzed a different group of men—not women, Custis's "maids and matrons"—starting with indignant Washington family members, to form a monumental committee and initiate a fundraising campaign. Although motivated by the local concerns over who would get to claim Mary, like Custis they "went national" in their rhetoric and ultimately tapped a faraway source of funding. This was a stroke of fortune because when they turned to the community to raise funds, none were forthcoming; yet a monument went forward. It would have to *create* unity in the community, state, and in the nation, not issue from it.

When George Washington Bassett, husband of George Washington's grand-niece Betty Burwell Lewis, got wind of the Presbyterians' plan, he felt usurped and was astonished and dismayed to learn of the "scheme," as he termed it. In March 1831 he wrote to an unknown recipient, almost certainly his cousin Lawrence Lewis: "The publication in the Advertiser of Friday last has been copied into the papers of this town and doubtless you have seen the same before this." In the face of this displeasing revelation, Bassett had taken it upon himself to write to the *Advertiser* and set the matter straight—namely that the people of Fredericksburg "had no knowledge of the proceedings of this committee" and "the feeling produced on these by the Publication in the Advertiser is one of disapprobation."[14] Regardless of whether or not the entire town disapproved of a plan to link a monument to Mary Washington to the erection of a new Presbyterian church, he certainly did.

Members of the extended Washington family were no strangers to conversations over remains and what to be done with them. George Washington's will made very clear his wishes to be buried at Mount Vernon, and they were respected. But into the nineteenth century, some in the federal government lobbied for a mausoleum that would contain his remains to be built in Washington, D.C. Others wanted an equestrian statue in the capital as a fitting memorial tribute while the state of Virginia wanted him too. The approaching 1832 centennial of the founding father's birth spurred the erection of a new tomb at Mount Vernon, a family vault bearing a marble slab reading (should there be any doubt) "Washington Family."[15] But in the case of Mary, the Washingtons were not speaking with one voice. In fact, Bassett had reason to believe that the Presbyterians had enlisted Custis in their plan—"Mr. Custis was made the organ," in Bassett's words. Claiming to speak for the family of Washington, Custis had in turn approached Samuel Gordon, on whose property Mary lay buried, about disinterring and acquiring the remains. Gordon, for his part, could not "surmise from Mr C's letter that his was not a personal application for the remains of a venerated connection," according to Bassett. Hoping to further set the record straight, in an edited draft of this lengthy missive that remains in Bassett's papers, he averred that "a respectable portion of the relatives of Mrs Washington will not agree to the exhumation of her bones for the purpose contemplated by the Presbyterian community here—and that Mr Gordon will not consent to their removal for such a purpose in violation of their filial wishes," attempting to don the "family of Washington" mantle more broadly and effectively than Custis. Of his meddling relative he had to say only, "I do most sincerely and deeply lament the participation of Mr. Custis in this matter."[16]

It is possible that Custis acted out of frustration generated by lack of action on the monument front. According to another of Bassett's letters, a proposal had gone before the Fredericksburg town council to create a subscription for a monument, but it was never seconded. Whether Custis approached the Presbyterians or vice versa in response to the town's apparent lack of will, once the plan became public it did have the effect of catalyzing Bassett and others. Bassett's uncle-in-law, George Washington's nephew Lawrence Lewis, married to Custis's sister Eleanor "Nelly" Custis Lewis, wrote, "I entirely agree with Mr. Gordon, in thinking if any Monument is erected, it had better be upon the spot where she now is, + for this purpose I will contribute liberally, and obtain as many of the relatives as possible to aid us." Failing that, he would only agree to have her remains removed to Mount Vernon "with that of my Mothers . . . at my own expense." Lewis felt that his "knowledge of the spot where my Grandmother was deposited, + an examination of her bones will enable me to identify her remains, as for many years before her death she had no teeth, or at least not more than one fore tooth," whereas "others deposited in that place were all much younger, therefore it is not likely a mistake will be made." He concluded, "altho it may be attended with some trouble . . . I shall not mind on such an occation."[17]

Although Lewis was not quite as exercised about the Presbyterians' plan as Bassett, and indeed wrote in a couple of places that he wished to keep clear of any controversy, his willingness to exhume and identify forty-year-old remains is suggestive. Facing an attempt by a group outside the Washington family circle (an increasingly wide one, it should be said) to lay claim to Mary, perhaps in order to gain attention, traffic, and congregants, Lewis touted his insider standing and intimate knowledge to keep her in place, both literally and figuratively. He essentially implied that the Presbyterians should back off because they would not know Mary's remains from, well, a hole in the ground—but he would. His preference seemed to be that she be kept on the property that had been his parents Betty and Fielding Lewis's estate. Named Kenmore in 1819, it was no longer owned by anyone in the Washington family but rather the Gordon family, of Scots origin (although not, Bassett noted, Presbyterians). Rather, Mr. Gordon had been "a liberal supporter of our own church, indeed his very ample subscription to our own church edifice and large annual supply to our pastor he told me were the ostensible grounds upon which he declined subscribing to the New Presbyterian church."[18] Perhaps Gordon felt inclined toward the Presbyterians' plan to exhume and relocate Mary out of guilt over his lack of support for his natal church.

Relative to the Episcopalians, the dominant church in the region, the Presbyterian Church was new to Fredericksburg, the first building erected in 1808. But it was a denomination on the rise and, according to church historian Edward Alvey Jr., "dissatisfaction with the state of the Episcopal church" led many prominent families to defect, including a Mrs. Robert Lewis, a Washington family connection. Others who claimed "family of Washington" status may have felt some threat, as the 1820s were a time of high spirit and growth for the Presbyterians, as the congregation outstripped its original home. In Alvey's loaded words, "as plans for the erection of the church went forward, George Washington Parke Custis gave his permission for the removal of the remains of Mary Ball Washington from the cornfield . . . where they were resting almost forgotten and uncared for, to an appropriate place in the new edifice." The Episcopalians were "aghast" and claimed she could not possibly rest in peace there.[19]

Thus were the bones of Mary Washington becoming the site of a local, sectarian, and family conflict; but the conflict did get things moving, and, paradoxically, produced some consensus that she be memorialized. At issue for Bassett and others was not only that her remains would be removed from the spot of her own choosing and without any family support (save Custis), but to a Presbyterian site. Although Bassett described them as "respectable Presbyterians," both he and Lewis clearly found their actions presumptuous. Yet Lewis was more pragmatic and hoped to avoid the controversy he saw brewing. Although he thought the Episcopalians should have her, given that they had not expressed interest, "the question then is, is it better Mrs Washingtons remains should continue where they are, unattended to, + when a few years more may for ever obliterate the spot." Perhaps it was preferable to allow "a most respectable religious community, to pay that honour prompted along by feelings of the most profound respect for her, who was the mother of the Father of his country?" Here Lewis "went national," subtly shaming Bassett—would you rather have her remain unmemorialized, he implied, and her grave "obliterated?" To assuage Bassett's denominational concerns, he claimed, "I do not think placing the remains in a Presby.^{an} Church will be any evidence of her being of that sect, the Monument will only be in memory of her who was Mother of the father of his country." Furthermore, calling on what he viewed as common knowledge of the past, he claimed that everyone knew she was Episcopalian. Finally, her relationship to George superseded all other associations in his mind, and in the public's, he felt certain. He concluded that it was best to "let them proceed quietly in their plans."[20] To Lewis's mind, securing the legacy of the Washington family on the literal landscape was important enough to make some allowances, even across denominational lines.

But Bassett had no intention of doing that. He sent representatives to deliver a counter notice to the *New York Advertiser,* whose editor deemed the letter "sectarian" and refused to publish it on the grounds that it would destroy the proposed subscription "in toto." Bassett's first courier to New York, Lucius Minor, then took it to another paper, who pledged to publish it. When a second representative, Silas Wood, followed up, the editor claimed his paper was too full at present to permit the inclusion of Bassett's missive. Wood then asked to see the correspondence and was none too pleased. He worried that its publication would make trouble, especially with Custis, which might be unnecessary given that the original plea for a subscription has been a "perfect failure" and received no attention. Why risk an ugly family quarrel in public? Wood simply wanted the conflict resolved and the matter reintroduced and "divested of conflicting feelings and excitements" so people could come together in support of a monument. He imagined a monument to Mary Washington as a unifying project.[21]

Although accused of "sectarianism" (and tarring the Presbyterians with the same brush), Bassett likewise deployed the language of unity, local and national. He wrote that he "suggested a plan in which I humbly trust all will unite corresponding with Mr Gordons your own and my view of the proper course in this matter." Furthermore, he had "little doubt of its adoption by the Nation as a substitute for the more private and particular scheme heretofore entertained by a religious Society of this place," a plan instead commencing "under united auspices of the nation."[22] Lawrence Lewis too wanted all to be "united" and "in harmony" concerning a memorial. He, Bassett, and Custis all agreed that publicly, materially commemorating Mary Washington was in the national interest; but who got to decide how this project would proceed and appear? Bassett claimed to speak not only for the Washington family but also the town of Fredericksburg and a broader public. Custis was also family but claimed to represent the nation as well, his "Recollection" of Mary establishing the discursive terrain on which Bassett had to fight. But Bassett could then claim that such a figure belonged not to one "particular" group but to all. Finally, both men, in championing Mary's commemoration and claiming authority to direct it, implied that the family of Washington was synonymous with the nation.[23]

With the local public now aware that Mary Washington remained unmemorialized, Bassett felt satisfied "there is now not the slightest ground for doubt that the contemplated monument will be erected and that too in a more enlarged and splendid style" than originally anticipated.[24] He was expecting, perhaps, a flood of subscriptions. But in May 1831 Silas E. Burrows of Connecticut and New York wrote to the mayor of Fredericksburg offering to fund the monument himself. Having seen the original notice, "It would be one of the most happy events of my life," he claimed, "if my means are adequate and your citizens would allow an individual to furnish the funds for erecting a monument agreeable to their wishes."[25] Burrows was a wealthy merchant and ship owner who, according to a later article in the San Francisco newspaper the *Call*, had exhibited surprising generosity before. His "remarkable instances of philanthropy" included sending one of his ships to help the Greeks in their independence struggle in the late 1820s and, upon learning that the children of a "Prince of the Ethiopians" had been captured by traders and sold into slavery in America, sending money to support their purchase. In addition, and more akin to his support for the monument, in 1829 (or perhaps earlier) he "deposited in bank $1200 to the credit of the ex-President Monroe to pay a sum of money due, and to prevent the sale of his estate."[26] On the heels of this act came his offer to fund the Mary Washington monument.

Lawrence Lewis, for one, felt it best to decline the support. "I admire the generous offer of Mr. Burrows of New York," he wrote to Bassett in May 1831, "but think you ought not to avail yourselves of it unless compelled to it." He further explained, "I view the subject as a national one, in which thousands will like to contribute, and to deprive them of the opportunity will be offending against those feelings so dear to every true American." He had no doubt that the sum "will be easily raised if unaccompanied by any other scheme."[27]

And so, having consulted Lewis, Bassett drafted a circular letter dated June 1, 1831, a surviving copy of which was sent to John Thompson, Esq., of Culpeper. The document establishes a "Monumental Committee" of fifteen members drawn from Fredericksburg and three surrounding counties and refutes the Presbyterian plan in lawyerly fashion. In the main, it was "not national or universal," whereas a "public monument . . . should occupy some conspicuous and public place; that it should not only be accessible to all but accessible by an equal and common propriety." Furthermore, "the relatives of Mrs. Washington, resident in this town and vicinage, decidedly, but calmly, disapprove," and of course — the pièce de résistance — Mary herself had chosen the spot in her "dying injunctions," a "favorite" which she frequently visited. Having dispensed with the Presbyterians, among the resolutions was "that this is and ought to be a national measure, and that we will pursue it as such."[28] Perhaps most importantly, the letter put out a call for subscriptions, monetary pledges toward the erection of a monument that Lawrence Lewis had all but assured Bassett would be forthcoming.

But Lewis was too optimistic, put too much faith in the feelings and generosity of his countrymen. Two letters to Bassett, chairman of the monumental committee, describe their authors' inability to solicit subscriptions. In July 1831 George Washington Lewis lamented, "it is a subject of sore regret to me that I have been so entirely unfortunate as to procure a solitary subscriber to the monument." With disdain, he continued, "whenever I have mentioned the subject . . . I have received nothing in return but repulsive indifference and apathy." Feeling "mortified" at his failure, he himself pledged two dollars — although he did not enclose it.[29] Nine months later, George Fayette Washington wrote to provide "a detail of my proceedings as Agent in procuring a subscription for the erection of a Monument of Mrs. Mary Washington, the mother of our good old relative." Although he had expended great effort in "this patriotic and praiseworthy cause," he explained that, apparently, providing relief in the wake of a local fire had drained people's charity. He then posted a "conspicuous" notice but had not managed to snare one subscriber. In any case, he concluded this portion of the letter, "Mr. Burrows has forestalled us . . . which affords another evidence that republics are ungrateful. After the wanton neglect evidenced in the case of the Son, we could not rationally anticipate national Union."[30] Washington wanted the monument to be the work of the people of the nation, and in particular local Virginians, not just one wealthy donor. But it was not to be. The public just did not seem to care—not enough, anyway, to loosen their purse strings. If the son, the founding father himself, had suffered "wanton neglect" by the public, still unmemorialized, what could be expected toward Mary? It was a time of economic uncertainty, of booms and busts. Ultimately, if the men of the Washington family and Fredericksburg wanted to build a monument, it was going to have to be with Burrows's money. "National union," in his phrase, had not gotten the monument off the ground, but might ensue from its existence, a tribute to the Mother of Washington.

National union, however, was increasingly hard to come by in the early 1830s. Since at least the contested presidential election of 1824, national politics had been divisive and had not grown less so with Andrew Jackson's ascendance. White Americans were on the move, and people espoused widely different opinions on the prospect of forcibly dislocating several Native American nations from their ancestral lands in the Southeast. The issue tested the nature of federalism and pitted the state of Georgia (and Jackson) against the Supreme Court. Also connected to national expansion, the "slavery question" grew increasingly vexed—always the case for African Americans, free and enslaved, and increasingly so for white Americans. New antislavery forces confronted (and perhaps helped to create) a robust proslavery ideology. Even unity within a state was in short supply; Virginia was riven by social and political division and rocked by violent upheaval.

First, elite white women were organizing around various causes. The early nineteenth century saw their engagement in benevolent activity expand across the state, with Mary Washington's last home of Fredericksburg as an important node. Initially their work, framed always as a pious extension of domestic and maternal duties, stood a comfortable distance from the public world of politics, and for many this remained the case, hewing closely to the rhetoric of domesticity and subservience.[31] But by the late 1820s, a white women's antislavery movement, frankly colonizationist and racist, was coalescing in Virginia. Many of these women, covering a broad political spectrum, had come to regard slavery as a "canker" that bred domestic chaos and immoral behavior in everyone associated with the institution. In Fredericksburg, women organized a female auxiliary chapter of the American Colonization Society in 1829, which became "the state's most active female society," a robust public presence.[32]

At around the same time, Virginia held a Constitutional Convention chiefly to address issues of malapportionment embedded in the original frame of 1776. Many recognized that the document disadvantaged western counties; correction had been a long time coming and finally seemed at hand in the fall of 1829. Also nominally on the table was gradual emancipation, but the issue never made it out of committee and onto the floor for debate. More pressing, and related to the competition of regional interests in the state, was the question of universal white manhood suffrage. Extending the vote to all adult white men regardless of wealth or property failed by two votes, as did popular election of the governor. Although there was some reapportioning of delegates in the House to reflect western settlement, the Convention was a "triumph of traditionalism" in a state divided, east and west.[33]

Alongside the growing public presence of white antislavery women and political challenges by smallholding white men in the west, free Black men and women were asserting their right to exist in Virginia. An 1806 "expulsion" law held that no emancipated adult African American could remain in the state for more than a year, yet many stayed in violation as whites looked the other way, while others sought counsel to sue for their right to remain. Although unevenly enforced, the law suggests how dangerous many white Virginians considered the presence of free Black people in a slave society, even 50,000 relative to 450,000 enslaved. They were, in the minds of slaveholding whites in particular, kindling in a fire that required only a lighted match to spark the conflagration of revolt. Additional fuel may have arrived in the form of David Walker's *Appeal to the Colored Citizens of the World;* he sent thirty copies to Thomas Lewis of Richmond in 1829.[34]

White fears and enslaved hopes were realized in August 1831 when Nat Turner led more than seventy enslaved and free Blacks in Southampton County in a revolt intended to free slaves and kill whites who stood in the way. Virginia's white militia suppressed the rebellion within a few days, but retaliation by the militia as well as white civilians continued and extended far beyond Virginia. The climate of panic, rage, and vigilantism that ensued resulted in the deaths of as many as 148, in addition to the accused who were convicted and executed.[35]

The Turner Revolt brought the question of slavery's existence to the fore in the Old Dominion and further spurred white women's antislavery activism in the form of petitions to the Assembly.[36] The following spring the body debated the institution's future, and for a moment it looked as if emancipation, however grudging and gradual, might become the law of the land. The debates were lengthy and spirited, showing just how divided legislators were on slavery, if not on race—most agreed that freed Blacks should not long remain. But proslavery forces prevailed. Not only would the institution persist, but its strictures were strengthened. Newly robust Black codes forbade literacy, pamphlet distribution, firearms, preaching, and religious gatherings unsupervised by whites, with broad language extended to "slaves, free blacks and mulattos" in each instance of the bill.[37] If there had ever been doubt about the views of Virginia legislators, their fear and contempt of all African Americans, and their commitment not only to slavery but to racial hierarchy, the new laws left no question. They situated the Old Dominion firmly on one side of the debate over the existence and legitimacy of slavery, but they also reveal the various forces pressing on the institution.

The fault lines in Virginia were many in the 1820s and early 1830s, a time of upheaval and uncertainty. In some sense, it served as a microcosm of issues facing the republic. Perhaps that made it all the more important to look to the past to unify white Virginia and the nation. A monument to the Mother of the Father could perform important cultural work in a climate of social and political division, the "unity" and "union" about which men of the Washington family wrote and spoke.

Sources are silent as to what transpired between the flurry of correspondence about the location of and funding for the Mary Washington monument in 1831 and 1832 and the elaborate ceremony that marked its beginnings in the spring of 1833. Given the dearth of contributions from the local community, Silas Burrows's money must have supported the endeavor and, indeed, he was prominently featured in the procession to

the site. Although Washington family and denominational conflict catalyzed the monument's creation, Virginia and national politics animated
its meaning. The monument aimed to foster national unity by recalling
the achievements of the revolutionary era through George Washington,
championing maternalism through Mary Washington, and linking the
two inextricably.

The monumental committee invited President Andrew Jackson to lay
the cornerstone "of the monument proposed to be erected to the Mother
of Washington," and he graciously accepted. Despite the divisions in
the state over the Nullification Crisis in South Carolina and Jackson's
handling of it, he had easily carried Virginia in his reelection bid of 1832
and certainly enjoyed popularity in this region. The president's presence
gave the undertaking great weight and provided it with a national stage.
For Jackson's part, attending was perhaps a way of rewarding the area for
its loyalty, as well as an opportunity to publicly connect himself to the
revolutionary past and a general-turned-executive. A town meeting ensued to discuss his visit and the proceedings, out of which a committee
formed to organize the events, all of which featured men.[38]

The whole thing possessed, and kicked off with, a distinctly martial
flavor. Jackson arrived by steamboat the day before, received by "a large
party" that included members of the monumental committee, a "military company," and the marine band. Fredericksburg's newspaper, the
Political Arena, lauded the "imposing military array" that included local
guards, "volunteers," and national cadets. For its part, the *Virginia Herald* detailed "Captain Moore's company of National Cadets from Washington, Capt. Kinsey's company of Riflemen and Capt. Brockett's Light
Infantry of Alexandria, the Marine Band from the Navy Yard," met by
the "Fredericksburg Guards, the Rifle Company and the Fredericksburg
Blues Junior." Finally, a troop of Light Horse from Fauquier County arrived that evening.[39] All amounted to a military parade par excellence,
an impressive display for the commander in chief. In addition to honoring Jackson, the martial cast gestured more to George Washington than
to Mary.

The following morning Jackson received "ladies and gentlemen" before the procession formed to begin its march to Kenmore. It was led by
the monument's architect, Colonel Joseph B. Hill and his assistants, followed by donor Silas Burrows and the monumental committee. Listed

fourth in the enumerated order published in the *Virginia Herald* came President Jackson, curiously given his status, followed by "clergy and relations of Mrs. Washington," the mayor, naval and military officers, masonic societies, the band, "military" (presumably rank-and-file men), "teachers and their pupils," and finally "citizens and strangers." Presumably, anyone could join the parade, but they had to adhere to the script and choreography. The *Herald* also noted the "company of boys, handsomely uniformed and well drilled" whose "appearance attracted much attention and called forth expressions of interest and admiration from the President."[40] Even youth—young men at least—had a part to play.

In addition to publicizing (and helpfully enumerating) the order of procession, the *Herald* detailed the timing, the route, and where each group would end up upon arrival at the monument site. Its language reflects a near-obsession with order—perhaps unsurprising given not only the presence of the president, other dignitaries, and the number of participants, but also because of recent disorderly events to the South. The masonic societies, military, and "band of music" would gather in front

Sketch of the unfinished monument to Mary Ball Washington. (From *Frank Leslie's Illustrated Newspaper*, New York, June 14, 1862)

of the courthouse at ten in the morning and walk to the town hall where they were to be joined by the remaining numbers. The parade "will then move, at precisely half past ten o'clock, each division in its proper order, the citizens and strangers marching six abreast, down Princess Anne Street to the corner of Wolf Street," and so on until reaching Kenmore. Numbers 1 through 6 were then to approach the base of the monument, encircled by number 8 (masons), while number 9 (musicians) was to line up behind the masons, and number 10 would "form upon the south, east, and west of the position occupied by the antecedent numbers, making three sides of a square." Finally, numbers 11 and 12 "will then be thrown in rear of the whole reserving the space within the enclosure upon the west for the ladies"—the audience.[41]

Once all were in proper place, the ceremony itself began. It opened with a prayer, then George Washington Bassett took the pulpit. He opened with expressions of gratitude toward and flattery of "General Jackson," but may have also been directing comments about the lessons of history toward him, given how polarizing a figure he was compared with Washington (or narratives of Washington that had calcified over time): "frail man is ever apt to forget the past . . . and seldom learns from the experience of others the means of attaining what he aims at." More directly addressing sectional tensions, and connecting their repair directly to the monument, he hoped that "the citizens of these states will remember that they are brothers. They will remember that here lies the ashes of the Mother of the Father of his Country."[42] Mary Washington was the national brotherhood's grandmother.

Both Bassett's address and Jackson's remarks were tinged with high maternalism and lessons for the ladies about their primary role of motherhood and its stakes for the nation. Waxing philosophical about monuments, Bassett called them "lasting incentives . . . to imitate the virtues they commemorate," deeming the one at hand a "just tribute to the merits of her who . . . encouraged and fostered the dawning virtues of her illustrious son . . . the ornament and glory of her waning years." Jackson, who, in his turn opened with references to George, said of the phrase and inscription, "Mary the Mother of Washington . . . no eulogy could be higher, and it appeals to the heart of every American." He went on with words of praise for her drawn from, in part, Custis's "Mother of Washington" essay, emphasizing the "domestic government" and "firm discipline" that formed her son's self-command. George Washington may have possessed inherent "greatness," but he had to be "guided and directed by maternal solicitude and judgment." Warming to his point and at least some of his intended audience, Jackson continued, "How important to the females of this country are these reminiscences of the early life of Washington and the maternal care of her upon whom its future course depended." From there he widened the lens to the "mothers and sisters and wives and daughters" who performed their duties so well, no doubt aware of the "importance of the maternal character and the powerful influence it must exert on the American youth." Happy for them to have the example of Washington, as well as his mother, as a reminder that "upon the mother must therefore frequently, if not generally, depend the fate of the son."[43]

The ceremony closed with the reading of a poem by Lydia Sigourney, a well-known and prolific writer from Connecticut, that emphasized similar themes. As historian Susan Hetzel puts it, "nor were the 'females' of the day silent." But Virginian women were, and Sigourney herself, whose published work included conduct literature informed by "separate spheres" ideology, did not deliver the verse. It was a sentimental paean to devotion, both Christian and maternal, and reiterated some of the material from Custis's recollections.

> Me thinks we see thee as in olden times,
> Simple in garb, majestic and serene
> Unmoved by pomp and circumstance, in truth
> Inflexible and with a Spartan zeal

Sigourney went on to emphasize Mary's serious approach to life and to motherhood in particular, and like Jackson, she lauded the results for Mary's son and the nation.

> For the might that clothed the "Pater Patriae"—for the glorious deeds
> That make Mount Vernon's tomb a Mecca shrine
> For all the earth, what thanks to thee are due

To mothers fell a "holy charge" and a "kingly power" to "rule the fountains of the unborn mind."[44] In motherhood was great responsibility and power, but only relational—an early version of the hand that rocks the cradle rules the world.

Yet on this influence the course of national union, which George Washington symbolized, depended. Making the connection explicit, the *Political Arena* likened the cornerstone-laying event to the "three days" of July, albeit without the "revolution and bloodshed." This was a generative moment, "forming an era in the history of our town," by locating it at center of revolutionary commemoration. In fact, "the concourse of people" was "much greater than when Lafayette visited," claimed the *Herald*.[45] Mary's generation of George and his of the nation papered over a host of fraught, present-day concerns facing Virginia, as the state anxiously doubled down on slavery and asserted white supremacy within long-standing status hierarchy. The eighteenth-century past and the dead mother that the monument memorialized was, simply, safer terrain.

Given the fanfare and the support of national figures, why did the Mary Washington monument languish incomplete? George Washington Parke Custis blamed "commercial reverses" while early twentieth-century historian Susan Hetzel cited bank failure—perhaps the same thing—but also the death of the contractor.[46] Burrows's donation only went so far, and dried-up funding certainly provides an explanation. But the lack of will and perhaps interest foreshadowed by the failed local subscription campaign suggests that although the monument went unfinished, the public attention and cornerstone-laying ceremony rendered some of its work complete: to thwart the designs of an "upstart" congregation; to chasten antislavery white women and reinforce slavery and racial order in Virginia without ever mentioning either; to admonish sectionalism and promote unity; and to demonstrate Andrew Jackson's magnanimity and connection to George Washington. Memorializing the Mother of the Father might serve many purposes. But did anyone really care about Mary Ball Washington?

Notes

I am grateful to Guy Nelson, Gautham Rao, members of my writing group at American University, the anonymous readers for UVA Press, and most especially the volume's editors for suggestions that strengthened this essay, and to Amy Pflugrad-Jackisch for generously sharing research in the Bassett family papers.

1. David Gobel and Daves Rossell, eds., introduction to *Commemoration in America: Essays on Monuments, Memorialization, and Memory* (Charlottesville: University of Virginia Press, 2013), 2–3. There has been much excellent work on Civil War, and especially Confederate, commemoration but not as much on how Americans publicly commemorated the American Revolution in the early nineteenth century. For the latter, see Sarah J. Purcell, *Sealed with Blood: War, Sacrifice, and Memory in Revolutionary America* (Philadelphia: University of Pennsylvania Press, 2002), and, more recently, Michael McDonnell, Clare Corbould, Frances M. Clarke, and W. Fitzhugh Brundage, eds., *Remembering the Revolution: Memory, History and Nation Making from Independence to the Civil War* (Amherst: University of Massachusetts Press, 2013). Most germane and related to this essay, on the creation of George Washington's birthplace as a historic site of memory and commemoration that, being a birthplace, gestures toward Mary Washington and motherhood, see Seth C. Bruggeman, *Here, George Washington Was Born: Memory, Material Culture, and the Making of a Monument* (Athens: University of Georgia Press, 2008), 15–18. On battlefields and commemoration, see Thomas A. Chambers, *Memories of War: Battlegrounds and Bonefields in the Early American Republic* (Ithaca: Cornell University Press, 2012). A collection that contends with "five critical methodologies," among them race and gender, for reading interpretations of the American past across periods is Jeffrey Lee Meriwether and Laura Mattoon D'Amore, eds., *We Are What We Remember: The American Past through Commemoration* (Newcastle: Cambridge Scholars Publishing, 2012). Near the end of his tour, Lafayette laid the cornerstone of the Bunker Hill monument. On it, and women's controversial fundraising efforts, see Amy Sopcak-Joseph, "The Fruits of Industry and Ingenuity: Politics, Gender, and the Bunker Hill Monument" (paper presented at the 40th Annual Meeting of the Society for Historians of the Early American Republic, July 20, 2018, Cleveland, OH, cited with permission of the author).

2. On the cult of George Washington in the early republic and his life as a civic sacred text, including his resonance as slaveholding, yet proto-abolitionist "father" of the nation, see Francois Furstenberg, *In the Name of the Father: Washington's Legacy, Slavery, and the Making of a Nation* (New York: Penguin Press, 2006). The fact that Mary Ball Washington is known chiefly as the mother of George has long obscured investigations into her life on its own terms (while, this essay posits, offering productive interpretive possibilities at the intersection of gender and the public history of the founding). A recent biography that accomplishes the goal of recovering her

experiences is Martha Saxton, *The Widow Washington: The Life of Mary Washington* (New York: Farrar, Straus, and Giroux, 2019).

3. On "dead body politics" and the ways in which corpses can transcend time, uniting past and present, see Katherine Vedery, *The Political Lives of Dead Bodies: Reburial and Postsocialist Change* (New York: Columbia University Press, 1999).

4. M. L. Weems, *The Life of George Washington* (Philadelphia, 1800), 30; 192–93.

5. Saxton, *The Widow Washington*.

6. Saxton, 23–73.

7. Saxton, 75–167.

8. Saxton, 139–41; 261–67.

9. Susan Riviere Hetzel, *The Building of a Monument: The Mary Washington Associations and Their Work* (Lancaster: Press of Wickersham Company, 1903). Hetzel's book recounts the efforts by women's organizations that resulted in the completion of the monument in 1894. The only other account of the monument, also a narrative treatment focusing on its completion, is Melissa Plotkin's "'Long Hast Thou Slept Unnoted': The Mary Washington Monument," *Virginia Cavalcade* 45, no. 1 (Summer 1995): 26–35, and see also Philip Levy, *Where the Cherry Tree Grew: The Story of Ferry Farm, George Washington's Boyhood Home* (New York: St. Martin's Press, 2013), 102–5; 138–42. It is accurate that Mary Washington's grave was more or less unmarked in the 1820s. According to the Virginia Museum of History and Culture website, George Washington ordered a memorial stone for the burial site soon after her death, but it was "ravaged by souvenir hunters" ("Mary Washington Monument," Virginia Museum of History and Culture, https://www.virginiahistory.org/collections-and-resources/garden -club-virginia/public-buildings-and-sites/mary-washington-monument).

10. The essay appeared in two parts in the *National Gazette* on May 13 and June 6, 1826. On Custis, see Seth C. Bruggeman, "'More than Ordinary Patriotism': Living History in the Memory Work of George Washington Parke Custis," in McDonnell et al., *Remembering the Revolution*, 127–43. As Bruggeman states, Custis "made a career of remembering his childhood" (12). Presaging his efforts surrounding Mary's memorialization, in 1815 he traveled to Virginia's northern neck to place a marker at George Washington's birthplace. On Parke Custis and the wider Custis family's display and use of objects connected to George Washington as cultural capital that established themselves as the "family of Washington," see Cassandra Good, "Washington Family Fortune: Lineage and Capital in Nineteenth-Century America," *Early American Studies* 18, no. 1 (Winter 2020): 90–133.

11. Custis embraced and crafted "physicalist" memory—loved spaces and stuff. See Bruggeman, "'More than Ordinary Patriotism,'" 135–40.

12. George Washington Parke Custis, *Recollections and Private Memoirs of Washington* (New York: Derby and Jackson, 1860), 148.

13. Custis, 148.

14. George Washington Bassett to Lawrence Lewis, March 12, 1831, Bassett Family Papers, Virginia Historical Society, Richmond, VA.

15. Matthew R. Costello, *The Property of the Nation: George Washington's Tomb, Mount Vernon, and the Memory of the First President* (Lawrence: University Press of Kansas, 2019), 19–38.

16. Costello, 19–38.

17. Lawrence Lewis to Bassett, May 5, 1831, Bassett Family Papers, Virginia Historical Society.

18. Bassett to Lawrence Lewis, March 12, 1831, Bassett Family Papers, Virginia Historical Society.

19. Edward Alvey Jr., *A History of the Presbyterian Church in Fredericksburg, 1808–1976* (Fredericksburg: Session of the Presbyterian Church, 1976), 8–9, 16.

20. Lawrence Lewis to Bassett, April 9, 1831, Bassett Family Papers, Virginia Historical Society.

21. Silas Wood to Bassett, May 17 and May 20, 1831, Bassett Family Papers, Virginia Historical Society.

22. Bassett to Lawrence Lewis, March 12, 1831, Bassett Family Papers, Virginia Historical Society.

23. On the importance of lineage as a source of "privilege, distinction, and power" in early America, see Good, "Washington Family Fortune," 91.

24. Bassett to Lawrence Lewis, March 12, 1831, Bassett Family Papers, Virginia Historical Society.

25. Silas Burrows to mayor of Fredericksburg, May 19, 1831, Bassett Family Papers, Virginia Historical Society.

26. "How Silas Burrows Bought Two Princes out of Slavery," *The Call*, August 8, 1897, available from California Digital Newspaper Collection, Center for Bibliographic Studies and Research, University of California, Riverside, https://cdnc.ucr.edu/cgi-bin/cdnc?a=d&d=SFC18970808.2.184.10.

27. Lawrence Lewis to Bassett, May 30, 1831, Bassett Family Papers, Virginia Historical Society.

28. Letter, printed, dated Fredericksburg, June 1, 1831: proposing a monument to the memory of the mother of George Washington, Rare Books o.s., Virginia Historical Society.

29. George Washington Lewis to Bassett, July 31, 1831, Bassett Family Papers, Virginia Historical Society.
30. George Fayette Washington to Bassett, April 25, 1832, Bassett Family Papers, Virginia Historical Society.
31. Cynthia Kierner, *Beyond the Household: Women's Place in the Early South, 1700–1835* (Ithaca: Cornell University Press, 1998), 189–211.
32. Elizabeth R. Varon, *We Mean to Be Counted: White Women and Politics in Antebellum Virginia* (Chapel Hill: University of North Carolina Press, 1998), 10–14; 41–70; quote on 46. See also Patrick H. Breen, "The Female Antislavery Petition Campaign of 1831–32," *Virginia Magazine of History and Biography* 110, no 3 (2002): 377–98.
33. William G. Shade, *Democratizing the Old Dominion: Virginia and the Second Party System* (Charlottesville: University Press of Virginia, 1996), 57–77; Ronald L. Heinemann et al., *Old Dominion, New Commonwealth: A History of Virginia, 1607–2007* (Charlottesville: University of Virginia Press, 2007), 171–73.
34. Ted Maris-Wolf, *Family Bonds: Free Blacks and Re-Enslavement Law in Antebellum Virginia* (Chapel Hill: University of North Carolina Press, 2015), 27–60.
35. Patrick H. Breen, *The Land Shall Be Deluged in Blood: A New History of the Nat Turner Rebellion* (New York: Oxford University Press, 2015), 98–99.
36. Breen, "The Female Antislavery Petition Campaign of 1831–32."
37. *Acts Passed at a General Assembly of the Commonwealth of Virginia, Begun and Held at the Capitol, in the City of Richmond* (Richmond, 1832), 20–22.
38. *Virginia Herald* (Fredericksburg), April 10, 1833.
39. *Political Arena* (Fredericksburg), May 10, 1833; *Virginia Herald,* May 8, 1833.
40. *Virginia Herald,* May 8, 1833.
41. *Virginia Herald,* May 8, 1833.
42. *Political Arena,* May 10, 1833. The *Arena* published the full text of Bassett's and Jackson's speeches.
43. *Political Arena,* May 10, 1833.
44. Lydia Huntley Sigourney, "The Mother of Washington," in Hetzel, *The Building of a Monument,* 16–17.
45. *Political Arena,* May 10, 1833; *Virginia Herald,* May 8, 1833.
46. Custis, *Recollections,* 149; Hetzel, *The Building of a Monument,* 19–21.

"SHE DID NOT COME UP TO 'OLE MISTIS' IN MAMMY'S EYES!"

Relationships between the Women, Enslaved and Free, of Mount Vernon

MARY V. THOMPSON

Starting about 1980, historians of women's history turned serious attention to the role played by women at the head of southern plantations and, somewhat later, began to examine both sides of the relationships between plantation mistresses and the enslaved women with whom they interacted most closely. Many of these studies tend to focus on plantations and women in the nineteenth century instead of the experiences of white and Black women one hundred years earlier, such as the white women of the extended Washington and Custis families and the enslaved women who worked for them. Examining the relationships between these women, both at Mount Vernon and other family homes, reveals not only the various tensions in these relationships but also the roles enslaved women played in raising younger generations of these families and passing along family traditions. The often fraught interactions of Martha Washington, Hannah Bushrod Washington, and other women of the Washington and Custis families with the enslaved women—named and unnamed—forced to work for them, such as Doll and Charlotte, demonstrate the complexity of female plantation relationships that women's historians have been analyzing over the last decades.

George Washington and Martha Dandridge Custis were married on 6 January 1759 at the bride's home in New Kent County, Virginia. The twenty-six-year-old groom had spent the previous decade trying to improve his station in life, starting out as a county surveyor before moving on to a career as an officer in the colonial military. Most recently, he had been elected to the Virginia House of Burgesses and left the army to take up life as a plantation owner. This was his first marriage. His bride was a twenty-seven-year old widow, whose life over the last decade had been very different from that of her second husband. Where he was primarily involved with business and war, she was focused on family and household. She had been married for seven years to Daniel Parke Custis, the sole surviving heir of John Custis, one of the wealthiest landowners in Virginia. Daniel's sudden death in the summer of 1757 left Martha with the responsibility of raising their two surviving children and protecting the sizable estate they would inherit, which included over 17,000 acres of land and almost two hundred enslaved workers.[1]

In cases where a husband died without making a will, both British common law and Virginia colonial law ensured that his widow would be taken care of by awarding her a life interest or dower rights in one-third of his estate, including the enslaved people, with the other two-thirds being reserved for any heirs after they reached adulthood or were married. Should the widow remarry, control of the dower property was transferred to her new husband, who also controlled any enslaved laborers while the heirs were minors. Upon the death of the widow, her dower property would be divided among the remaining heirs.[2]

Several months after the wedding, George Washington moved his new family to his own plantation in Fairfax County, Virginia. Among the enslaved people who, however unwillingly, accompanied them to Mount Vernon were eight dower slaves: two male waiters, Breechy (age twenty-four) and Mulatto Jack (forty-one); Doll, the thirty-eight-year-old cook, and Beck, her twenty-three-year-old assistant or scullion; Jenny (age thirty-nine), the laundress; Martha Washington's maid, Sally (fifteen); Betty, a twenty-one-year-old seamstress; and Phillis (twenty-five), a spinner. In addition, there were five other enslaved people from the Custis children's share of the estate: Julius, a ten-year-old boy, who "waits on Jacky Custis," Martha's son; Moll, who was nineteen and responsible for waiting on and sewing for both of the children; thirty-nine-year-old Mima, who ironed clothes; and a twelve-year-old girl named Rose, who served as maid to Martha's daughter, Martha Parke Custis, nicknamed Patsy.[3]

In the years to come, Doll would become the matriarch of a large and important family, whose collective experience provides a good example of the way jobs would often be passed along within enslaved families. In the next generation, Doll's daughter Lucy would follow her mother as one of the cooks in the kitchen after Doll became too old and frail to continue that strenuous work. Lucy married Frank Lee, the butler, who was the younger brother of George Washington's long-time valet, William Lee. William was injured in two accidents in the 1780s, which left him disabled and unable to perform his duties. At this point, the third generation of Doll's family came into the picture. Another of Doll's daughters, Alce or Alice, was a spinner, whose son Christopher Sheels eventually replaced William Lee, his uncle by marriage, as Washington's personal servant, while Alce's daughter Anna worked beside her to produce thread. Following the deaths of George and Martha Washington, the young man who served as valet to George Washington Parke Custis (the grandson raised by the Washingtons) was Philip Lee, the son of Lucy and Frank Lee, nephew to William Lee, cousin of Christopher Sheels, and grandson of Old Doll.[4]

Betty, the seamstress who came to Mount Vernon along with Doll, would also become the mother of a prominent family on the estate. She arrived with an infant son, Austin, who grew up to be a waiter in the mansion and later in the official presidential residences in New York and Philadelphia. Betty was the mother of Betty Davis, a spinner, and Tom Davis, a bricklayer, who were probably fathered by Thomas Davis, a hired weaver at Mount Vernon in the 1760s. Finally, Ona Judge and her younger sister Delphy (short for Philadelphia) were Betty's younger children, whose father is believed to have been indentured English tailor, Andrew Judge, who began working on the plantation in 1772. Like her parents, Oney, as she was known to the Washingtons, became very good at sewing and needlework, traits that made her a valuable ladies' maid to Martha Washington, for whom she began working at about the age of ten. Like her older half-brother Austin, Ona accompanied the Washingtons to New York and Philadelphia during the presidency. One of the most intriguing facts about Betty's family was that all of her children were described as mulatto or mixed race, as was she. The identity of Austin's father is not known, but the fathers of the other four children were white men who worked in textile trades, jobs that brought them

Unlike many of the artists who portrayed the first presidential spouse, James Peale captured the look of the sixty-four-year-old woman, who had been managing both hired and enslaved household staff for forty-five years. (Courtesy of the Mount Vernon Ladies' Association)

into contact with Betty. There is neither documentation nor family stories to suggest anything about the nature of these relationships, which may have ranged from love to rape. Betty may have been attracted to white men like her father or perhaps these white tradesmen saw sexual access to Betty as one of the perks of their jobs.[5]

In looking at the skills of the enslaved people she brought to her new home, and the roles expected of a plantation mistress, Martha Washington chose people with whom she had worked for years, who understood her expectations, and could help to make this new plantation a home. Thirty years later, as the Washingtons settled into a different way of life in the northern cities of New York and Philadelphia, enslaved people were once again called on to leave their own families in order to serve as living touches of home in a new location.

According to historian Elizabeth Fox-Genovese, one of the first things a new wife on a plantation needed was to "establish a tone for husband, children, and servants," something a significant number of women could not manage.[6] For Martha, who already had a decade of experience running the domestic side of a plantation, bringing domestic slaves she already knew, who were familiar with her personality, expectations, and proclivities made the transition to Mount Vernon easier; she would not immediately have to win the respect and bend the wills of an entirely new population of unwilling laborers to get breakfast on the table at seven o'clock in the morning, when her husband expected it.[7]

Historian Thavolia Glymph's insights into the world of the plantation mistress focused on a major difference between the management of European estates, where butlers and/or housekeepers ran the household, and American plantations, where household management fell completely to the mistress. While male planters in America, because of their frequent absences from home, typically had several layers of managers between themselves and their enslaved people, their wives, who were pretty much tied to the household, usually did not. Those layers provided distance between masters and the enslaved, which, in Glymph's words "reduce[d] the occasions for conflict" and direct confrontations with their domestic slaves. The lack of that distance led to violence between mistresses and slaves.[8] In contrast, the Washingtons employed both hired housekeepers and stewards/butlers for decades, beginning in the late 1760s and continuing until their deaths. The first housekeeper, Sarah Harle, who worked on the estate between September 1765 and May 1767, was probably hired because of the serious illness—likely epilepsy—of Martha's only surviving daughter, Patsy.[9] She died during a convulsion in the summer of 1773, at the age of seventeen.[10]

Whereas isolation was a cause of stress for many plantation mistresses, it was not such a problem at Mount Vernon. The plantation was situated about ten miles from the nearby city of Alexandria, not far from a major north-south road. In 1768, well before Washington became a household name, the family welcomed dinner guests on 82 and overnight guests on 130 of the 291 days for which there are records. By 1798, they entertained at least 656 dinner guests and 677 overnight guests at Mount Vernon.[11] As George Washington explained to his mother after the Revolutionary War, Mount Vernon was something of "a well-resorted tavern" because "scarcely any strangers who are going from north to south, or from south to north do not spend a day or two at it."[12]

While Martha's grandson George Washington Parke Custis would later write extensively about life with the Washingtons, including details

about several of the enslaved people working in and around these households, it was his oldest sister Eliza who wrote about her relationships
with the family's enslaved domestics when she was a small child—the
source of both affection and frustration. Eliza was especially close to
Moll, the nurse to Martha Washington's children and grandchildren. She
recalled that when she was separated from the two older women, she
would console herself by thinking about the times when her "Grand-
mama" Washington and "Mammy Molly, my old Nurse," would be reunited with her and the little girl would be "overwhelm'd . . . with ca-
resses, when I visited Mt Vernon, & from whom I was ever afflicted to
part." At one point in her childhood, Eliza recalled being very sick with
a "nervous fever" and unable to walk, when "Mammy Molly came to
nurse me, my Grandmother often visited me, & also I almost regretted getting well which was to take them from me." But she also remembered other enslaved "servants" laughing at her from the hallway when
her young father would stand her on the table when she was only three
or four years old to entertain his guests after dinner by singing "very
improper" songs he and a friend had taught her, although it is unclear
whether this embarrassed her or simply added to the fun. Several years
later, following her father's death in 1781, her mother's remarriage two
years later, and the birth of a new half-sibling (the first of many), other
"servants of the House [incited] some jealousy by making me observe
my [Mother's] fondness for her infant."[13] Where Moll and Martha were
both nurturing figures who were recalled with affection, the last two
recollections suggest that the enslaved people were trying to weaken ties
between members of the slaveholders' family.

Martha Washington took seriously her responsibility to teach the
next generation in the family to be good housekeepers. Of her three
granddaughters, Eleanor (Nelly) Parke Custis, the youngest, was especially close to the grandmother who raised her. Martha took advantage
of the opportunities available in New York and Philadelphia to ensure
that Nelly received one of the finest educations possible for a young
woman of the time.[14] After completing her schooling in her late teens,
Nelly was described as something of a paragon. Polish nobleman Julian
Ursyn Niemcewicz, who spent about two weeks at Mount Vernon in
1798, wrote that she was "one of those celestial figures that nature pro-
duces only rarely, that the inspiration of painters has sometimes divined

and that one cannot see without ecstasy. Her sweetness is equal to her beauty."[15] Following the family's return to Mount Vernon upon George Washington's retirement from the presidency in March 1797, Nelly began training for the next stage of her life—as a wife and plantation mistress. In a letter to a friend in Philadelphia, she boasted that she was now "deputy Housekeeper."[16] Surviving family documents show that Nelly developed into a good housekeeper, but the shift from life as the adored daughter in a prominent household to being the wife of a sickly and not terribly successful nephew of George Washington, mother to eight children (only four of whom survived childhood), on an isolated plantation, and having the responsibility of running her own household changed her lively, outgoing personality almost completely. No stories of her relationships with her own enslaved staff have yet been found.[17]

Within days of George Washington's retirement from the presidency, the family headed back to Mount Vernon in March 1797. Martha Washington readily admitted to friends and family members that she was not happy with the situation she found at home. To a younger sister, she explained that she was "obliged to be my [own] Housekeeper which takes up the greatest part of my time,—our cook Hercules went away so that I am as much at a loss for a cook as for a house keeper.—altogether I am sadly [plagued]."[18] Over the years, six white women worked closely with Martha Washington as hired housekeepers at Mount Vernon, as did two white men, variously described as housekeepers, butlers, or stewards. The last of these would be an English widow, Eleanor Forbes, who arrived at Mount Vernon in December 1797.[19] In addition, there were several relatives who filled in as mistresses at Mount Vernon during both the American Revolution and George Washington's presidency, when Martha Washington was away from home for long periods of time. These women faced a number of challenges in their relationships with both their own enslaved people and those of the Washingtons.

One of those earlier substitutes for Martha Washington was the wife of one of the most important and trusted management figures at Mount Vernon, Lund Washington, who was the farm manager on the plantation for twenty years (1765–1785), including the entire period of the Revolutionary War. A third-cousin of George Washington, Lund was a bachelor for the majority of his term of employment. That changed in 1779, when he married another cousin, Elizabeth Foote, and brought her to live at Mount Vernon, where she, too, won the respect of George Washington. She was one of three women described in his will as "my friends," to each of whom he left the sum of one hundred dollars to purchase a mourning ring in his memory. Known as Betsy, Lund's new wife was deeply religious but differed from most of the eighteenth-century women in the family by being an evangelical Anglican. She kept a spiritual journal for seventeen years, beginning shortly before her marriage to Lund, whom she described as her "dear partner and companion." Within the pages of this small work, which was initially intended as a guide to household management for any daughters she might have, she periodically confided her hopes and dreams for the future, her fears for her husband and children, and her relationships with the family's enslaved people.[20]

Several years after her marriage, while living at Mount Vernon, Betsy wrote about the kind of relationship she wanted to have with those African and African American women she supervised, who would have belonged to George and Martha Washington and her own family. In cases where she believed they had done something wrong, she wanted to

> talk to them in a kind & friendly way, pointing out their fault with calmness,—but at the same time with a steadiness that they may know I will not be impos'd upon—& I will endeavor to make them think I do not wish they should behave well for my sake, but because it will be pleasing in the eyes of the almighty—& that if they will do their business for his sake, I shall be well serv'd if they never think of me,—which is truly the case—I do most sincerely wish for their sakes—they may do their business with an earnest desire to please him—nothing would give me so great pleasure as having a truly religious family—not led away with Baptistical notions— but a religion that effectually touches the heart—no outside show.[21]

Betsy hoped that she would never rebuke the women she held in slavery in front of someone else. She never wanted to use "harsh expressions, because they are in my power—such as fool—Blockhead—vile wretches." Historian Lauren Winner notes that, although Betsy never mentions the names of slaveholders who did "deride their slaves with [such] epithets . . . it is reasonable to suppose that [she] may have been thinking about the mistress she would have seen up close during the five years of marriage she lived at Mount Vernon: Martha Custis Washington." Winner also observes that, while Martha Washington was away from Mount Vernon for most of this time, Betsy would still have seen her during her visits home, which added up to slightly more than a year through the end of the war, and then was with her for roughly nine months before she and Lund moved to Hayfield, a nearby plantation of their own.[22] It should be pointed out that Betsy was no inexperienced girl at the time of her marriage. Thought to have been about thirty-three years old when she moved to Mount Vernon, she would have had the opportunity to meet and observe many slave owners by the time she became a member of the Washington household, so Martha Washington was not the only plantation mistress Betsy would have seen interacting with enslaved people.[23]

In her efforts to bring the gospel to the enslaved women she directed, Betsy provided reading lessons and Bibles to them and also tried to conform to the Anglican tradition of holding family devotions and prayers twice a day. Several years after she and Lund moved to their own home a few miles from Mount Vernon, she wrote of her frustrations that their enslaved people were drawn to the more evangelical Baptists, who were welcoming to them and critical of slavery at this point. Betsy complained that they had "got so Baptistical in their notions, as to think they commit a crime to join with me in Prayer morning & evening," noting that they were disappearing when it was time for the devotional services and looking "quite angry" if they were forced to attend. She tried to discuss this issue with them individually but was hurt that nothing she said could convince them that there was nothing wrong about praying with her. She eventually gave up trying to have family devotions, something that gave her "great concern—but I trust as my gracious God knows the desire I had to serve him daily in my family—that I shall not be answerable for not having family Prayers—I persever'd in it as long as I could—until it was a mere farce to attempt it any longer."[24] By thwarting her attempts to draw them into worshiping with her, Betsy's domestic slaves were using passive resistance to keep her out of their private lives.

During an interview with Martha Washington's former enslaved ladies' maid, Ona Judge, about fifty years after her escape from the family in Philadelphia, the elderly woman noted that she had not received any "moral instruction" while she lived with the Washingtons, indicating that they did not have family devotions in their home and probably that she did not attend church services with them. She stated that she never heard George Washington pray, "and does not believe that he was accustomed to," while noting that "Mrs. Washington used to read prayers, but I don't call that praying."[25] This statement about Martha's prayer routine (she had private devotions each morning and at bedtime) suggests that reading a prayerbook was too staid and not heartfelt enough to appeal to Ona, which, in the eyes of the enslaved women at Hayfield, may also have been a problem with Betsy's family devotions.[26]

It may have been during her individual talks with the enslaved women in her household that Betsy learned they initially thought her inclusion of them in family devotions meant that she would "never find fault of them, nor ever reprimand them for anything at all." They eventually became disillusioned "and thought my religion was all preten[s]e," an explanation that made sense to her, because "where a person professes to be a believer in Jesus, there is no . . . charity extended to them, but rather all their words & actions will be sifted, their mistakes exaggerated, & if any part of their conduct will bear a double construction it will generally be viewed in [*illegible word*] most unfavourable light."[27] It is also possible that they considered Betsy as something of a hypocrite.

There may have been other tensions between Betsy Washington and her enslaved domestics. During the course of her marriage, she gave birth to two daughters, both of whom were named Lucinda. Described as "Lovely" and "healthy," the first child died at fourteen months of age and the second at thirteen months. Family recollections noted that both children died of "Convulsion fits," after being ill for "about the same number of days."[28] Lund was planning to emancipate his family's enslaved people, which a skeptical relative attributed to the fact that the "manumission delusion had commenced," but Lund was quoted as saying that "his Slaves should not serve anybody but himself and his Wife." While neither Lund nor Betsy suspected foul play in the deaths of their children, others in the family had doubts: "An opinion was entertained that his Slaves knew of this declaration [about freeing them upon his death] and had determined to remove [Lund's] Children in order to secure its fulfilment," perhaps through poisoning. Betsy ultimately followed Lund's wishes and freed those enslaved to him.[29]

As she came to the end of her spiritual journal late in 1796, Betsy

Foote Washington hinted at her distrust of the enslaved women who had served her for years. Having no surviving daughters with whom to leave it, she worried about the disposition of the little book and feared that her "female servants will take every manuscript Book they can lay their hands on, & many of my other religious Books—tho' it is my intention, if I am in my senses when on my death bed, [that] I should have a friend with me—to warn them of my servants."[30] As we will see, she would not be the only family member to express similar fears as she lay dying.

During the first half of George Washington's presidency, the Mount Vernon estate was managed by two younger relatives. A nephew, George Augustine Washington, took on George Washington's role, while his wife, who was Martha Washington's niece, Frances (Fanny) Bassett Washington, saw to the domestic duties that were the purview of her aunt. The chronic illness of Fanny's husband, who was dying of consumption (tuberculosis), and her own gentle personality interfered with the younger woman's ability to perform her duties in the household, particularly the management of the enslaved domestic staff and the orphaned children of the extended Washington family being raised there. Throughout their

Robert Edge Pine, who visited Mount Vernon in 1785, painted this portrait of Fanny Bassett just months before her wedding to George Augustine Washington. (Courtesy of the Mount Vernon Ladies' Association)

years at Mount Vernon, consumption plagued the younger couple and eventually led to both their deaths.

Fanny's mother was Martha's favorite sister, Anna Maria (Nancy), who was the wife of Burwell Bassett of Eltham Plantation. When Nancy died in late 1777, Martha wrote to her widower to say that her sister had "often mentioned my taking my dear Fanny if she [Nancy] should be taken away before she grew up—If you will let [sic] her come to live with me, I will with the greatest [pleasure] take her and be a parent and mother to her as long as I live." At the time, Martha was spending considerable time each year at her husband's various military headquarters in the North, and her daughter-in-law was about to give birth to another baby, so she could not then go to southern Virginia to pick up ten-year-old Fanny. It is also possible that the girl's father could not face losing another family member so soon after the death of his wife, so it was seven years before Fanny became a permanent member of the Washington household in 1784. Less than a year later, Fanny and George Augustine were married at Mount Vernon on 15 October 1785.[31] They would have four children in the eight years of their marriage, three of whom survived to adulthood.[32]

The closeness between Fanny and Martha grew into a strong working relationship during the presidency. Their regular correspondence documents the duties for which they were both responsible, many of which involved interactions with enslaved men and women: menu-planning; ensuring that meals got to the table on time; greeting and making guests feel comfortable; oversight of the poultry yard and kitchen garden; preserving fruits and vegetables for use in winter; ensuring that meats were properly salted, smoked, and stored; supervising the enslaved housemaids and butlers, so that the fireplaces were cleaned, the china and glassware sparkled and were ready for use, the beds had been scalded and scrubbed to keep them free of bedbugs; and clothing was cleaned and mended.[33]

Martha Washington was very close to the enslaved seamstresses who worked with her to provide clothing for their community, and she knew them well. One of these women was singled out in a surviving letter. After noting that she had been pleased to learn that domestic affairs at Mount Vernon were going so well, Martha remarked to Fanny that "sickness is to be expected and [Charlotte] will lay herself up for as little as any one will," a reference to a common form of enslaved people's passive resistance—feigning illness. This letter was written in the summer, the season when mosquitos brought malaria to both free and enslaved residents of Mount Vernon, and perhaps a non-rebellious reason why Charlotte might have been ill. Several years later, Martha noticed from a Mount Vernon report that Charlotte was sick again, and she asked that the doctor be brought in to care for her.[34] Early in 1793, Charlotte got into an argument with farm manager Anthony Whiting, which resulted in a thrashing (the immediacy of which was against the rules at Mount Vernon at that time), with a follow-up beating two days later, after she refused to work because she had been injured by the first punishment. She was furious, stating that she had not been whipped in fourteen years and threatened to get word to Martha Washington. The farm manager immediately wrote to the president to get his side of the story out first.[35]

Fanny came in for criticism as she tried to manage domestic affairs while also caring for a terribly ill husband and three small children. Martha complained in one letter to her about the supervision being given to her grandchildren's half-siblings by their mother's enslaved maid, writing that "it was a very careless trick in [Mrs. Stuart's] maid, to let the children break the Looking glass" and then asked Fanny to pick out a replacement mirror.[36] There was no understanding that the enslaved maid may well have felt unable to discipline the children in her charge. In a telling letter, Martha wrote to console her niece, following the death of a young enslaved child: "I am truly sorry that [anything] should happen in your family to give you pain. Black children are liable to so many accidents and complaints that one is [hardly] sure of keeping them[.] I hope you will not find in him much loss[.]" Martha then let slip her thoughts on the people with whom she spent so much of her life, "the Blacks are so bad in their nature that they have not the least [gratitude] for the kindness that may be [showed] to them."[37] This last remark suggests several things. Martha had had very little contact with free Black people and, to the best of our knowledge only had sustained relationships with those who were enslaved—a role that led to all sorts of resistance, such as stealing, breaking tools, feigning illness, procrastinating, and doing jobs poorly so they would never be asked to do them again, which she would have interpreted as behaving badly. She could not see that enslavement was the reason these things happened. Second,

Martha had probably been very angry—and even hurt—over the years, when trusted enslaved people, individuals for whom she had perhaps interceded or done a favor, later showed resistance by stealing, shirking work, or even running away (see the examples of Frank Lee, Charlotte, and Ona Judge in this chapter).

It is clear that Martha Washington thought that the mistress—or in Fanny's case, the acting mistress—should have custody of the keys used to lock up foods, textiles, and all manner of products in order to stave off theft. It was obviously a question of great importance when Martha wrote: "I do not know what keys you have—it is highly necessary that the beds and bed cloths of all [kinds] should be aired if you have the keys I beg you will make Caroline [an enslaved housemaid] put all the things of every kind out to air and Brush and Clean all the places and rooms that they are in . . . when the President comes down [to Mount Vernon] I beg you will get the key of my closet if you have not got it."[38] In the words of historian Thavolia Glymph, "Control, even symbolic, of the keys to smokehouses, corn cribs, and other stores of supplies constituted for many mistresses, the very essence of adherence to the ideology of domestic authority, the most 'obvious emblem of female domestic authority.'"[39]

After making a quick trip to Mount Vernon by himself, George Washington expressed surprise at finding that so much good wine had been served to plantation visitors. Martha, in turn, wrote to tell Fanny that it had "never been his intention to give wine or [go] to any Expence to entertain people that came to Mount [Vernon] out of curiosity to see the place." If the practice was continued, the family would "have but very little for ourselves if we should come home." Fanny should give them rum instead. Her aunt closed with an admonition that she "not give . . . another Bottle out of the vault" and a caution about Frank Lee, the enslaved butler, that she had "not the least doubt but Frank drinks as much wine as he gives to the visitors—and rum [both],—and wish you not to give more out unless the President should order it."[40]

George Washington's view of Fanny is revealed in a letter to another niece, Harriot, the orphaned daughter of his next youngest brother, Samuel Washington. After their father's death, Harriot and her two brothers were split up, with the boys coming to George and Martha Washington and Harriot bouncing between several family members.

During one of the times the awkward teenager was at Mount Vernon, she received some advice from her uncle George, in an attempt to help her understand the hard facts about her social and financial situation: "Your cousins [George Augustine and Fanny], with whom you live are well-qualified to give you advice, and I am sure they will if you are disposed to receive it. But if you are disobliging, self-willed, and untowardly it is hardly to be expected that they will engage themselves in unpleasant disputes with you, especially Fanny, whose mild and placid temper will not permit her to exceed the limits of wholesome admonition or gentle rebuke." He also suggested that Harriot "become the intimate companion of and aid to [Fanny] in the domestic concerns of the family. . . . The merits and benefits of it would redound more to your advantage in your progress thro' life, and to that person with whom you may in due time form a matrimonial connection . . . but to none would such a circumstance afford more real satisfaction, than to Your affectionate Uncle." In other words, it was time for her to start learning how to be the mistress of a plantation.[41]

As in the case of Elizabeth Foote Washington, the end of life could be full of tension for a dying widow surrounded primarily by the enslaved people with whom she had spent the majority of her life. That was also true of another relative, Hannah Bushrod Washington, the widow of George Washington's favorite younger brother, John Augustine Washington I. Like Betsy, Hannah was someone George Washington considered a friend and to whom he left money to purchase a mourning ring in his memory.[42] In the spring of 1801, Hannah lay on her deathbed as she drew up her last will and testament. Then sixty-five years old, Hannah was the daughter and sole heir of John and Jenny Corbin Bushrod of Bushfield Plantation, in Westmoreland County, Virginia. Except for the few years she and Jack lived at Mount Vernon as newlyweds, looking after the plantation while George was with the army during the Seven Years' War, Bushfield had always been Hannah's home. It was there that she and Jack raised their six children. It was there that she buried her parents, youngest son, and beloved husband. Now, after seventeen years as a widow, she needed to deal with her possessions.

Mixed in with various bequests and instructions were several telling references to the enslaved people who had served Hannah over the years. As she chose which furnishings and household goods would go to various family members, Hannah abruptly shifted gears and began to discuss "a negro woman [called] Judy who is a very good cook, my daughter in law Hannah [Lee] Washington is by me left at liberty to sell the said Judy if she thinks it most for her [son's] advantage and put the money received for her to Interest. . . . That she was a very good cook— her age I suppose to be about forty and a very healthy hearty woman, she also spins, washes and Irons extremely well."[43] Hannah clearly respected Judy for her skills in the kitchen and her talents at various textile chores. This expertise, together with the fact that she was still young and healthy enough to work, meant that Judy would be a valuable addition to another household—and a means of leaving cash to Hannah's eleven-year-old grandson, Richard Henry Lee Washington.

Returning to the division of various possessions, Hannah came once more to the issue of the family's enslaved workers. She began by noting that her late husband had bequeathed to her "the following slaves to dispose of as I chose at my death provided I gave them to our own children[.] [The] slaves are as follows—Billey WHO IS dead since [John Augustine's will was written,] his wife [Jenny,] their daughter [Venus] who has brought a daughter since [John Augustine's death] called Bettey, these three slaves I give to my beloved grandson Richard Henry Lee Washington."[44]

There was another member of this small family with whom Hannah was particularly concerned: "a lad called West, son of Venus, who was born before my husband's will was made and not therein mentioned, I offered to buy him of my dear sons Bushrod and Corbin Washington, but they generously refused to sell him but presented the boy to me as a gift." Hannah noted that she most earnestly wished and desired that West "be inoculated for the small pox" as soon as possible, and then he was to be "bound to a good tradesmen [sic] until the age of twenty one years, after which he is to be free the rest of his life."[45] Her granddaughters were bequeathed "all my wearing apparel of every sort, to be entirely and equally divided among the three." Almost as an afterthought, Hannah directed that "some of my most indifferent things" her daughter-in-law, Hannah Lee Washington, and granddaughter, Anne Aylett Robinson, "may at their own discretion, give [to several enslaved house servants] Letty, Jenny, Suck & Venus though the two last mentioned treated me with great disrespect in my last hours," indicating perhaps long-standing tensions with Suck and Venus.[46]

Family records do not reveal what issues there were with Suck, but there is little doubt about the cause of tension between Hannah and Venus—it was most likely Venus's son, West Ford, whose story is widely known at this point. He was brought to Mount Vernon when Hannah's oldest son, Bushrod Washington, inherited the estate after Martha Washington's death in 1802. Following his manumission, in about 1805, Ford was hired for positions of responsibility and trust by several generations of Washingtons at Mount Vernon. One referred to him as "my venerable Lieutenant," and he became a familiar figure to the thousands of visitors who came to the estate each year. In his will, Bushrod Washington left 160 acres of land to Ford, who later sold them in order to purchase a slightly larger tract of 214 acres, the nucleus of a free Black community known as Gum Springs. Ford's descendants believe that his father was either George Washington or Hannah's eldest son, Bushrod Washington. My own belief is that Ford was the son of George Washington's nephew William Augustine Washington—Hannah's youngest son, who died in a shooting accident at his school in early 1784.[47] Conflict or competition between West Ford's mother, Venus, and his paternal grandmother, Hannah, who may well have seen him as the last link to the son she lost as a teenager, could easily account for the fraught emotional situation at Hannah's deathbed.

For later generations of the Washington-Custis family, those elderly enslaved people, who had served the family for decades, played a role in passing along the family's oral history. The woman known at Arlington as "Mammy" had a close relationship with Martha Washington's great-great-granddaughters and told them stories about life at Mount Vernon. According to Agnes Lee, the fifth of seven children born to Robert E. Lee and his wife, Mary Anna Randolph Custis, Mammy was born about 1777 or 1779, making her somewhere between seventy-five and seventy-seven years old in the mid-1850s, when Agnes began keeping a journal. Mammy died a little before Christmas in 1855.

Several months later, fifteen-year-old Agnes noted that the elderly woman had been a great storyteller: "What tales she could tell of 'those good old times' of Mrs. Washington's beauty & good management." As a girl or young woman, Mammy had been "one of the out-door gals & would run to open the gate for the Gen[eral]." One of the biggest family events in the last year of George Washington's life was the wedding of Martha Washington's youngest granddaughter, Nelly Custis, to George

Washington's nephew, Lawrence Lewis, which took place on 22 February 1799—George Washington's final birthday. Mammy told Agnes that "when my beautiful Aunt Lewis was married . . . ole Mistis [Martha Washington] let all the servants come in to see it & gave them such good things to eat." She recalled "how Ole Mistis was dressed so splendid, in a light flowered satin your Aunt Lewis all in something white, beautiful too." But though a celebrated beauty Nelly "did not come up to 'ole Mistis' in Mammy's eyes!" The elderly woman also recalled something about George Washington: "she could not see why so much fuss was made over 'the gen[era]l, he was only a man!', a very good master he was sure, but she didn't suppose he was so much better than anyone else." She went on to say, "O those nice talks! we [sic] won't have any more."⁴⁸ In praising Mammy's long-term faithfulness, Agnes was exhibiting the paternalism so common in the American South, both prior to and after the Civil War. And in telling her tales of long-ago life at Mount Vernon, the elderly woman was helping to preserve and pass on the oral history and traditions of the family that enslaved her.

For all the affection Agnes felt toward Mammy, it appears that the younger woman may not have known her given name, but only knew her by a title relating to her job, which involved caring for several generations of children in the family. Likely, the work done by the enslaved people on the plantation was considered their primary purpose for being. Alternatively, it might have been considered rude for a young teenager to refer to someone so much older than herself by her given name, rather than a title, even if she were enslaved. Many years ago, Arlington's long-time curator, Agnes Mullins, noted that the nurse or "Mammy" at that plantation was originally known as "Nurse Judy" and later as "Old Mammy."⁴⁹ The most likely candidate to have been "Mammy" was Judy or Judith, who was the granddaughter of "Old Doll," the cook brought to Mount Vernon in the spring of 1759, as well as the daughter of Alce or Alice, and the sister of Christopher Sheels.⁵⁰

Judy gave birth to at least two children of her own—a daughter named Louisa, born about 1801 at Mount Vernon, and a son she called John, who was probably born at Arlington in 1804. Louisa was freed on 1 March 1803, when she was two years old, while John had to wait for freedom until 1818, when he was fourteen. Both of the children were thought to be the offspring of Martha Washington's grandson, George

Washington Parke Custis, who was the owner of Arlington.[51] Judy's children were both conceived when Custis was a bachelor, prior to his marriage at the age of twenty-three on 7 July 1804.[52] These were not, however, the only enslaved children believed to have been fathered by Custis, whose only legitimate daughter, Mary Anna Randolph Custis Lee, was said to have forty mulatto half-siblings in the Washington area; those children were often freed or otherwise cared for by Custis.[53]

In conclusion, Martha Washington's experiences as a plantation mistress were both similar to and different from those of other women in the extended Washington-Custis family. What they had in common was a complicated mix of thoughts and emotions about the enslaved people who were their closest neighbors, and especially the enslaved women who were bound to serve them for life, who often worked beside them, and were there during both good times and bad.

Several months before his death, George Washington made arrangements in his will to free those people who were enslaved to him after the death of his beloved wife. About a year later, however, following the advice of several men in the family, Martha Washington decided to free them on 1 January 1801.[54] Following a visit to Martha about that time, Abigail Adams wrote that the emancipation was taking place because of fears for Martha's safety: "[W]hat could she do. [In] the state in which they were left by the General, to be free at her death, she did not feel as tho her Life was safe in their Hands, many of whom would be told that it was [in their] interest to get rid of her—She therefore was advised to [set] them all free at the close of the year." Noting that this action involved a bit less than half of those enslaved on the plantation, Adams wrote that those who would soon be manumitted were anxious about what freedom would mean for themselves and their families. She confided that Martha was "[distressed] for them . . . and very many of them are already [miserable] at the thought of their Lot. . . . She feels a parent and a wife [to them]."[55] Martha's words about herself, feeling like a parent, suggest both the responsibility she felt for feeding, clothing, and caring for her formerly enslaved people, while feeling like a wife suggests affection and a sense of duty.

While some of those who were about to be freed may have been telling Martha what they thought she wanted to hear, still others undoubtedly had very real misgivings because they were married to Custis dower slaves who could not be freed by the Washingtons, and their families would consesquently be divided among her four grandchildren. Many were probably concerned about supporting their families. What, for example, was a newly freed woman like thirty-six-year-old Silla, who lived with her six children at Mount Vernon's Dogue Run Farm, going to do? Would anyone hire her to plow their fields, as she had done for the Washingtons for years? How often would she and the children be able to see her husband Joe, a dower slave who would remain enslaved to the Custises?

Martha Dandridge Custis Washington died on 22 May 1802, surrounded by her grandchildren, their families, and long-time friends. The division of the Custis dower slaves would take place not long afterward. Other women in the family, in life and as they were dying, experienced fears and tension with those enslaved to them, based on isolation, religious expression, personality, and sexual exploitation. George Washington's reputation drew hundreds of people to his plantation each year, greatly reducing the stress of isolation and providing an incentive for the family, including the mistress, not to behave badly. While Martha had to know how to run the domestic side of a plantation, and did so, there were many years when hired white stewards and housekeepers directly supervised the enslaved domestic staff, further reducing the possibility of conflict between the mistress of Mount Vernon and the enslaved people of the household. There is evidence of closeness and respect between Martha, Charlotte, and Mammy. Still, Martha Washington, the other women of the extended Washington-Custis family, and the enslaved women forced to work for them, faced considerable conflict over the years that often came to a head at the end of the slaveholders' lives, when they found themselves at the mercy of the women whose labor they coerced.

Notes

I would like to thank Charlene Boyer Lewis and George W. Boudreau for recognizing the need for a book on the women in George Washington's world, the University of Virginia Press for agreeing to publish it, and my little family, Anthony Bates (husband) and Shalimar (cat), for their patience in dealing with my frustration at trying to tell this story in the pages required.

1. For background on Daniel Parke Custis's family, including their fraught relationship with those enslaved to them, see William Byrd II, *The Secret Diary of William Byrd of Westover, 1709–1712*, ed. Louis B. Wright and Marion Tinling (Richmond: The Dietz Press, 1941), 34–35, 205, 216, 240, 249n, 307, 338, 481, 494, 533, 579. For historians who have tackled the issue of plantation mistresses and their enslaved property, see Catherine Clinton, *Plantation Mistress: Woman's World in the Old South* (New York: Pantheon, 1982); Elizabeth Fox-Genovese, *Within the Plantation Household: Black and White Women of the Old South* (Chapel Hill: University of North Carolina Press, 1988); Thavolia Glymph, *Out of the House of Bondage: The Transformation of the Plantation* (Cambridge: Cambridge University Press, 2012); Stephanie E. Jones-Rogers, *They Were Her Property: White Women as Slave Owners in the American South* (New Haven: Yale University Press, 2019).

2. For Virginia law concerning issues relating to enslaved people in intestate estates and other estate issues pertaining to slavery faced by the Washingtons, see Virginia, *The Statutes at Large: Being a Collection of All the Laws of Virginia, from the First Session of the Legislature, in the Year 1619*, 13 volumes, ed. William Waller Hening (Richmond: Samuel Pleasants, Jr., 1809–23), 5:445, 446, 464; 11:39–40; 12:145–46, 150.

3. George Washington (hereafter GW), "The Estate of Daniel Parke Custis," [circa 1759], in Martha Washington (hereafter MW), *"Worthy Partner": The Papers of Martha Washington*, comp. Joseph E. Fields (Westport, CT: Greenwood Press, 1994), 126.

4. See GW, "A List . . . of All My Negroes," 18 February 1786, in GW, *The Diaries of George Washington*, ed. Donald Jackson and Dorothy Twohig (Charlottesville: University Press of Virginia, 1978), 4:277–83 (hereafter 1786 Slave List), and "Negroes Belonging to George Washington in His Own Right and by Marriage," [June 1799], and "A List of Negroes Hired from Mrs. French," [15 July 1799], *The Writings of George Washington* (Washington: US Government Printing Office, 1940), 37:256–68, 308–9 (hereafter 1799 Slave Lists); Murray H. Nelligan, "'Old Arlington': The Story of the Lee Mansion National Memorial" (unpublished report prepared for the U.S. Department of the Interior, National Park Service, Washington, DC, 1953), 214.

5. For a fuller treatment of Ona's story, see Erica Armstrong Dunbar, *Never Caught: The Washingtons' Relentless Pursuit of Their Runaway Slave, Ona Judge* (New York, NY: 37INK/Atria Books, 2017) and Mary V. Thompson, *"The Only Unavoidable Subject of Regret": George Washington, Slavery, and the Enslaved Community at Mount Vernon* (Charlottesville: University of Virginia Press, 2019), 285–90. The current convention is to call this young

woman by the name she used as a free woman, Ona Judge (or Ona Judge Staines after her marriage). At Mount Vernon, both she and a young niece were called Oney, and it is by that name that they appear in the Washington papers.

6. Fox-Genovese, *Within the Plantation Household,* 114–15.

7. For breakfast, see Mary V. Thompson, "'Served up in Excellent Order': Everyday Dining at Mount Vernon," in *Dining with the Washingtons: Historic Recipes, Entertaining, and Hospitality from Mount Vernon,* ed. Stephen A. McLeod (Mount Vernon, VA: Mount Vernon Ladies' Association, 2011), 37–38.

8. Glymph, *Out of the House of Bondage,* 50–52.

9. For the hire of Sarah Harle, see GW, *The Papers of George Washington, Colonial Series,* ed. W. W. Abbot and Dorothy Twohig (Charlottesville: University Press of Virginia, 1990), 7:430n1.

10. MW to Mrs. Margaret Green, [29 September 1760], *"Worthy Partner,"* 131. For more on Patsy's illness and death and their effects on the family, see Mary V. Thompson, *"In the Hands of a Good Providence": Religion in the Life of George Washington* (Charlottesville: University of Virginia Press, 2008), 54, 58, 94, 117–18, 121, 136–37.

11. Mary V. Thompson, "'That Hospitable Mansion': Welcoming Guests at Mount Vernon," in McLeod, *Dining with the Washingtons,* 11–12, 216n8.

12. GW to Mary Ball Washington, 15 February 1787, *The Papers of George Washington, Confederation Series,* ed. W. W. Abbot and Dorothy Twohig (Charlottesville: University Press of Virginia, 1997), 5:35.

13. Eliza Parke Custis Law, "Self-Portrait: Eliza Custis, 1808," ed. William D. Hoyt Jr., *Virginia Magazine of History and Biography* 53, no. 2 (April 1945): 93–94, 97, 99.

14. MW to Mercy Otis Warren, 26 December 1789, in MW, *"Worthy Partner,"* 224.

15. Julian Ursyn Niemcewicz, *Under Their Vine and Fig Tree: Travels through America in 1797–1799,* trans. and ed. Metchie J. E. Budka (Elizabeth, NJ: The Grassmann Publishing Company, 1965), 97.

16. Nelly Custis to Elizabeth Bordley, 18 March 1797, in *George Washington's Beautiful Nelly: The Letters of Eleanor Parke Custis Lewis to Elizabeth Bordley Gibson, 1794–1851,* ed. Patricia Brady (Columbia: University of South Carolina Press, 1991), 32.

17. For Nelly as a household manager, see Eleanor Parke Custis Lewis, *Nelly Custis Lewis's Housekeeping Book,* ed. Patricia Brady Schmit (New Orleans: Historic New Orleans Collection, 1982). For more on that topic, as well

as the sharp change in Nelly's life and personality after her marriage, see Brady, *George Washington's Beautiful Nelly*, 5–9, 17–73. For her adult ideas about slavery and the need for gradual emancipation, see Brady, 199.

18. MW to Elizabeth Dandridge Henley, 20 August 1797, in MW, *"Worthy Partner,"* 307.

19. Thompson, *"The Only Unavoidable Subject of Regret,"* 79, 382n11.

20. For the identification of Lund and Elizabeth Foote Washington and a basic description of her journal, see Sheridan Harvey et al., eds., *American Women: A Library of Congress Guide for the Study of Women's History and Culture in the United States* (Washington, DC: Library of Congress, 2001), 149. For more on the contents of the journal, see Thompson, *"In the Hands of a Good Providence,"* 98–99, 103–6; Thompson, *"The Only Unavoidable Subject of Regret,"* 38, 208, 209–10, 274, 373n38. For Elizabeth Foote Washington's relationship with George Washington and his bequest to her, see *The Writings of George Washington*, 37:287, 287n36.

21. Thompson, *"The Only Unavoidable Subject of Regret,"* 208.

22. Lauren F. Winner, *A Cheerful and Comfortable Faith: Anglican Religious Practice in the Elite Households of Eighteenth-Century Virginia* (New Haven: Yale University Press, 2010), 112, 213n60.

23. For Betsy Washington's age at the time she married Lund, see "Elizabeth Washington," Geni, last updated 1 December 2014, https://www.geni.com /people/ElizabethWashington/6000000004047287768.

24. Thompson, *"In the Hands of a Good Providence,"* 104; Thompson, *"The Only Unavoidable Subject of Regret,"* 209–10.

25. "Washington's Runaway Slave, and How Portsmouth Freed Her," *Frank W. Miller's Portsmouth, New Hampshire, Weekly*, 2 June 1877.

26. For Martha Washington's daily schedule, including her religious devotions, see George Washington Parke Custis, *Recollections and Private Memoirs of Washington, by His Adopted Son, George Washington Parke Custis, with a Memoir of the Author, by His Daughter; and Illustrative and Explanatory Notes, by Benson J. Lossing* (1860; reprint edition, Bridgewater, VA: American Foundation, 1999), 514. Augusta Blanche Berard, "Arlington and Mount Vernon 1856 as Described in a Letter of Augusta Blanche Berard," ed. Clayton Torrence, *Virginia Magazine of History and Biography* 57, no. 2 (April 1949): 162. Eliza Ambler Brent Carrington, "A Visit to Mount Vernon—A Letter of Mrs. Edward Carrington to Her Sister, Mrs. George Fisher," *William and Mary College Quarterly Historical Magazine*, 2nd ser., 18, no. 2 (April 1938): 201. For the context of Marth Washington's activities, see Clinton, *Plantation Mistress*, 20.

27. Thompson, *"The Only Unavoidable Subject of Regret,"* 209–10.
28. Lund Washington, *Lund Washington's History of His Family* (Bristol: Frank Milton; Greenville, SC: E. D. Sloan, Jr., 1998), 12–13.
29. Washington, *Lund Washington's History,* 12–13.
30. Harvey et al., *American Women,* 149.
31. MW to Burwell Bassett, 22 December 1777, in MW, *"Worthy Partner,"* 175; GW, entries for 1 January, 14 and 15 October 1785, in GW, *The Diaries of George Washington,* 4:72, 72n, 206, 206n.
32. For the children of George Augustine and Fanny Bassett Washington (hereafter FBW), see GW, entries for 10, 24, and 25 April 1787, GW, *The Diaries of George Washington,* ed. Donald Jackson and Dorothy Twohig (Charlottesville: University Press of Virginia, 1979), 5:131, 142, 143; MW to FBW, 19 April 1791, and MW to Mary Stillson Lear, 3 November 1796, in MW, *"Worthy Partner,"* 230, 231n2, 293, 294n2, 294n6.
33. See, for example, MW to FBW, 1 July 1792, in MW, *Worthy Partner,* 238–39.
34. MW to FBW, [July 1789], in MW, *Worthy Partner,* 217; and GW to William Pearce, 12 January 1794, in GW, *The Writings of George Washington,* 33:242.
35. Thompson, *"The Only Unavoidable Subject of Regret,"* 54–56, 269.
36. MW to FBW, 22 April 1792, in MW, *"Worthy Partner,"* 237.
37. MW to FBW, 24 May 1795, in MW, *"Worthy Partner,"* 287.
38. MW to FBW, 2 June 1794, in MW, *"Worthy Partner,"* 267. For another letter dealing with keys, see MW to FBW, 30 November 1794, in MW, *"Worthy Partner,"* 281. For more on Fanny having control of the keys in Martha's absence, see GW to Tobias Lear, 12 December 1794, in GW, *The Writings of George Washington,* 34:53.
39. Glymph, *Out of the House of Bondage,* 84.
40. MW to FBW, 30 November 1794, in MW, *"Worthy Partner,"* 281. For George Washington's own statements about this issue, including what categories of visitors should be served what types of wine, see GW to William Pearce, 23 November 1794, in GW, *The Writings of George Washington,* 34:41–2, 53.
41. GW to Harriot Washington, 30 October 1791, in GW, *The Writings of George Washington,* 31:408. Harriot's name also appears as "Harriet" in sources.
42. For Hannah Bushrod Washington's relationship with George Washington and his bequest of one hundred dollars to her, to be spent on a mourning ring in his memory, see GW, *The Writings of George Washington,* 37:287, 287n32.

43. Hannah Bushrod Washington, Last Will and Testament, [prior to 26 April 1801], (typescript, Fred W. Smith National Library for the Study of George Washington, Mount Vernon, VA) (hereafter FWSNL), 4, 6.

44. Hannah Bushrod Washington, Last Will and Testament, 5–6.

45. Hannah Bushrod Washington, Last Will and Testament, 5–6.

46. Hannah Bushrod Washington, Last Will and Testament, 6. For the fact that Jenny, Suck, and Venus were enslaved domestic servants, see List of John Auge. Washington [sic] Negroes 3d March 1783, From J. A. Washington's Ledger C, RM-73, MS-2166 (typescript, FWSNL).

47. Thompson, "The Only Unavoidable Subject of Regret," 146–48, 151, 403–4nn108–9.

48. Agnes Lee, Sunday morning, 23 March 1856, Growing Up in the 1850s: The Journal of Agnes Lee, ed. Mary Custis Lee deButts (Chapel Hill: Published for the Robert E. Lee Memorial Association by The University of North Carolina Press, 1984), 80–81.

49. Conversation of the author with Agnes Mullins, 7 July 1995.

50. See 1786 Slave List and 1799 Slave Lists.

51. For Louisa's manumission, see Timothy J. Dennee, comp., "Slave Manumissions in Alexandria Land Records, 1791–1863," http://www .freedmenscemetery.org/resources/documents/manumissions.shtml, 2001. John's manumission can be found in C. B. Rose Jr., Arlington County Virginia: A History (Baltimore: Arlington Historical Society, 1976), 72n.

52. Murray H. Nelligan, Arlington House: The Story of the Robert E. Lee Memorial (Burke, VA: Chatelaine Press, 2001), 78.

53. For the documentation on these other children, see "Virginia F. F's.," Cleveland Daily Leader, 20 September 1865; interview with Maria Syphax, "Lovely Arlington," Atchison [Kansas] Daily Globe, 15 September 1888. See also Mary G. Powell, "Scenes of Childhood," The Fireside Sentinel: The Alexandria Library, Lloyd House Newsletter (January 1990): 9.

54. Thompson, "The Only Unavoidable Subject of Regret," 294, 309–10.

55. Abigail Adams to Mary Smith Cranch, 21 December 1800 (typescript, PS-605/R-102, FWSNL).

SERVICE AND SACRIFICE

Martha Washington

LYNN PRICE ROBBINS

On June 16, 1775, George Washington accepted the role of commander-in-chief of the newly formed Continental army. On June 18, he wrote to his wife, Martha, to inform her of the news. Indeed, he confided, he had not sought this weighty responsibility and did not believe himself up to the task. Nevertheless, his main concern was leaving Martha. He pleaded with her to keep his uneasy feelings at bay by not "complaining at what I could really not avoid." He asked her to summon her "whole fortitude & Resolution" to keep busy in order to survive without him. In the end, however, Martha Washington had no difficulties with her husband's absence during the Revolutionary War. At the first winter encampment in 1775, it was he who requested her presence with him in New Jersey. Despite worsening health, threats to her safety, and the loss of her last living child, Martha ultimately attended all eight winter encampments of the Revolutionary War. Rather than living out her dreams of domestic tranquility at Mount Vernon, she spent nearly half of the war with or near her husband. The initial invitation for Martha to join her husband in an army encampment may have stemmed from loneliness or from a need to recapture some of his home life. However, she would soon prove invaluable to General Washington and the war effort. Martha was the competent partner and confidante that he needed, and she was acutely aware of military matters and concerns throughout the war. She lent both her name and her time and efforts to raise money for soldiers when supplies and morale were low. She interacted with officers and foreign dignitaries, translating her domestic duties from

Mount Vernon to the battlefield. The most difficult new role for Martha Washington was undoubtedly that of national celebrity. The Virginia woman who had not left her home colony in her life was suddenly thrust into the public eye and celebrated for her role as His Excellency's Lady. Throughout the Revolutionary War, however, she proved she was so much more than an officer's wife.

Martha Washington's story highlights the experience of a white, wealthy, socially elite woman. While this perspective is valuable to analyze independently, it also must be compared to women of other social classes, races, and cultures of the time to ensure a complete narrative.

Martha Dandridge Custis Washington had seen loss in her life. Born on June 2, 1731, at Chestnut Grove in New Kent County, Virginia, she belonged to a family who could afford to teach her reading and writing skills at an early age. As was common for the era, Martha spent her early years close to home and family. She married Daniel Parke Custis in May 1750 when she was eighteen years old and Custis was thirty-eight.[1] By

The earliest known portrait of Martha after her marriage to George Washington. Capturing her at forty-one years of age, this image illustrates that she was not always the matronly elder woman remembered throughout history. (Courtesy of the Mount Vernon Ladies' Association)

the time she was twenty-six years old, she had lost her husband to illness and two of her four children: Daniel Parke Custis Jr. and Frances Parke Custis. She had also become a sought-after widow with her husband's large estate, which consisted of 17,779 acres of land; a furnished house in James City County; approximately 289 enslaved workers; liquid assets at £8,500 sterling; and £1,650 in the Bank of England.[2]

Martha acted as executrix of Daniel Parke Custis's will (he died intestate); she also took over business matters that had previously been her husband's domain. On August 20, 1757, Martha wrote to Robert Cary & Company, a London mercantile firm, to announce that her husband had died and "all his Affairs fall under my management." She added, "I think it wil[l be] proper to continue the Account with you in the same [man]ner as if he was living, as most of the Goods I shall send for will be for the use of the Family."[3] Martha sent a similarly worded letter to another London mercantile firm, John Hanbury & Company, on the same date. She again announced her husband's death and the need to continue correspondence as though he were still living. Martha then displayed her business savvy by continuing, "I now inclose the Bill of Lading for the Tobacco which I hope will get safe to your Hands, and as I have reason to believe it is extremely good I hope you will sell it at a good Price."[4] She would continue to hold control over the Custis estate as long as she remained unmarried, or a feme sole.

Several gentlemen, hoping for an advantageous marriage, attempted to woo the wealthy widow Martha Dandridge Custis. One of her suitors, Charles Carter of Cleve, was a member of the House of Burgesses, fifty years old, and a wealthy widower with twelve children. Another suitor had considerably less wealth, prestige, and years behind him: George Washington. George was leasing the Mount Vernon estate from his brother Lawrence's widow in 1758 when his first recorded meeting with Martha occurred at her home in New Kent County, Virginia. He was also the commander of the Virginia Regiment and seen as the hero of the French and Indian War's General Edward Braddock campaign. Martha, a wealthy widow searching for a father figure for her remaining two children, had a freedom of choice more than a middling, or poorer, woman would. She had the wealth and experience to remain a feme sole. She could also choose a marriage partner based on more than just his income. Forgoing a marriage for money, she chose George Washington to be her life partner. They married in 1759.[5]

Prior to the outbreak of the Revolutionary War, Martha Washington had not traveled outside of Virginia. She was forty-five years old, the mistress of Mount Vernon, a wife, and a mother. In 1773, her beloved daughter Patsy died at the age of seventeen from a seizure, leaving her with one remaining child, John "Jacky" Parke Custis.[6] Nineteen-year-old Jacky married Eleanor Calvert in 1774. He then divided his time at several homes: his properties White House and Abingdon, his in-laws' home of Mount Airy, and Mount Vernon.

Martha Washington's personality and physical attributes were described by some of her contemporaries during the war. Mercy Otis Warren wrote in a 1776 letter to Abigail Adams, "I think the Complacency of her Manners speaks at once the Benevolence of her Heart, and her affability, Candor and Gentleness Quallify her to soften the hours of private Life or to sweeten the Cares of the Hero and smooth the Rugged scenes of War."[7] In 1777, she was described as having "a hospitable disposition, always good-humoured and cheerful," and in 1780, as being "the most amiable woman upon Earth."[8] Such descriptions of Martha focus on her outward charm and abilities as a hostess; however, her stubbornness and resilience hid just below the surface. It was these strengths that kept her going during many years of war.

Elizabeth Schuyler Hamilton wrote of Martha after first meeting her in 1779 or 1780, "She was then nearly fifty years old, but was still handsome. She was quite short: a plump little woman with dark brown eyes, her hair a little frosty, and very plainly dressed for such a grand lady as I considered her. She wore a plain, brown gown homespun stuff, a large white handkerchief, a neat cap, and her plain gold wedding ring, which she had worn for more than twenty years. She was always my ideal of a true woman."[9] The Revolutionary War centered around the pursuit of self-governance, to be achieved by throwing out the tyrannical British monarchy and establishing a new republic. As the opulence of European fashion and goods became associated with the enemy and lost favor, new ideals were established for women in the budding United States. Homespun goods were associated with patriotism and practicality. A plain or simple appearance assumed a political stance of the rejection of European extravagance. Later in 1789, when Martha's new role was that of the president's wife, Abigail Adams said of her, "If I was to speak sincerly, I think she is a much better figure, her manners are modest and unassuming, dignified and femenine, not the Tincture of ha'ture about her."[10] Martha embodied the new American woman.

The Marquis de Chastellux wrote about Martha, "I found there Mrs. Washington, who had just arrived from Virginia, and was on her way to join her husband, as she does at the end of every campaign. She is about forty or forty-five, rather plump, but fresh and with an agreeable face."[11] In 1782, Frenchman Claude Blanchard noted, "Mrs Washington is a woman of about fifty years of age; she is small and fat, her appearance is respectable. She was dressed very plainly and her manners were simple in all respects."[12] Again, Martha's simplicity and plain manners are highlighted by contemporaries as complimentary.

Martha's grandson, George Washington Parke Custis, published his recollections many years after her death. Custis focused on his grandmother's example as a model of domesticity and femininity, attributes considered admirable in the antebellum era. For example, he wrote, "Mrs. Washington, an accomplished Virginia housewife of the olden time, gave her constant attention to all matters of her domestic household, and by skill and superior management greatly contributed to the comfortable reception and entertainment of the crowds of guests always to be found in the hospitable Mansion of Mount Vernon."[13] The perception of Martha Washington that had fit into the role of the ideal woman of the revolutionary era thus transformed to become the ideal woman for a later generation.

Martha Washington's life as a wife, a mother, and the mistress of Mount Vernon came to an end on June 15, 1775, when the Continental Congress named George Washington the commander-in-chief of all colonial forces.[14] He responded with a letter to his "Dearest" Martha, making it clear that he was concerned with her well-being without him: "My unhappiness will flow, from the uneasiness I know you will feel at being left alone—I therefore beg of you to summon your whole fortitude & Resolution, and pass your time as agreeably as possible—nothing will give me so much sincere satisfaction as to hear this, and to hear it from your own Pen."[15] The couple had not been apart for an extended period of time since their wedding. Although Martha could not have anticipated that she would be away from Mount Vernon for almost half of the eight years of war, or the hardships she would endure in those years, it is clear that she envisioned something very different for her life. Years later, when her life again was thrust into a public arena when George Washington was elected president, Martha described her feelings to Mercy Otis Warren: "I little thought when the war was finished, that any circumstances could possible have happened which would call the General into public life again. I had anticipated, that from this moment we should have been left to grow old in solitude and tranquility together: that was, my dear madam, the first and dearest wish of my heart; but in *that* I have been disappointed."[16] Nevertheless, Martha assured her friend that her husband had a duty to public life and service, and that she, as his partner, also had a duty and role to undertake.

George did not silence his concerns after informing Martha of them. To her brother-in-law Burwell Bassett, he wrote on June 19, 1775, "I must Intreat you & Mrs Bassett, if possible, to visit at Mt Vernon as also my Wife's other friends—I could wish you to take her down, as I have no expectations of returning till Winter & feel great uneasiness at her lonesome Situation."[17] He likewise wrote to Jacky, imploring him to visit his mother to stave off loneliness: "I have I must confess very uneasy feelings on her acc[oun]t . . ."[18] George's concerns also may have amplified any anxieties that Martha experienced. After confessing to Mount Vernon's caretaker, Lund Washington, that he had considered the possibility of Virginia royal governor Lord Dunmore having Martha kidnapped, George received the following response from Lund: "Mrs Washington I believe was under no apprehension of Lord Dunmores doing her an injury until your mentiong it in several of your last Letters."[19] Martha's safe domestic role at Mount Vernon and her life as a Virginia woman had begun its rapid transformation.

As the winter of 1775 approached, the Continental army prepared to cease military activity until the spring. Despite George's oft-expressed concern for Martha's loneliness, it was he who requested her company. He wrote to his brother John Augustine on October 13, 1775, "seeing no great prospect of returning to my Family & Friends this Winter I have sent an Invitation to Mrs Washington to come to me, altho' I fear the Season is too far advanced . . . to admit this with any tolerable degree of convenience—I have laid a state of the difficulties however which must attend the journey before her and left it to her own choice."[20] Lund assured George that Martha "often declared she would go to the Camp if you would permit her," and sent the request to New Kent where Martha was visiting family.[21] She agreed to travel to Cambridge, Massachusetts, and arrived in December, fulfilling her role as a dutiful wife.[22] The role would soon get much more challenging.

Martha's journey from Virginia to Massachusetts marked her entry into public life. Her first visit outside of her home commonwealth was met with public enthusiasm. A stop in Philadelphia on the way to Cambridge resulted in an announcement in the November 21, 1775, *Pennsylvania Evening Post*: "This day the Lady of his Excellency General Washington arrived here, upon her way to New-England. She was met at the Lower Ferry by the officers of the different battalions, the troop of light horse, and the light infantry of the second battalion, who escorted her into the city."

The attention Martha's travel received came as a surprise to her. She wrote to her friend Elizabeth Ramsay on December 30, 1775, to inform her she had safely arrived in Cambridge. Martha described her welcome in Philadelphia in the letter: "I dont dout but you have seen the Figuer our arrivel made in that Philadelphia paper—and I left it in as great pomp as if I had been a very great some body."[23] Her status of celebrity would only grow as the Revolutionary War dragged on for eight years. This new role added a greater weight of responsibility onto her shoulders. She became a symbol of compassion and nurturing to balance out her battle-tested warrior husband.[24] She also represented the patriot cause and hope for a new nation. As early as 1776, a Philadelphia resident named his twin son and daughter George Washington and Martha Dandridge.[25]

Martha's initial experience at a military camp was not pleasant. Several months before she arrived in Massachusetts, General Washington had complained about his enlisted men in a letter to Lund, in which he described them as lacking discipline and "an exceeding dirty & nasty people."[26] Regarding his officers, George wrote, they were "the most indifferent kind of People I ever saw."[27] In her letter to Elizabeth Ramsay, Martha confessed her early nervousness: "Every person seems to be chearfull and happy hear—some days we have a number of Cannon and shells from Boston and Bunkers Hill, but it does not seem to surprise any one but me; I confess I shuder every time I hear the sound of a gun." She also shared that she had been to dinner with Major Generals Charles Lee and Israel Putnam.[28]

Despite any fear or uncertainty on her part, Martha remained beside her husband, the General, for roughly half of the conflict. She attended all eight winter encampments of the war: Cambridge, Mass. (December 1775–April 1776); Morristown, N.J. (March–June 1777 and December 1779–June 1780); Valley Forge, Pa. (January–June 1778); Middlebrook, N.J. (February–June 1779); New Windsor, N.Y. (December 1780–June 1781); Yorktown, Va. (Williamsburg and Eltham, October–November 1781); and Newburgh, N.Y. (March–July 1782 and November 1782–October 1783). Each year the travel took a greater toll on her health and extended the time she had to spend away from her beloved Mount Vernon. Martha suffered from exhaustion and other illnesses throughout the war. Yet she continued to endure the hardships for her husband, fulfilling the role of loyal and dutiful wife.

Martha did not travel throughout the war just to keep her husband company. Nevertheless, in this role she was effective. Several extant letters reveal the positive impact her presence had on George Washington. For example, Major General Nathanael Greene wrote on April 8, 1777, from Morristown, "Mrs Washington and Mrs Bland from Virginia are at Camp, happy with their better halves. Mrs Washington is excessive fond of the General and he of her. They are very happy in each other."[29] The feeling was mutual. According to Martha Bland, also writing from Morristown, George's "Worthy Lady seems to be in perfect felicity while she is by the side of her *Old Man* as she calls him."[30]

In addition to lifting the spirits of George, Martha did her part to advance the war effort as the support behind the commander-in-chief. She acted as hostess in a similar manner in which she would at her home, Mount Vernon. Elizabeth Drinker recorded Martha's importance in her diary. In April 1778, Drinker visited Valley Forge to request a meeting with General Washington. She described her experience: "We requested an audience with the General, and sat with his wife, (a sociable, pretty kind of woman), until he came in."[31] Later in her diary, upon hearing of Martha's death, she recalled, "dined with her [Martha] at Valley Forge when G. Washington's camp was there. Ye General and 22 officers also dined there."[32]

Good communication is essential in a time of war, and Martha bolstered the patriot cause by acting as a secretary to her husband when needed. Several Martha Washington letters exist that were drafted by her husband and then copied by her before being sent. In a letter from George to James McHenry on May 14, 1783, enclosures included an excerpt from a Robert R. Livingston letter and a letter from James Madison, both in Martha's hand. Martha's assistance appears to have extended beyond this timeframe, however, as a surviving draft letter of April 7, 1796, from George Washington to Andrew Parks is also in her handwriting.[33] The letter discusses George's niece Harriot and his expectations of a successful suitor for her, a topic on which Martha undoubtedly had strong opinions. Harriot went on to marry Parks in July of that year.[34] Martha also communicated military information to the camps. On February 5, 1778, Nathanael Greene wrote to General Alexander McDougall from Valley Forge: "Mrs. Washington arrivd in Camp this evening, and brings the agreeable intelligence that 5000 Volunteers engag'd for six or twelve months from April next are to join us from Virginia under the command of Col Spotswood now made a Brigadier General."[35]

Fundraising was a crucial activity throughout the war, and women played key roles in the efforts. In 1780, Esther De Berdt Reed created the Ladies Association of Philadelphia to raise money to aid Washington's troops. Reed then wrote a broadside titled "Sentiments of an American Woman" to encourage support. Martha joined the effort, returning home that summer with a copy of the broadside and sharing it with her acquaintances. Martha Wayles Skelton Jefferson wrote a letter to several of her prominent friends in support of the effort:

> Mrs Washington has done me the honor of communicating the inclosed proposition of our sisters of Pennsylvania and of informing me that the same grateful sentiments are displaying themselves in Maryland. Justified by the sanction of her letter in handing forward the scheme I undertake with chearfulness the duty of furnishing to my countrywomen an opportunity of proving that they also participate of those virtuous feelings which gave birth to it. I cannot do more for its promotion than by inclosing to you some of the papers to be disposed of as you think proper.[36]

The campaign raised more than $300,000 in paper currency.[37]

Martha Washington's correspondence illustrates her knowledge regarding the Revolutionary War and military information. In January 1776, Martha wrote to her sister, "a few days agoe General Clinton, with

several companyes Sailed out of Boston Harbor to what place he is di-
stand for, we cannot find out. some think it is to Virginia he is gon, others to New York . . . If General Clinton is gon to new York—General Lee
is thare before him and I hope will give him a very warm reception."[38]
In August, Martha told her that George had informed her of upcoming
military actions: "the General . . . wrote to me yesterday and informed
me that Lord dunmore with part of his fleet was come to General Howe
at Staten Island, that an other devisian of Hessians is expected be fore
they think, the regulars will begen thare attack on us, some hear begen
to think thare will be noe Battle after all."[39] In 1778, she wrote to Mercy
Otis Warren, "in virginia we have had no British troops since the cruel
Dunmore left us—but how soon we shall, is not at this time known; I
hope, and trust, that all the states will make a vigorious push early this
spring, if every thing can be prepard for it, and there by putting a stop to
British cruelties."[40] Martha was also aware of the leaders of the opposition. In the same letter to Warren, Martha referenced British Lieutenant
General John Burgoyne's surrender in 1777 in Saratoga, New York, adding, "would bountifull providence aim a like stroke at Genl Howe, the
measure of my happyness would be compleat."[41] Although Martha filled
the role of ideal woman and dutiful wife throughout the war, she also
understood the military aspects of the revolution and consequences of
their results. She, like other women of the time, took a broader view than
her previous domestic roles had allowed and became more engaged in
the act of nation making.

Mount Vernon remained on Martha's mind during the many months
she spent away during the war, and she continued her role of plantation
mistress from afar. She kept track of her enslaved workers' progress and
activities through correspondence. For example, in 1781, Martha wrote
to caretaker Lund Washington, "M. Washington will be glad to know if
the Cotton for the counterpins was wove . . . she desired milly Posey to
have the fine peice of linning made white[,] how is Betty has she been
spinning, all winter—is charlot done the worke I left for her to do."[42] She
would repeat this concern for her home later in life when she resided in
New York and Philadelphia with President George Washington.

Martha Washington's contributions to the Revolutionary War did not
come without a cost. Leaving home meant separation from family and
friends, a key source of support in Martha's life. Her desperate letters to

her sister and son, demanding updates from Virginia, highlight her anxiety. While in her first winter encampment in Cambridge in the winter of 1775–1776, Martha pitifully complained to her sister Anna Maria: "I have wrote to you several times in hopes, that would put you in mind of me, but I find it has not had its intended affect. I am realy very uneasy at not hearing from you and have made all the Excuses for you that I can think of, but it will not doe much longer, if I doe not get a letter by this nights post I shall think myself quite forgot by all my Freinds the distance is long yet the post comes in very regularly every week."[43] In 1779, she resorted to threats to convince her son and his wife to write to her: "If you doe not write to me—I will not write to you again or till I get Letters from you."[44]

Martha missed special events with her family due to her travels and time away from Virginia. Her son Jacky wrote to her excitedly in August 1776 announcing the birth of a daughter: "I make not the least Doubt but you will heartily join us in the Pleasure We feel on this Happy Event; I wish You were present, You would be much more pleased."[45] She also had at least one letter to Mount Vernon, to caretaker Lund Washington, intercepted by the British. The letter, written in 1781, inquired about the work being done by enslaved people at Mount Vernon. Despite her absence from the plantation, she attempted to continue her watch over productivity and Lund's management. Her domestic roles as the mistress of Mount Vernon remained important to her, and she continued them whenever possible.

The home of Martha and George Washington, Mount Vernon, found itself in peril in 1781. In early April, a sloop of war, the *Savage*, commanded by Captain Thomas Graves, sailed up the Potomac and threatened the destruction of Mount Vernon if they were not given provisions. Consenting to Graves's wishes, Lund Washington furnished the ship with sheep, hogs, and a variety of supplies. Seventeen enslaved workers—fourteen men and three women—also took the opportunity to seek freedom with the British.[46] The Marquis de Lafayette informed General Washington about the situation: "You Cannot Conceive How Unhappy I Have Been to Hear that Mr Lund Washington Went on Board the Ennemy's vessels and Consented to give them provisions."[47] George was infuriated. He wrote to Lund Washington, acknowledging that Lund had acted from his best judgment, but that he nevertheless

was disappointed in the news: "It would have been a less painful circumstance to me, to have heard, that in consequence of your non compliance
with their request, they had burnt my House, & laid the Plantation in
Ruins."[48] Whether or not Martha would have agreed with her husband's
preference of a destroyed homestead is a matter of conjecture, although
it is not difficult to presume that her feelings would lean toward the preservation of Mount Vernon over a patriotic performance.

In order to travel safely to military camps, it was necessary for Martha to be inoculated for smallpox, a highly contagious disease threatening the Continental army and the war effort. The process involved
the patient being infected with a weak strain of the disease and, if all
progressed as hoped, surviving a shorter and milder bout of symptoms
such as fever, muscle pain, and pustules covering the skin.[49] Despite the
necessity of immunity to smallpox, George Washington was not confident that Martha would voluntarily accept inoculation. Because he had
contracted smallpox while in Barbados in 1751, George was already immune. He wrote to his brother in April 1776, "Mrs Washington is still
here, and talks of taking the Small Pox, but I doubt her resolution."[50]
Martha, however, certainly understood that her husband needed her by
his side, and the only way to ensure that possibility was to be immune
from smallpox. She continued with the procedure and only experienced
mild symptoms.[51] Her loyalty superseded any fear or concern she may
have had concerning an inoculation that was by no means promised to
be simple or painless.[52]

The miles Martha traveled to join General Washington and the Continental army for eight years took their toll on her emotionally and physically. She wrote of her first journey to a winter camp—Cambridge—in
1775: "This is a beautyfull Country, and we had a very plasent journey
through new england."[53] In 1780, her exhaustion was apparent: "I got
home on Fryday—and find myself so much fatigue with my ride that
I shall not be able to come down to see you this summer . . . I suffered
so much last winter by going late that I have dtermind to goe early in
the fall before the Frost set in."[54] Almost a year later, George informed
his brother-in-law that Martha had been "in a very low and weak state
having been sick for more than a month with a kind of Jaundice."[55] By
the last months of the war in 1783, Martha's health had significantly
worsened since the start of the conflict. George explained to a friend,

"Mrs Washington enjoys an incompetent share of health; Billious Fevers & Cholic's attack her very often, & reduce her low. at this moment she is but barely recovering from one of them."[56]

Martha experienced loss throughout the war. Her sister, with whom she was close, Anna Maria "Nancy" Dandridge Bassett died in December 1777 at her home, Eltham. Undoubtedly the most difficult time in the Revolutionary War for Martha was when she lost her last remaining child. After losing three of her four children with Daniel Parke Custis, Martha was anxious to protect John "Jacky" Parke Custis. In 1771, Jacky was inoculated for smallpox, and George Washington kept the matter a secret from Martha until Jacky was recovered because her "anxiety & uneasiness is so great."[57] Naturally, Martha did not wish for her son to risk fighting in a war. However, in October 1781, she felt comfortable allowing Jacky to join George in Yorktown as a civilian aide-de-camp, away from the front lines of battle. Jacky had been ill that month, but he assured his mother that he had since recovered.[58] The next month, November, Martha traveled southward to reunite with her son and husband unaware that Jacky had again become ill. She arrived at a family member's home to discover that Jacky was clinging to life. By November 5 he was dead.

The loss of her son came after years of difficult travel, worsening health, and living in the public spotlight. General Henry Knox wrote, "His Excellency the General & Mrs Washington amidst flattering public prospects have Received the most fatal blow to their domestic felicity—the amiable Mr Custis, Mrs Washingtons only child has just been obliged by the rigid hand of fate to pay his last Debt to nature."[59] General Nathanael Greene lamented that Martha needed more support from a present husband to handle the overwhelming grief, writing to George, "I sincerely condole with Mrs Washington in the loss of her amiable son—a loss which will be more sensibly felt from your continual absense."[60] Greene may have been hinting to General Washington that his duties as a husband and a father were not being entirely met.

The events of Martha Washington's life during the Revolutionary War, whether illness, family concerns, or domestic matters, took on a greater importance as she was forced to live in the gaze of the public eye. Newspapers followed Martha on each difficult journey to the winter encampments, and towns celebrated her arrival along the way. She became more than a woman. She was a symbol. Martha became the embodiment of the female experience during the war—despite her unique situation. The public expected her to retain the ideals of an American woman, and it was her patriotic duty to both her husband and her homeland to attempt to live up to that role. It was not an experience or a role that she had chosen, but one that had been thrust upon her.

At the conclusion of the Revolutionary War, General Washington illustrated the importance of Martha's contributions by invoicing Congress for her travel expenses. He had refused a salary for his role as commander-in-chief but asked Congress at the beginning of the war if he could submit his expenses for reimbursement so that he would not "make any proffit" from war.[61] The total amount George requested for reimbursement solely for Martha's travels added up to £1064.1.—.[62] While a hefty sum of money, no amount of currency could soothe the years

"The Washington Family," by Edward Savage, 1796. After Martha's son John "Jacky" Parke Custis died in 1781, the Washingtons raised two of his four children, George Washington "Washy" Parke Custis and Eleanor "Nelly" Parke Custis. (Courtesy of the Mount Vernon Ladies' Association)

of worsening illnesses, exhausting trips, and unending public scrutiny that Martha Washington had endured. Martha certainly anticipated her return to Mount Vernon following the war and the domestic bliss that she had sought—and would continue to chase—throughout her lifetime.

The commander-in-chief of the Continental army, General George Washington remains a household name in the United States. His life partner's name may be known, but the extent to which Martha Washington contributed to the Revolutionary War has remained hidden. Her account not only reflects additional light onto essential details of the conflict but it also deepens the historical context of the era by including the experience of a white, wealthy, socially elite woman—a perspective by which to analyze independently as well as to compare to women of other social classes, races, and cultures. Her story is but one of many.

Notes

I wish to thank Charlene Boyer Lewis for her helpful comments on this essay, and thank Boyer Lewis and George Boudreau for their tireless work on this volume.

1. Patricia Brady, *Martha Washington: An American Life* (New York: Penguin Group, 2005), 32.
2. See Editorial Note, Report of the Commissioners to Settle the Estate [c. October 1759], and Combined County Inventory of Slaves and Personal Property in the Estate [1757–58], in *The Papers of George Washington, Colonial Series*, ed. W. W. Abbot (Charlottesville: University Press of Virginia, 1988), 6:201–9, 215–17, 220–32.
3. Martha Washington to Robert Cary & Company, August 20, 1757, Virginia Historical Society (hereafter ViHi): Custis Family Papers.
4. Martha Washington to John Hanbury & Company, August 20, 1757, ViHi: Custis Family Papers.
5. For an excellent study of the Washingtons' marriage, see Flora Fraser, *The Washingtons: George and Martha: Partners in Friendship and Love* (New York: Anchor Books, 2015).
6. George Washington to Burwell Bassett, July 20, 1773, in *The Papers of George Washington, Colonial Series*, ed. W. W. Abbot and Dorothy Twohig (Charlottesville: University Press of Virginia, 1994), 9:243–44.
7. Mercy Otis Warren to Abigail Adams, April 17, 1776, in *Adams Family Correspondence*, ed. L. H. Butterfield (Cambridge: Belknap Press of Harvard, 1963), 1:385.

8. Nicholas Cresswell, *The Journal of Nicholas Cresswell, 1774–1777* (New York: Dial Press, 1924), 255; John Steele to William Steele Jr., June 14, 1780, in *A Salute to Courage: The American Revolution as Seen through Wartime Writings of Officers of the Continental Army and Navy*, ed. Dennis P. Ryan (New York: Columbia University Press, 1979), 187.

9. Hugh Howard, *Houses of the Founding Fathers: The Men Who Made America and the Way They Lived* (New York: Artisan, 2007), 147.

10. Abigail Adams to Mary Smith Cranch, June 28, 1789, in *Adams Family Correspondence*, ed. Margaret A. Hogan (Cambridge: Belknap Press of Harvard, 2007), 8:379.

11. Marquis de Chastellux, *Travels in North America in the Years 1780, 1781 and 1782* (Chapel Hill: University of North Carolina Press, 1963), 1:134.

12. Gilbert Chinard, ed. and trans., *George Washington as the French Knew Him: A Collection of Texts* (New York: Greenwood Press, 1969), 67.

13. George Washington Parke Custis, *Recollections and Private Memoirs of Washington by G. W. Parke Custis, of Arlington* (Washington, DC: William H. Moore, 1859), 82. The perception of Martha Washington as an ideal woman for each era continued into the twentieth century. For example, the August 22, 1918, issue of the *Wilkes-Barre [Pa.] Times* published the following "rarebit": "Martha Washington must have been a wonderful woman. We would all be George Washingtons if our wives didn't ask us so many damn fool questions."

14. Worthington Chauncey Ford et al., eds. *Journals of the Continental Congress, 1774–1789*, 34 vols. (Washington, DC: Library of Congress, 1904–37), 2:91.

15. George Washington to Martha Washington, June 18, 1775, Tudor Place Foundation.

16. Martha Washington to Mercy Otis Warren, December 26, 1789, Maine Historical Society.

17. George Washington to Burwell Bassett, June 19, 1775, in *The Papers of George Washington, Revolutionary War Series*, 1:13.

18. George Washington to John Parke Custis, June 19, 1775, in *The Papers of George Washington, Revolutionary War Series*, ed. W. W. Abbot and Dorothy Twohig (Charlottesville: University Press of Virginia, 1985–87), 1:15.

19. George Washington to Lund Washington, August 20, 1775, and Lund Washington to George Washington, October 15, 1775, in *The Papers of George Washington, Revolutionary War Series*, 1:335, 2:174–75.

20. George Washington to John Augustine Washington, October 13, 1775, in *The Papers of George Washington, Revolutionary War Series*, 2:162.

21. Lund Washington to George Washington, October 29, 1775, in *The Papers of George Washington, Revolutionary War Series*, 2:256.

22. Martha Washington arrived in Cambridge on December 11, 1775, with Jacky, his wife Eleanor, and George's nephew George Lewis.

23. Martha Washington to Elizabeth Ramsay, December 30, 1775, Pierpont Morgan Library (hereafter NNPM): Literary and Historical Manuscripts.

24. Martha's grandson, George Washington "Wash" Parke Custis, wrote in his recollections that her "kindness to the sick and wounded" made her annual arrival in camp a celebration, "hailed as an event that would serve to dissipate the gloom of the winter-quarters" (Custis, *Recollections*, 403).

25. *New-York Journal*, May 2, 1776.

26. George Washington to Lund Washington, August 20, 1775, in *The Papers of George Washington, Revolutionary War Series*, 1:336.

27. George Washington to Lund Washington, August 20, 1775, 1:335.

28. Martha Washington to Elizabeth Ramsay, December 30, 1775, NNPM.

29. Nathanael Greene to Mrs. Catharine Greene, April 8, 1777, in Richard K. Showman, ed., *The Papers of Nathanael Greene*, [1980], 2:54.

30. George Washington to Capt. Caleb Gibbs, May 1, 1777, in *The Papers of George Washington, Revolutionary War Series*, ed. Philander D. Chase (Charlottesville: University Press of Virginia, 1999), 9:322, source note.

31. Henry D. Biddle, ed., *Extracts from the Journal of Elizabeth Drinker, from 1759 to 1807, A.D.* (Philadelphia: J.B. Lippincott Company, 1889), 93.

32. Biddle, 371. The Drinkers were Quakers, and Henry—Elizabeth's husband—had been arrested for refusing to swear allegiance to the new government. Elizabeth visited Valley Forge to request his release from prison. For more on the topic, see Wendy Lucas Castro, "'Being Separated from My Dearest Husband, in This Cruel Manner': Elizabeth Drinker and the Seven-Month Exile of Philadelphia Quakers," *Quaker History* 100 (2011): 40–63.

33. Library of Congress: Papers of George Washington.

34. Library of Congress: Papers of George Washington. For the sent version of the letter, see George Washington to Andrew Parks, April 7, 1796, Founders Online, National Archives, accessed April 11, 2019, https://founders.archives.gov/documents/Washington/05-20-02-0016. Harriot's name also appears as "Harriet" in sources.

35. Nathanael Greene to Alexander McDougall, February 5, 1778, in Showman, *The Papers of Nathanael Greene*, 2:276.

36. Martha Wayles Skelton Jefferson to Eleanor Conway Madison, August 8, 1780, in *The Papers of Thomas Jefferson*, ed. Julian P. Boyd (Princeton: Princeton University Press, 1951), 3:532.

37. Esther De Berdt Reed to George Washington, July 4, 1780, in *The Papers of George Washington, Revolutionary War Series*, ed. Benjamin L. Huggins

and Adrina Garbooshian-Huggins (Charlottesville: University of Virginia Press, 2019), 26:649. "Sentiments of an American Woman" has been misattributed to Martha and was even published under her name in European newspapers. George Washington applauded the effort of women fundraisers, noting that "this fresh mark of the patriotism of the Ladies entitles them to the highest applause of their Country." He later wrote that "a taste of hard money may be productive of much discontent, as we have none but depreciated paper for their [the soldiers'] pay," resulting in using the money raised to purchase shirts for the men rather than sending them the money. George Washington to Esther De Berdt Reed, July 14, 1780, Bristol Historical and Preservation Society, and August 10, 1780, John Carter Brown Library.

38. Martha Washington to Anna Maria Dandridge Bassett, January 31, 1776, Morristown National Historical Park (hereafter NjMoHP).

39. Martha Washington to Anna Maria Dandridge Bassett, August 20, 1776, NNPM: Literary and Historical Manuscripts.

40. Martha Washington to Mercy Otis Warren, March 7, 1778, Warren-Adams Papers, Massachusetts Historical Society.

41. Martha Washington to Mercy Otis Warren, March 7, 1778.

42. Martha Washington to [Lund Washington], [c.31 May 1781], Henry Clinton Papers, William L. Clements Library, University of Michigan. The date of this letter is estimated based on context; in addition, it was intercepted by the British.

43. Martha Washington to Anna Maria Dandridge Bassett, January 31, 1776, NjMoHP.

44. Martha Washington to John Parke Custis and Eleanor Calvert Custis, March 19, 1779, Mount Vernon Ladies' Association of the Union (hereafter ViMtvL): Martha Washington Collection.

45. John Parke Custis to Martha Washington, August 21, 1776, ViMtvL: Martha Washington Collection.

46. Lund Washington reported a list of the enslaved people who joined the British: "Peter. an old man. Lewis. an old man. Frank. an old man. Frederick. a man about 45 years old; an overseer and valuable. Gunner. a man about 45 years old; valuable, a Brick maker. Harry. a man about 40 years old, valuable, a Horseler. Tom, a man about 20 years old, stout and Healthy. Sambo. a man about 20 years old, stout and Healthy. Thomas, a lad about 17 years old, House servant. Peter. a lad about 15 years old, very likely. Stephen. a man about 20 years old, a cooper by trade. James. a man about 25 years old, stout and Healthy. Watty. a man about 20 years old, by trade a weaver. Daniel. a man about 19 years old, very likely. Lucy.

a woman about 20 years old. Esther. a woman about 18 years old. Deborah. a woman about 16 years old." John C. Fitzpatrick, ed. *The Writings of George Washington from the Original Manuscript Sources, 1745–1799*, 39 vols. (Washington, D.C.: U.S. Government Printing Office, 1931–44), 22:14n20.

47. Marie-Joseph-Paul-Yves-Roch-Gilbert du Motier, Marquis de Lafayette to George Washington, April 23, 1781, Papers of George Washington, Library of Congress.

48. George Washington to Lund Washington, April 30, 1781, Papers of George Washington, Library of Congress.

49. For more on smallpox, see George Henry Fox, S. D. Hubbard, S. Pollitzer, and J. H. Huddleston, *A Practical Treatise on Smallpox, Illustrated by Colored Photographs from Life*. Part 1 (Philadelphia: J. B. Lippencott Company, 1902); and Elizabeth A. Fenn, *Pox Americana: The Great Smallpox Epidemic of 1775–82* (New York: Hill and Wang, 2001).

50. George Washington to John Augustine Washington, April 29, 1776, in *The Papers of George Washington, Revolutionary War Series*, ed. Philander D. Chase (Charlottesville: University Press of Virginia, 1991), 4:173.

51. George Washington to Burwell Bassett Sr., June 4, 1776, in *The Papers of George Washington, Revolutionary War Series*, 4:435. For more on smallpox in the eighteenth century, see Fenn, *Pox Americana*.

52. Martha's positive experience with the smallpox inoculation led her to recommend it to family members. In 1777, she cared for the sons of her sister Anna Maria "Nancy" Dandridge Bassett after they were inoculated. She then wrote to Nancy, "I have often wished for my Dear sister and Fanny [Nancy's daughter and Martha's niece], as the small pox was so trifleing with the Boys—believd that it would have been as slight with them." Martha Washington to Anna Maria Dandridge Bassett, November 18, 1777, Washington Family Collection, Library of Congress.

53. Martha Washington to Elizabeth Ramsay, December 30, 1775, NNPM: Literary and Historical Manuscripts.

54. Martha Washington to Burwell Bassett Sr., July 13, 1780, NjMoHP.

55. George Washington to Fielding Lewis Sr., June 28, 1781, Van Pelt-Dietrich Library, University of Pennsylvania.

56. George Washington to George William Fairfax, July 10, 1783, Papers of George Washington, Library of Congress.

57. George Washington to Jonathan Boucher, April 20, 1771, in *The Papers of George Washington, Colonial Series*, ed. W. W. Abbot and Dorothy Twohig (Charlottesville: University Press of Virginia, 1993), 8:448.

58. John Parke Custis to Martha Washington, October 12, 1781, ViMtvL: Martha Washington Collection.

59. Henry Knox to Clement Biddle, November 11, 1781, Gilder Lehrman Collection.

60. Nathanael Greene to George Washington, November 22, 1781, Papers of George Washington, Library of Congress.

61. Address to the Continental Congress, June 16, 1775, in *The Papers of George Washington, Revolutionary War Series*, ed. W. W. Abbot and Dorothy Twohig (Charlottesville: University Press of Virginia, 1985), 1:1.

62. George Washington's Account of Martha Washington's Revolutionary War Travel Expenses, July 1, 1783, ViMtvL: George Washington Collection.

"THE TENDER HEART OF THE CHIEF COULD NOT SUPPORT THE SCENE"

General Washington, Margaret Arnold, and the Treason at West Point

CHARLENE M. BOYER LEWIS

On September 25, 1780, in the upstairs bedroom of a large house near West Point, a patriot fort in the Hudson Highlands of New York, George Washington faced his most dangerous loyalist woman of the American Revolution, though he did not know it. Downstairs, just minutes before, his aide-de-camp Alexander Hamilton had handed him a packet of documents that made clear that Benedict Arnold, one of Washington's favorite officers, had committed treason by providing detailed information about the fort at West Point and other army matters to the recently captured John André, British General Sir Henry Clinton's adjutant general and spymaster. The news shook Washington to the core, and he trembled as he announced to Hamilton, General Henry Knox, and the Marquis de Lafayette that "Arnold has betrayed us!" and then forlornly wondered: "Whom can we trust now?"[1] Soon after Washington ordered Hamilton to ride off in hopes of intercepting the traitor, one of Benedict's aides-de-camp, Richard Varick, came rushing up to the General and told him that "Mrs. Arnold [had] request[ed] to see him." Varick escorted Washington upstairs to her bedroom. There, the General encountered, in Varick's words, a "poor[,] distressed, unhappy, frantic, and miserable lady," who was "in the most alarming distress of mind" and "had lost her reason."[2]

For the few hours between Benedict's escape and Washington's arrival at Robinson House, where the Arnolds lived, Margaret had been, according to Varick, "raving distracted" with a "wild look." Weeping, shrieking, and delusional, and, as Varick scandalously noted, "with her hair dishevelled and flowing about her neck; her morning gown with few other clothes remained on her, too few to be seen even by a gentleman of the family much less by many strangers." Margaret had cried out to him that her husband "will never return" and that he was "gone forever," pointing to the ceiling and shouting "*there, there, there*, the spirits have carried [him] up there; they have put hot irons in his head." She had already grabbed Varick by his hand and asked: "'*Colonel Varick, have you ordered my child killed.*'" Then, Varick reported, she "fell on her knees at my feet with prayers and intreaties to spare her innocent babe."[3] Greatly alarmed, Varick had "felt apprehensive of something more than ordinary having occasioned her hysterics and utter frenzy" and had summoned a doctor. When she eventually shouted that only General Washington could remove the "hot iron on her head" and that she "wanted to see the General," Varick quickly brought Washington to her. When the commander-in-chief entered her bed chamber and Varick told her "there was General Washington," she held her baby in her arms and shrieked that the man was not Washington, and even after Washington assured her that he was, she cried at him "that is the man who was agoing to assist Colonel Varick in killing my child."[4] According to another source, "the tender Heart of the Chief could not support the Scene [and] he was obliged to leave her" to the care of Major David Franks, another of Benedict's aides-de-camp, and her housekeeper.[5] Washington returned downstairs to Hamilton, Knox, and Lafayette, who all remained desperately worried about Margaret even as their rage at Benedict grew. Later that afternoon, Washington received a letter from Benedict, now safely on a British ship, attempting to explain his motives and asking his former commander to protect his wife since she was "as good and as innocent as an angel and is incapable of doing wrong."[6] Washington reportedly threw the letter away from him "with Indignation, saying, 'Wretch, did he think I would treat Mrs. Arnold with Humanity for his sake, no, she is far above him & Every Tenderness in my Power shall be shown her.'"[7]

The next morning, Lafayette described the distressing scene in a letter to the French minister: "Her husband told her before going away that he was flying never to come back, and he left her lying unconscious. When she came to herself, she fell into frightful convulsions, and completely lost her reason. We did everything we could to quiet her; but she looked upon us as the murderers of her husband, and it was impossible to restore her to her senses. The horror with which her husband's conduct has inspired her, and a thousand other feelings, make her the most unhappy of women."[8] Hamilton, in a letter to his fiancée Elizabeth Schuyler, called it "the most affecting scene I ever was witness to" as "one moment she raved; another she melted into tears; sometimes she pressed her infant to her bosom and lamented its fate . . . in a manner that would have pierced insensibility itself." He then added, "We have every reason to believe she was intirely unacquainted with the plan."[9]

Lafayette, Hamilton, and the rest were all relieved when Margaret "recovered her reason" the next morning, and Lafayette was especially pleased when Margaret "sent for me to go up to her chamber" since he was "on very good terms with her."[10] Hamilton also "paid her a visit" while she was still abed, when she was "more composed," and "endeavoured to sooth her by every method in my power."[11] What Margaret thought about the whole scene we will never know.

Beginning on September 25, 1780, Margaret Shippen Arnold became known as the traitor's wife. Though the stories told about the treason— at the time and later—rarely included her as a significant player, Margaret had definitely played an active part in the treachery and had consciously made a number of choices with her husband that ended up placing her in this dangerous situation at West Point.

Margaret's father, Edward Shippen, a wealthy Philadelphia judge from a long-established Pennsylvania family, had worked diligently to avoid choosing a side since the revolution began, a stance which caused many patriots to think of him as a loyalist. His children, including Margaret (called Peggy), the youngest, kept knocking the family off the delicate line he was attempting to walk. During the British occupation of Philadelphia in the winter of 1777–78, Edward's daughters and their girlfriends had relished the social whirl created by the British officers, especially John André. The lively officers staged plays for them, went sleighing with them, established a Dancing Assembly, and regularly drank tea in the women's drawing rooms and parlors. These young ladies happily played the role of loyalist flirts. André and his friends especially enjoyed visiting the Shippen household on Fourth Street with its four vivacious daughters, and Peggy seems to have become their favorite Shippen sister. She and André became especially good friends, though apparently not romantically involved. He even sketched her in a costume he designed for the most magnificent of his Philadelphia entertainments—the Meschianza Ball, which was held in honor of General Howe's departure and was an amazing spectacle of jousting knights, costumed ladies, decorated barges floating down the Schuylkill, and a grand illuminated ball with fireworks at the end of the evening. There were fourteen young ladies who were particularly honored by the knights, which included Peggy and two of her sisters. They wore dazzling "Turkish costumes," that were not as skimpy as that description suggests. The ladies' long white dresses flowed back like a robe, with pink sashes covered in spangles, and each woman donned a small turban that held the favors—pearls, jewels, and feathers—they intended to award to the knights who were to joust in their honor.[12] It must have been one of the highlights of Peggy's young life.

In mid-June 1778, when the British decided to leave Philadelphia and concentrate their resources in New York City, the young women had been disappointed. They knew the returning patriots would not be nearly so entertaining and attentive—nor so approving of frivolities during wartime. Yet, eighteen-year-old Peggy quickly became the focus of the amorous attentions of the new commanding military governor of Philadelphia, Major General Benedict Arnold, who was thirty-seven.

The dashing hero of Saratoga, still limping from the injuries of that battle, intrigued her, and her beauty captivated him. Supposition says that they probably met through Robert Morris and his wife. Benedict soon began sending her love letters, declaring by September that he possessed "a tender and ardent passion" for her and that "on you alone my happiness depends."[13] And he visited her regularly enough to fuel gossip about their future in the city and beyond. The gossips could not resist using military analogies. One wrote about how the general "lays close siege to Peggy." Another, a female cousin, had heard that Peggy intended "to surrender soon" and was not surprised since, in her view, "the fort could not hold out long; after all, there is nothing like perseverance [in] a regular attack."[14] Peggy kept his ardent passion at bay for many months but finally accepted his marriage proposal and wed him at her family

John André's sketch of Peggy Shippen for the Meschianza Ball, 1778. (Image courtesy of the Yale University Art Gallery)

home in April 1779. The loyalist flirt had chosen to become a patriot bride. By that time, however, some of Benedict's glory had faded as he faced growing problems and tensions with officers in the Continental army, with members of the Continental Congress, and, especially, with Joseph Reed, the president of Pennsylvania's Supreme Executive Council, who heartily despised him.

After her wedding, Margaret (like other newlywed women, she seems to have adopted her more formal name at marriage) moved into one of the grandest houses in Philadelphia, Richard Penn's mansion. That was where Benedict had taken up residence upon his entrance into the city—an action that provoked a lot of criticism from patriot quarters. Here, with the help of her sister-in-law, Margaret became the mistress of a large household, a role she had assuredly been groomed for but one that would have been immensely difficult to perform well in the middle of a war and in a home that also served as a military headquarters. During their engagement and the first weeks of their marriage, she must have listened to Benedict's constant complaints about his unfair treatment by just about everyone he had encountered. The couple was also anxiously awaiting the verdict of Benedict's court martial on several charges dealing with the misuse of his power and military stores. In addition, the pair soon faced money problems because of their high style of living and Benedict's difficulties in getting repayment from Congress for military expenses he had regularly covered out of his own pocket dating back to the Quebec campaign of 1775.[15] As a daughter of a neutral father who had been harassed by patriot officials and, more significantly, as a devoted wife, Margaret increasingly shared her husband's resentments toward Continental and Pennsylvania authorities, a "set of men," according to Benedict, "void of principle" who had placed the Arnolds in such a "cruel situation."[16] With his honor and reputation under attack, Benedict's frustrations became hers.

As the Arnolds worked their way toward their eventual decision to turn to the British, Margaret's previous friendship with John André proved immensely useful to the couple. It was André—now serving as adjutant general for the British commander-in-chief of North America, Sir Henry Clinton, while secretly acting as his spymaster—who ultimately received the couple's initial proposal in the early summer of 1779 that Benedict was ready to help the British, either by coming over to them immediately or working with them on "Concerting the means of a blow of importance." André's first correspondence with the Arnolds already used code names for the key players and suggested that they all use a secret code and invisible ink to write between the lines of seemingly normal letters. André's letter clearly indicated that Margaret would be involved in whatever plans developed: "The Lady [meaning Margaret] might write to me at the Same time [as] one of her intimates[.] She will guess who I mean [he meant Peggy Chew], the latter remaining ignorant of [the invisible] interlining and sending the letter" unknowingly on to André. He then suggested that "the letters may talk of the Meschianza & other nonsense."[17] Only Margaret, not Benedict, could write such letters.

The conspiracy was slow to develop, with Benedict and Margaret wavering and waiting to see how he would ultimately be treated by both sides. By the summer of 1780, however, after their first son's birth in March, both the couple's financial difficulties and their frustrations with the patriots, both military and civilian, had increased to such a point that going over to the British seemed to be the best answer to all of their problems. After lengthy negotiations between Benedict and André and Clinton, the Arnolds moved forward with a plan to commit treason. Before the summer was over, Benedict managed to convince General George Washington to appoint him commander of West Point—a strategically valuable fort that defended the Hudson Highlands of New York and had been long coveted by the British. New York congressman Robert Livingston had recommended Benedict for the post, stating that it could be "most safely confided to Genl. Arnold whose courage is undoubted [and] who is the favourite of our militia."[18] Livingston was also an admirer of Margaret, who may have pursued a friendship with him in order to gain the congressman's support for her husband. Indeed, their flirtations caused Benedict's sister Hannah to write her brother, warning him that Livingston was "a dangerous companion for a particular lady in the absence of her husband" and adding that "I could tell you of frequent private assignations and of numberless billets-doux, if I had an inclination to make mischief, but as I am of a very peaceable temper, I'll not mention a syllable of the matter."[19]

In August, Benedict moved into a nicely appointed house near the fort that had been confiscated from the loyalist Beverly Robinson; Margaret and their infant son, Edward, joined him there in mid-September.

By that time, the plot to turn over West Point to the British was in place, with the possibility that General Washington, who had scheduled a visit to the fort at the end of September, would provide an even greater prize. Benedict demanded £10,000 (over $2.2 million today) for his efforts and his defection. Clinton promised only £6,000, but André said he could get Benedict the larger sum if everything succeeded according to plan.[20] The couple's hopes for their future must have been high. But, then, on September 25 everything fell apart.

That morning, at Robinson House, Benedict and Margaret were expecting Washington, his aides-de-camp Alexander Hamilton and the Marquis de Lafayette, General Henry Knox, and some others to join them for breakfast. Then, a message arrived from one of Benedict's officers that André had been arrested at a nearby army camp with detailed maps and papers about West Point hidden in his boots. At that moment, no one knew Benedict had given the information to André—except for Margaret. Benedict raced upstairs to Margaret's bed chamber to tell her that their plot had been discovered. We can only imagine their furtive and frantic conversation. Benedict ordered his horse, gave a quick excuse to his aide David Franks, and fled to a British ship anchored in the Hudson, beyond the reach of the patriots' guns. With her little boy still in his crib, Margaret now had to face all alone the exposure of their treachery and the looming presence of Washington and his officers. The pressure proved too much. By the time Washington, Knox, Hamilton, and Lafayette, now all at the Arnolds' house, had been informed of André's arrest and Benedict's treachery, Margaret had broken down.

Much of what took place during those few days in Robinson House at West Point—in fact, much of the story of Benedict Arnold and his treason—is shrouded in legend and outright fiction. Since the mid-nineteenth century, various writers have concocted details to make these events even more dramatic, with little care for separating fact from fiction. Jared Sparks's 1835 *The Life and Treason of Benedict Arnold* and Isaac Arnold's 1905 *The Life of Benedict Arnold: His Patriotism and His Treason* provided much of the narrative *and many of the conclusions* for later historians, even though those two biographers did not have access to the British side of the correspondence concerning the treason (which was not available until 1941) and were far more committed to teaching the lessons of treachery to good patriotic Americans than to carefully analyzing sources and explaining historical context. In the 1950s, James Flexner, in one of the most popular and still influential twentieth-century histories of the treason, criticized earlier histories where "legend is mixed with useful fact," but then he continued to do the same, making up, for example, entire scenes in Robinson House with absolutely no evidence.[21] His telling, as well as Sparks's and Arnold's earlier ones, have shaped much of the way historians—popular and academic—view the treason and, especially, Peggy Arnold. For over two centuries, including as recently as 2018, fictional elaborations and unsubstantiated stories have been propagated from one history to the next, many times almost word-for-word. The treason at West Point has been told in a number of ways—as a morality tale, a patriotic tale, or just a thumping good story—with only the rare scholar going back to the primary sources and sifting the fact from the fiction in the existing accounts.

Some mysteries will always surround this episode; it involved spies, conspiracies, and secrets. Like the Salem Witch Trials or the Burr Conspiracy, some key documents are missing and some of the key players never chronicled what they actually thought or did. While most of us know the story of Benedict Arnold's treason, few of us know the story of Margaret's treason. We think we know Benedict's motivations: some combination of greed, frustration, revenge, hatred of the French alliance, and concern for his family's welfare. We think of Benedict as the most notorious traitor in American history, and historians have spent reams of paper chronicling every step of the treason and trying to explain Benedict's motives. But, we still know little about his wife Margaret (or Peggy), the role she played, and her possible motivations.[22] Some of Benedict's biographers have basically left her out of the narrative altogether; some have declared her fully innocent; some have even placed all of the blame for Benedict's treachery at her feet. Most recent works that have discussed her, though not all, see her as certainly part of the plot, but differ regarding how fully she was involved.

If we change our focus on the Arnolds' actions to include Margaret and not just Benedict, the narrative and significance of the treason and its context change. And, more importantly, so much more about revolutionary America is revealed. When we shift the focus of our usual examinations of the Revolutionary War from men's experiences to include women's, much can be learned about this era more broadly—not just about women. Even with Linda Kerber's and Mary Beth Norton's path-breaking works in 1980 and the works of other historians since then, there is still so much to understand about women's lives during the revolution and so much to learn about the broader picture of this time period from their gendered experiences of the war.[23] Looking at the responses to Margaret's and Benedict's actions reveals Americans' views about patriotism, citizenship, and loyalty as well as gender, marriage, and wifely fidelity during this unstable era.

Rewriting the treason at West Point with a focus on Margaret as well as Benedict transforms that story and its significance in multiple ways. First, this retold story makes clear how the political became so personal and the personal became so political during the American Revolution. A narrative equally centered on Margaret and Benedict becomes a narrative centered around a married couple, not simply a disgruntled and ambitious war hero. Much of the action in my rewritten story takes place not on battlefields and in war rooms, but in households and families — key spaces of change during the revolution. As Dallett Hemphill argued, the sweeping transformations involved in turning away from a patriarchal, monarchical culture and forming a new republican nation were "first felt in families." Similarly, Lorri Glover has stated that "in the revolutionary age, family values transformed alongside political culture" as adults "nurtured egalitarianism and individualism in their households no less than in government."[24] The Arnold household, first in Philadelphia and then at West Point, served as a site of political and personal negotiation as husband and wife figured out what to do and, then, how to play their strategic cards with André, Clinton, and their go-betweens. Since few sources about their lives together during this period survive (beyond those held by the British about the treason), it is hard to discern the level of conflict or agreement between Benedict and Margaret during these years. Yet, we can assume that there must have been much back and forth over means and goals.

Further, a focus on Margaret instead of Benedict also provides another example of women as strong actors during the revolution, not just passive spectators or occasional participants.[25] Multitudes of women, like Margaret Shippen Arnold, made choices — sometimes carefully, sometimes rashly — about loyalty, patriotism, and duty. These choices helped to determine their identities. During the American Revolution, as Margaret Arnold or Martha Washington demonstrate, women, like men, calculated odds and tried to figure out what was best for their families and their own desires.[26] Knowing about other active women during the revolution, it makes good sense to argue that the treason at West Point involved both of the Arnolds fully. Margaret was an important player in the betrayal. She certainly does not seem to be solely responsible for Benedict's decision to turn and probably was not an equal partner in their treachery, but it could not have been set in motion nor could Benedict have escaped so successfully without her help.

Assuming Margaret supported and aided her husband in his turn to the British is not a shocking conclusion. We already know of many other wives in revolutionary America who readily took their husband's side in disputes and were quick to defend his (and, therefore, their own) reputation. We only need to think of Martha Washington and Abigail Adams to prove the point. Surely, Margaret Arnold can fall into this category of supportive wife as well. The key difference is that those women were praised as patriotic wives for aiding their husbands, not condemned as the wife of a traitor. If Benedict had chosen to stay "the hero of Saratoga," Margaret would have joined the illustrious group of exemplary patriot wives.

Reorienting the narrative around Margaret also highlights the importance of gender constructions to not only private but also public identity during the revolution. And the day of her breakdown is a perfect illustration of this. Most historians who include an account of this episode have firmly declared that Margaret was simply acting, as one put it, in "an apparently prearranged delay of several hours" in which she used a calculated display of hysterics to buy time for her husband to escape to safety.[27] They have accused Margaret of knowingly "distracting the commander in chief at this critical juncture" and of "decid[ing] that insanity was her best defense."[28] Another account portrays her behavior on September 25 as "the grandest theatrical performance of her life," when she "successfully deceived Washington and Hamilton" and "hoodwinked" Lafayette through her "feigned fits."[29] Similarly, one of her biographers has labeled her emotional response "a calculated piece of theater" and "a distraction aimed to give Arnold time to make good his escape" that ended up "fool[ing]" the American officers.[30] Another writer has granted that her hysterics may have "at first been genuine," but then asserts that she soon "was consciously playing a role" for the men present.[31] This scene can be understood very differently, however, if we look at the sources in different ways, ways that place Margaret at their center.

If this was a performance, it was a performance of ingrained gender roles, in which not only Margaret but also the gentlemen who witnessed her breakdown played their well-learned roles of refined gentlemen and ladies. These genteel roles included more than just knowing how to sit a horse correctly, dance the minuet expertly, and wear clothing fashionably. All of the key players at Robinson House that day were products of an elite culture that prized displays of emotion, sensitivity, and sympathy for others—what they called "sensibility"—as appropriate signs of well-bred men and women. As Nicole Eustace has shown, the American Revolution was not just a political upheaval but an emotional one, as colonists developed new ideas about who was entitled to express anger, grief, and love. During the revolution, as historian Sarah Knott concludes, the culture of sensibility actually helped create bonds among citizens who were struggling to shape a new nation.[32] The events at Robinson House reveal these changes perfectly. The late eighteenth-century culture of sensibility and refinement provided the context for these people's reactions; in fact, it dictated how this scene at Robinson House would play out in its broad outlines. Those gendered cultural strictures guided the responses of these men and that woman during the crisis of the treason's exposure.

While Washington seems to have left no record of this scene, Margaret's brother-in-law reported just over a week after her breakdown that the General "certifies [and here he used direct quotes] 'that he has every Reason to believe she is innocent, & Requests all persons to treat her with that Humanity & Tenderness due to her Sex & Virtues.'"[33] The words here matter tremendously: "humanity," "tenderness," and "due to her Sex & Virtues." Those words are loaded, and everyone who read them in the 1780s would have understood their cultural and gendered significance.

Margaret's "sex and virtues"—and, crucially, her elite status—dictated that she would respond as a lady in distress, even if they did not determine her specific words and actions. And the studied humanity and tenderness of the gentlemen who witnessed her breakdown meant that they read her actions, and her physical appearance, in very particular ways. Some earlier writers have made much of the fact that this scene occurred in Margaret's bedroom and that Washington, Hamilton, and Lafayette all visited her there, imbuing the moment with something of a sexual overtone (a few even have added the fictional detail that her gown slipped off her shoulder while Washington was present, which embarrassed him and caused him to quickly retreat). However, these chroniclers forget that women's bed chambers were semi-public spaces in the eighteenth century; it was not at all unusual for gentlemen to visit ladies there. In this story, it is not the bedroom visits that are remarkable; it is Margaret's appearance and outcries.

Even though gentlemen often visited women in their bed chambers in this era, ladies did not greet them in only their morning gown and with their hair in disarray, as Richard Varick noted with apparent shock. Ladies did not weep and wail in front of gentlemen, let alone seem to lose their senses and shout out that they saw their husband in the ceiling and declare that one of them, George Washington no less, was there to murder her child. It was precisely because Margaret so transgressed the boundaries of appropriate genteel conduct for ladies that Washington, Hamilton, and Lafayette wholly believed in her innocence. It was the only way for them to explain her behavior. For these honorable men, the hysterics proved her ladylike delicacy—and her innocence. The presence of baby Edward also mattered in the retelling of this scene, emphasizing the growing cultural importance of women as mothers. Seeing Margaret as a mother desperately trying to protect her child also showed her vulnerability. This fact just added to these gentlemen's sense of her innocence. Given their ingrained ideas about refined behavior and women, the three gentlemen regarded Margaret with pity, rather than suspicion, and sought ways to ease her difficulties.

As importantly, her distress also gave them a chance to display their own sensibility, their manly sympathy for her plight. While this woman in her grief and fear breached the standards of genteel behavior and appearance, these respectable men were not about to breach their own. We can see this in both Lafayette's and Hamilton's long letters, detailing her agonies as well as their efforts to soothe her and help her. Her extreme emotions, typical of a delicate female, allowed them to express their own correct, manly emotions to others. Writing to the Chevalier

Margaret Shippen Arnold
and one of her children,
painted in London, by
Daniel Gardner. (Philadelphia History Museum at the
Atwater Kent/Bridgeman
Images)

de La Luzerne, for example, Lafayette framed his account of his efforts
to calm and reassure Margaret, by insisting that "the unhappy Mrs. Arnold's" situation "must touch every humane heart." He also "implore[d]"
Luzerne "to use your influence in her favor" in Philadelphia, adding that
"it would be exceedingly painful to General Washington if she were not
treated with the greatest kindness"—note the "painful."[34]

Hamilton decided that Margaret's breakdown was a chance to prove
himself to his fiancée, Elizabeth Schulyer. He penned her a long letter
during the evening of September 25, finishing it the next morning. In
it, he described Margaret in all the appropriate terms, revealing how
this sympathetic gentleman understood the scene: "All the sweetness
of beauty, all the loveliness of innocence, all the tenderness of a wife
and all the fondness of a mother showed themselves in her appearance
and conduct." "Her sufferings were so eloquent," he continued, "that I
wished myself her brother, to have a right to become her defender." The
letter was a perfect performance by an impassioned gentleman who
made clear that he would dutifully do his utmost to protect not only
the distressed Margaret in the present, but also—and importantly—his
own beloved Elizabeth in the future. After condemning Benedict for

his ungentlemanly behavior in abandoning his wife, Hamilton ardently concluded: "indeed my angelic Betsey, I would not for the world do any thing that would hazard your esteem. 'Tis to me a jewel of inestimable price & I think you may rely I shall never make you blush."[35]

Ladies could be damsels in distress; gentlemen were expected to face adversity with courage. The response to the hanging of John André in early October 1780 offers a fascinating juxtaposition to Margaret's breakdown, further illuminating the gendered nature of this culture of sensibility. Both events provided perfect scenes for the display of sensibility and genteel manners by each of the participants—the sufferer and the witnesses—but the expectations for appropriate behavior were different for men than for women.[36] There were far more witnesses to André's hanging, and they told and retold the story in multiple forms. André's remarkable composure and comportment as he walked to the gallows became the center of these stories, just as Margaret's remarkable hysterics were the center of the stories about her. Benjamin Tallmadge related that André "met death with a smile, chearfully marching to the place of execution," and bowing to the men he recognized in the crowd.[37] Margaret's shouting and wailing and her dishabille had elicited tender feelings from the men who watched her. Except for one brief moment when he saw the gallows, a moment that proved André was a man of feeling, André's fortitude and his elegance brought forth exactly the same feelings amongst the American officers who witnessed the hanging. Many of the stories about André noted how the officers held back tears as they listened to him declare: "'You will all bear witness that I met my fate like a brave man,'" and then watched the honorable officer swing.[38] In a letter to John Laurens, Hamilton went on for pages praising all of André's admirable qualities and lamenting his demise: "he united a peculiar elegance of mind and manners, and the advantage of a pleasing person. . . . His sentiments were elevated and inspired esteem. they had a softness that conciliated affection."[39] It was with "compassion" and "esteem" that these patriot officers viewed this particular honorable enemy, just as they had viewed Margaret. Their reactions also proved that patriot men were men of refinement and feeling, that they were gentlemen fighting for the cause of freedom, not some rebellious rabble rousers.

The officers at Robinson House demonstrated not only that they had learned and completely accepted the ways in which genteel men and women thought and behaved, but also that they had consciously mastered the intricate protocols of war adhered to by professional armies in Great Britain and Europe that patriot officers, especially Washington, so desperately wanted to follow. They "prided themselves" on "playing by the same rules" as the British.[40] Washington seems to have regularly sought out moments when he could display his sense of himself as a consummate gentleman and an officer, and Margaret's pitiful situation gave him plenty of opportunities. For example, when Benedict had written to Washington after fleeing to the British, he had enclosed a letter for Margaret, which Washington accordingly had a messenger deliver to her upstairs, along with the news "that, although his duty required him to do all that was possible to arrest [General] Arnold, he was glad to inform her that [Arnold] had found safety on board a British ship." The French soldier who had arrived with Lafayette considered these "Noble words, which only a noble nature could have uttered!"[41]

This desire to follow English military protocols as well as to act as gentlemen also helps to explain Hamilton's, Lafayette's, and Varick's responses to Margaret's breakdown. It also explains Washington's motives in ultimately releasing Margaret. During war, such men believed that officers should be gentlemen, showing civility and respect to women and children. Seeing Margaret as innocent, treating her with extra care, and then letting her go all proved that Washington was a gentleman general. On September 27, after Margaret was far more composed, Washington offered her the choice of returning to her family in Philadelphia or crossing enemy lines and joining her husband in New York City. Interestingly, she chose her family, probably because they promised more security for her and her baby. Escorted by a solicitous Major Franks, they left for Philadelphia. Apparently, not one of the officers had questioned her about anything. The scene at Robinson House was a performance. But it was a performance because gender roles are inherently performances and, as Richard Bushman has shown, so was the display of gentility in the late eighteenth century.[42] Margaret and the American officers were all performing that day, but they were not faking their parts.

Washington and his fellow officers' treatment of Margaret reveals even more. From their actions, it is clear that patriot gentlemen had a very hard time thinking of ladies as traitors or dangerous enemies. As Linda Kerber has claimed, "there was little room in the patriot position for the admission that women might make political choices that were distinct from—and at odds with—those of their husbands."[43] During the American Revolution, most men (and women) assumed women's loyalties were whatever their husbands' or fathers' were, even if women's actions time and again proved that was not the reality. The concept of coverture, that a married woman's legal identity was "covered" by her husband's, combined with the long-held belief that women did not possess political identities probably explains much of this view. At times, both the military and civilians certainly could regard wives as loyalists, and frequently punished them as such by confiscating their property or exiling them once patriots gained control of an area. They also categorized wives as occasional writers of letters to the enemy, smugglers of goods, or even concealers of suspected persons. And they took action against women who were believed to have persuaded men to desert from the military. Washington frequently complained about women committing these kinds of actions, which could have been considered treasonous since the general understanding of treason during the American Revolution included any act that gave aid or comfort to the enemy.[44] But, while patriots sometimes labeled loyalist women's actions treasonous, they rarely called them traitors, an important distinction and a gendered one. The standard punishments for traitors included death, exile, or "enforced service on a naval vessel." Reluctant to hang women and not able to place them in the navy, patriots turned to exile, property confiscation, fines, and, rarely, imprisonment for treasonous women. Importantly, extremely few women during the war were formally accused of being traitors, though many engaged in traitorous actions, and none were hanged.[45]

Under this contemporary definition, Margaret, just like her husband, committed treason. She certainly knew of the plot and talked with Benedict and the intermediaries who called at the Arnolds' Philadelphia home. Her correspondence with André definitely aided the enemy. The letters she conveyed to her husband from the British helped move the plot forward. And when Benedict fled from Robinson House to a British ship, she did not share this information with anyone, allowing him to get away. Yet none of those American officers considered her, unlike her husband, a traitor. Suspecting Margaret Arnold of being a traitor, of playing a major role in the potentially devastating treachery of her husband, was too far outside the gendered thinking of those gentlemen who witnessed her breakdown (and of many others who later heard of the treason). As other women discovered during the revolution, Margaret's elite status as a lady and her legal status as a wife saved her; that is, until she returned to Philadelphia.

With Margaret safely ensconced in her family's home, her father had hoped that she would remain with them, but Joseph Reed and the Executive Council considered her presence a dangerous threat to the patriot cause and to the "public safety" of the state. Even though she promised not to correspond with Benedict, the Council ordered her exiled from Pennsylvania and to "not return again during the continuance of the present war."[46] After freely choosing her family, Margaret was forced by the patriots to go to her husband in New York City. Her father reluctantly took her to him two weeks later. In November, Margaret left her Shippen family, little knowing what the future held for her or her child but certainly aware that she was now a committed loyalist and that her husband had barely escaped with his life.

Most Americans during and in the initial decades after the American Revolution seemed to have agreed with Washington, Hamilton, and Lafayette in considering Margaret innocent. Yet, some harbored doubts about her influence on Benedict, and their comments attest to the significance of women's roles during the revolution. In the early 1780s, the Marquis de Chastellux related that "it [was] generally believed" that Edward Shippen, "being himself a tory, had inspired his daughter with the same sentiments, and that the charms of this handsome woman contributed not a little to hasten to criminality a mind corrupted by avarice, before it felt the power of love."[47] Charles Thomson, the secretary of the Continental Congress, made the same link, writing soon after the treason was discovered that Benedict "was brave but avaricious, fond of parade and not very scrupulous about the means of acquiring money to defray the expence of it." He then ended with the more damning factor: "He had married a young woman who had been distinguished by genl Howes' Meschianza knights and her father was not remarkable for his attachment to the American cause."[48] Such a man, with such a wife, from such a family should have been long suspected. It would take until the late 1930s for her role in the treason to be fully discovered.

Concentrating on Margaret's life in these years underscores how fluid identity and loyalty could be during the war for men *and* for women, as this one woman moved from loyalist flirt to patriot bride to traitor's wife. The nature of the war often forced a recognition that women might have a political consciousness as some wives found themselves called upon to define their loyalties (which might or might not differ from their husbands'). Loyalist wives were viewed with great suspicion by the patriots as were patriot wives by loyalist officials. And many loyalist women were forced to abandon their property because their husbands, as well as themselves, were regarded as the enemy. When Margaret Arnold agreed to work with her husband in the plot to turn over West Point, she (and Benedict) abandoned a once-firm commitment to the patriots. They both became loyalists—and very active ones at that. Yet, as a wife, her loyalist identity and actions were lost on George Washington and most of the patriots. Only Joseph Reed and a few others regarded Margaret, as they did many other loyalist women, as a dangerous threat to the cause of liberty.

As so many of the Founders well understood at the time, many Americans vacillated in their support and sentiments depending on the fortunes of war in their immediate area. These vacillations mattered tremendously to the patriots' cause. Margaret seems to have decided to reject the neutral path of her father when she chose to marry Benedict and then made a second choice to identify as a British subject when she helped her husband commit treason. Yet, once the jig was up, she seems to have switched again, deciding that she could return to her family and safety, if not as a republican mother, then at least as a neutral citizen like her father. (Her father maintained the delicate balance so well that, after the war, he became chief justice of the Supreme Court of Pennsylvania in spite of his treasonous son-in-law and exiled daughter.) Patriot, loyalist, and British authorities all seemed to have trouble deciding how to label wives when they acted as if they had separate identities from their husbands. When a woman's husband was obviously a patriot or a loyalist and she seemed to act accordingly, it was easy to categorize her. But when a woman declared a different loyalty than her husband or, like Margaret, found herself forced into that decision, it became trickier for those authorities. Yet, many wives challenged those gender notions and enraged authorities when they made distinct political choices ranging from their fashions to their property.[49] Some women desperately tried to convince patriot authorities through petitions that they were separate beings from their husbands, that they held different political views and identities from their husbands and were patriots and not loyalists, and, then, that they deserved to have their confiscated property back. Some were successful; others were not. While never formally declaring herself separate from her husband, Margaret's choice to return to Philadelphia and her offer to have no communication with Benedict suggests that she may have thought of herself separately, at least for a time. Establishing a separate identity from a traitorous husband would certainly have better protected her and her son.

British documents from the planning of the treason and its disastrous aftermath make clear that they understood Margaret's shifting identities after September 1780. The British not only considered her a key player in the traitorous plot but also praised her loyalty to the crown. From the beginning, as already noted, John André's letters regularly referred to her or were even addressed to her, not just to Benedict. Moreover, an intermediary, Joseph Stansbury, stressed Margaret's crucial role when he alerted André in August 1780 that "things are so poorly arranged" with "Mr. Moore" (Benedict) at West Point that André's "last important Dispatches are yet in *her* hands."[50] And after the war was long over, when Benedict sought more money from King George or Parliament for his services, he commented on "the eminent danger [Margaret] had experienc'd" and reminded them that "the Pension given to Mrs. Arnold" by the king "was expressly given in consideration of the sufferings she endured, *the hazards She run*, and her being banished from her Friends, and Country in Consequence of her Loyalty."[51] "Running hazards" were words regularly used for risky and dangerous actions taken during the war; these were not words to describe a wife who had done nothing to help her husband commit treason. Margaret obviously had engaged in hazardous behavior. Furthermore, a deeply indebted British government would not have bestowed £500 per year in 1782 to an American woman for her "very meritorious" services, as Sir Henry Clinton called them, if she had done nothing beyond simply remaining loyal to her husband and, through him, to her government.[52] In fact, few female loyalists who petitioned the British government after the war received full compensation for their damaged or confiscated property, let alone a generous annuity as well as annuities for each of her children. In her active role as the traitor's wife, through the "hazards she run" and her "very meritorious" services, Margaret had served faithfully as a loyal subject on her own and, like her husband, reaped financial rewards for her choices, even if the rewards never met her expectations.

The war had been a revolution and there were a range of political choices to make and stances to take for both men *and* women. Many, such as Margaret Shippen Arnold, shifted loyalties and, therefore, identities multiple times during the war. As she moved from loyalist to patriot and then firmly back to loyalist, her decisions and behavior raised questions for authorities and others about whether women could be as political as men, how women could best serve the patriot cause, and whether their actions could be as threatening as men's. She forced many, including General George Washington, to consider whether married women should be viewed solely as extensions of their husbands or as separate entities. Margaret ultimately caused many to wonder how threatening women could be to the republican experiment. Moving Margaret Shippen Arnold from the margins to the center of an analysis of the West Point treason essentially rewrites the history of the American Revolution.

Notes

For their close readings of and insightful suggestions for this essay in its many versions, I would like to thank Craig Friend, Lorri Glover, Richard Godbeer, Dena Goodman, David Hancock, Cindy Kierner, James Lewis, Holly Mayer, John McCurdy, Barbara Oberg, and Ami Pflugrad-Jackisch. For their help with research and good ideas, I would also like to thank Linda August, Adam Erby, Sarah Heim, Connie King, Jim Green, and Samantha Snyder.

1. Jared Sparks, *The Life and Treason of Benedict Arnold* (Boston: Hilliard, Gray, 1835), 108.

2. Richard Varick, *The Varick Court of Inquiry to Investigate the Implication of Colonel Varick (Arnold's Private Secretary) in the Arnold Treason*, ed. Albert Bushnell Hart (Boston: The Bibliophile Society, 1907), 181–82; and Richard Varick to his sister Jane, 1 Oct. 1780, reprinted in *Varick Court of Inquiry*, 192.

3. Varick to his sister Jane, 1 Oct. 1780, in Varick, 191.

4. Varick, 191–92.

5. Edward Burd to Jasper Yeates, 5 Oct. 1780, in "Notes and Queries," *Pennsylvania Magazine of History and Biography* 40 (1916): 381.
6. Benedict Arnold to George Washington, 25 Sept. 1780, *Founders Online*, National Archives, https://founders.archives.gov/documents/Washington/99-01-02-03372.
7. Burd to Yeates, 5 Oct. 1780, in "Notes and Queries," 381.
8. Marquis de Lafayette to Chevalier de La Luzerne, 25–26 Sept. 1780, in Charlemagne Tower, *The Marquis de Lafayette in the American Revolution* (Philadelphia: J. B. Lippincott Co., 1901), 2:167–68.
9. Alexander Hamilton to Elizabeth Schuyler, 25 Sept. [1780], in *The Papers of Alexander Hamilton*, ed. Harold C. Syrett (New York: Columbia University Press, 1961), 2:441.
10. Lafayette to La Luzerne, 25–26 Sept. 1780, in Tower, *Marquis de Lafayette*, 2:167–68.
11. Hamilton to Schuyler, 25 Sept. [1780], in Syrett, *Papers of Alexander Hamilton*, 2:442.
12. John André, "Particulars of the Mischianza exhibited in America at the departure of Gen. Howe," *Gentleman's Magazine* 48 (Aug. 1778): 353–57. See also David S. Shields and Fredrika J. Teute, "The Meschianza: Sum of All Fêtes," *Journal of the Early Republic* 35 (Summer 2015): 185–214.
13. Benedict Arnold to Peggy Shippen, 25 Sept. 1778, in Lewis Burd Walker, "Life of Margaret Shippen, Wife of Benedict Arnold," *Pennsylvania Magazine of History and Biography* 25 (1901): 30.
14. Edward Shippen to James Burd, 2 Jan. 1779, Shippen Papers, 595a, Historical Society of Pennsylvania, Philadelphia (hereafter HSP); Elizabeth Tilghman to Elizabeth Shippen Burd, 29 Jan. 1779, Balch Shippen Papers, HSP.
15. See Nathaniel Philbrick, *Valiant Ambition: George Washington, Benedict Arnold, and the Fate of the American Revolution* (New York: Viking Press, 2016), chap. 9; and Stephen Brumwell, *Turncoat: Benedict Arnold and the Crisis of American Liberty* (New Haven: Yale University Press, 2018), chaps. 4 and 5.
16. Benedict Arnold to George Washington, 14 May 1779, reprinted in *A Hero and A Spy: The Revolutionary War Correspondence of Benedict Arnold*, ed. Russell M. Lea (New York: Heritage Books, 2006), 339.
17. John André to Joseph Stansbury, [10 May 1779], in Carl Van Doren, *Secret History of the American Revolution* (New York: Viking Press, 1941), 439–40.
18. Robert Livingston to George Washington, 22 June 1780, in Paul H. Smith et al., eds., *Letters of Delegates to Congress, 1774–1789* (*American Memory Online*, accessed Jan. 20, 2020), 15:364.

19. Hannah Arnold to Benedict Arnold, 4 Sept. 1780, in Van Doren, *Secret History*, 303–4.

20. Philbrick, *Valiant Ambition*, 290.

21. James Thomas Flexner, *The Traitor and the Spy: Benedict Arnold and John André* (Boston: Little, Brown, 1975), 419.

22. There are two popular biographies of Margaret Arnold: Mark Jacob and Stephen H. Case, *Treacherous Beauty: Peggy Shippen and the Woman Behind the Plot to Betray America* (Guilford, CT: Lyons Press, 2012) and Nancy Rubin Stuart, *Defiant Brides: The Untold Story of Two Revolutionary-Era Women and the Radical Men They Married* (Boston: Beacon Press, 2013). Both present her as actively a part of the conspiracy. Two of the most recent biographies of Benedict divide over her role. Steven Brumwell, in his impressive *Turncoat*, considers her an active player, while Joyce Lee Malcolm, in *The Tragedy of Benedict Arnold: An American Life* (New York: Pegasus Books, 2018), insists on her innocence.

23. Linda K. Kerber, *Women of the Republic: Intellect and Ideology in Revolutionary America* (Chapel Hill: University of North Carolina Press, 1980) and Mary Beth Norton, *Liberty's Daughters: The Revolutionary Experience of American Women, 1750–1800* (Ithaca: Cornell University Press, 1980). For more recent works, see Cynthia A. Kierner, *Beyond the Household: Women's Place in the Early South, 1700–1835* (Ithaca: Cornell University Press, 1998); Rosemarie Zagarri, *A Woman's Dilemma: Mercy Otis Warren and the American Revolution* (Wheeling, IL: Harlan Davidson, 1995) and *Revolutionary Backlash: Women and Politics in the Early American Republic* (Philadelphia: University of Pennsylvania Press, 2007); and Carol Berkin, *Revolutionary Mothers: Women in the Struggle for America's Independence* (New York: Knopf, 2005).

24. C. Dallett Hemphill, *Siblings: Brothers and Sisters in American History* (New York: Oxford University Press, 2011), 4–5; Lorri Glover, *Founders as Fathers: The Private Lives and Politics of the American Revolutionaries* (New Haven: Yale University Press, 2014), 132.

25. See works cited above and Joy Day Buel and Richard Buel Jr., *The Way of Duty: A Woman and Her Family in Revolutionary America* (New York: Norton, 1984); Zagarri, *A Woman's Dilemma*; Edith B. Gelles, *Portia: The World of Abigail Adams* (Bloomington: Indiana University Press, 1992); and Woody Holton, *Abigail Adams* (New York: Free Press, 2009).

26. For two informative discussions of Philadelphia women making a wide range of choices during the American Revolution, see Judith Van Buskirk, "They Didn't Join the Band: Disaffected Women in Revolutionary Philadelphia," *Pennsylvania History* 62 (Summer 1995): 306–29; and Kimberly

Nath, "Left Behind: Loyalist Women in Philadelphia during the American Revolution," in *Women in the American Revolution: Gender, Politics, and the Domestic World*, ed. Barbara B. Oberg (Charlottesville: University of Virginia Press, 2019), 211–28.

27. Philbrick, *Valiant Ambition*, 311.

28. Philbrick, 312.

29. Rubin Stuart, *Defiant Brides*, 100, 99, 96.

30. Jacob and Case, *Treacherous Beauty*, 164–65.

31. Flexner, *The Traitor and the Spy*, 373–74. See also Willard Sterne Randall, *Benedict Arnold: Patriot and Traitor* (New York: William Morrow and Company, 1990).

32. See Nicole Eustace, *Passion is the Gale: Emotion, Power, and the Coming of the American Revolution* (Chapel Hill: University of North Carolina Press, 2008) and Sarah Knott, *Sensibility and the American Revolution* (Chapel Hill: University of North Carolina Press, 2009), especially 153–93. Her understanding of Margaret's breakdown and Alexander Hamilton's response is similar to mine.

33. Burd to Yeates, 5 Oct. 1780, in "Notes and Queries," 381.

34. Lafayette to La Luzerne, 25–26 Sept. 1780, in Tower, *Marquis de Lafayette*, 2:168.

35. Hamilton to Schuyler, 25 Sept. [1780], in Syrett, *Papers of Alexander Hamilton*, 2:441–42.

36. Sarah Knott presents a similar understanding of the response to André's hanging in *Sensibility and the American Revolution*, 158–84.

37. Benjamin Tallmadge to Colonel Wadsworth, 4 Oct. 1780, in *Correspondence and Journals of Samuel Blachley Webb*, ed. Worthington C. Ford (New York: Arno Press, 1969), 2:294.

38. Knott, *Sensibility and the American Revolution*, 159.

39. Hamilton to John Laurens, 11 Oct. 1780, in Syrett, *Papers of Alexander Hamilton*, 2:467.

40. Andrew O'Shaughnessy, *The Men Who Lost America: British Leadership, the American Revolution, and the Fate of the Empire* (New Haven: Yale University Press, 2013), 354; Charles Royster, *A Revolutionary People at War: The Continental Army and American Character, 1775–1783* (Chapel Hill: University of North Carolina Press, 1979).

41. Gaston Maussion de la Bastie to his mother, 15 Oct. 1780, in *They Knew the Washingtons: Letters from a French Soldier with Lafayette and from His Family in Virginia*, trans. Princess Radziwill (Indianapolis: Bobbs-Merrill Company, 1926), 98–99.

42. Richard Bushman, *The Refinement of America: Persons, Houses, Cities* (New York: Vintage, 1992).

43. Kerber, *Women of the Republic*, 51.

44. See Bradley Chapin, *The American Law of Treason: Revolutionary and Early National Origins* (Seattle: University of Washington Press, 1964), especially chaps. 3 and 4.

45. Linda K. Kerber, *No Constitutional Right to Be Ladies: Women and the Obligations of Citizenship* (New York: Hill and Wang, 1999), 16–18. See also Kerber, *Women of the Republic* and Berkin, *Revolutionary Mothers*. Virginian Mary Willing Byrd faced a formal charge of treason in 1781, but whether her case actually went to trial is unclear. See Ami Pflugrad-Jackisch, "'What Am I but an American?': Mary Willing Byrd and Westover Plantation during the American Revolution," in Oberg, *Women in the American Revolution*, 176–81.

46. *Minutes of the Supreme Executive Council of Pennsylvania, From Its Organization to the Termination of the Revolution* (Harrisburg: State of Pennsylvania, 1853), 12:520.

47. Marquis de Chastellux, *Travels in North-America in the Years 1780-81-82* (New York, 1828), 1:114.

48. Charles Thomson to John Jay, 12 Oct. 1780, in *The Selected Papers of John Jay*, ed. Elizabeth M. Nuxoll (Charlottesville: University of Virginia Press, 2012), 297.

49. For the furor caused by fashionable women during the war, see Kate Haulman, *The Politics of Fashion in Eighteenth-Century America* (Chapel Hill: University of North Carolina Press, 2011), chap. 5.

50. Joseph Stansbury to Jonathan Odell, 14 Aug. 1780, in Henry Clinton Papers, William Clements Library, University of Michigan (emphasis in the original).

51. Benedict Arnold to William Pitt, 15 Nov. 1792, PRO 30/8/108, folio 197, and Benedict Arnold to George Rose, 29 July 1792, PRO 30/8/108, folio 210, Chatham Papers, National Archives, Kew, England (emphasis mine). My deepest thanks to Stephen Brumwell for bringing these letters to my attention.

52. Sir Henry Clinton, notes on conversation with William Pitt, 14 Nov. 1792, Henry Clinton Papers, William Clements Library, University of Michigan.

GEORGE WASHINGTON AND PHILLIS WHEATLEY

The Indispensable Man and the Poet
Laureate of the American Revolution

JAMES G. BASKER

In mid-December 1775, just five months after he arrived in Cambridge, Massachusetts, to take command of the American forces, General George Washington received one of the most surprising letters he would ever receive, certainly in the course of the war, perhaps of his lifetime. The letter arrived from Providence, Rhode Island, dated October 26. Had he opened it himself, he probably would not have recognized the letter writer's name. But fortunately, standard procedures meant that aides in his headquarters fielded all mail and dispatches and screened them for proper presentation to the commander-in-chief. This meant that several senior New England officers, all likely to be familiar with the story of Phillis Wheatley, including Henry Knox who until the war broke out owned a Boston bookstore through which her published works would have passed, would have been able to brief Washington on Phillis Wheatley's background and celebrity, as they presented her letter to the General during a lull in the action in mid-December. That background briefing would have been necessary for Washington to appreciate the extraordinary life and achievement of his correspondent, and the significance of her letter to him, because he almost certainly had never encountered anyone like her before.

As General Knox and all literate New Englanders knew, Phillis Wheatley embodied one of the most heroic life stories of the eighteenth century. Captured as a child in Africa and carried via the Middle Passage to New England, Phillis arrived in Boston in July 1761 as a seven-year-old girl, parentless, speaking no English, naked and terrified, being offered for sale on the Boston docks.[1] Something of the horrors of her experience on that slave ship are indicated by the fact that of ninety-six Africans taken on board, twenty-one died en route to Boston—some 25 percent of Phillis's fellow captives died at sea, more even than the usual mortality rate of 10 to 15 percent on slave-trading voyages. If such a thing can be said about the life of any enslaved person, Phillis was relatively lucky. She was purchased by John Wheatley, a merchant, and his wife Susannah, a well-off couple in their fifties, who took Phillis into their home, intending her to be educated and brought up as a household servant for them and their two eighteen-year-old children, Nathaniel and Mary. Wheatley's biographer, Vincent Carretta, has speculated that for the elder Wheatleys, Phillis was also, at another level, a kind of surrogate replacement for their daughter Sarah, who had died at age seven a few years earlier.[2] Certainly they treated her with kindness and Phillis grew up to feel an emotional closeness, especially to the motherly Susannah, that would endure for the rest of her life.

To everyone's surprise, Phillis also proved to be a prodigy. She quickly learned English, becoming fluent in less than sixteen months. The Wheatleys schooled her at home and she pursued her studies eagerly in reading, writing, religion, history, classics, and other subjects. By age eleven she was writing poems, the earliest of which—a short elegy on the death of a family friend—survived because it so impressed the prominent clergyman and man of letters Jeremy Belknap that he recorded it in his diary, twice.[3] By age fourteen she was publishing occasional poems in local newspapers, and countless others of her writings were circulating in manuscript, as was the practice of the time. By early 1772, when she was still only nineteen, she had produced so much poetry that her local supporters and patrons were working with her to publish it as a collection in book form.

Initially there was a proposal to publish her book of poems in Boston, but nothing came of it, probably because a much greater prospect emerged. Wheatley had achieved transatlantic fame in 1770 for her celebrated "Elegiac Poem on the Death of George Whitefield," the renowned evangelist who had led revivals on both sides of the Atlantic for more

than thirty years. On the strength of it, Wheatley had begun a correspondence with Whitefield's patroness and follower, the Countess of
Huntingdon, a wealthy evangelical and frequent patron of Black writers
in England. With the help of the countess and others in her circle, and
a group of prominent supporters in Boston, the manuscript of Wheatley's book *Poems on Various Subjects, Religious and Moral* was sent off to
London in November 1772. Ten months later it was published, to rave
reviews, in September 1773. The *Critical Review* of London called her "a
literary phenomenon," and the *London Magazine* gushed that "we cannot
suppress our admiration."[4] Glowing reviews of her book appeared in
ten different London periodicals, and in just the two year period from
1772 to 1773 Wheatley was mentioned in almost one hundred different
articles across the colonial and British press.[5]

A trip to England was arranged for Phillis that summer while her manuscript was in the press, and in May 1773 she departed for London with
much fanfare, in the company of Nathaniel Wheatley, her owner's son
who at age thirty was now fully in charge of the family business. In London
Wheatley was treated as a celebrity, hosted by many prominent people,
including the abolitionist Granville Sharp and the not-yet-revolutionary
Benjamin Franklin, given a tour of all the sights, from Westminster to the
Tower of London, and mentioned in all the newspapers. She stayed in
London enjoying this heady experience for six weeks before sailing back
to Boston where she arrived in mid-September, at about the same mo-
ment that her book was being published and acclaimed back in London.

But the most important outcome of Wheatley's celebrity visit to England was that it enabled her to achieve her own emancipation from
slavery. The *Somerset* decision of 1772 in the London courts had established that no enslaved person, once landed in England, could be compelled to leave—thus granting de facto freedom to any enslaved person
who could manage to get there. The decision was widely reported in the
press throughout the Anglo-American world, including all the colonial
newspapers.[6] Wheatley and her family were well aware of it and her biographers have concluded that on the basis of the *Somerset* precedent—
which meant that Wheatley would essentially be free once she arrived
in England and no one could compel her to return—she extracted from
her master a written promise of manumission, a copy of which she also
deposited with a London friend as a safeguard. In this extraordinary

way, Wheatley used her literary achievements and fame to negotiate her own freedom, one of the most unusual instances of self-emancipation in all of American history. It also means that when she got on that ship and sailed back to Boston in the late summer of 1773, she not only arrived a free woman, she effectively became the first person of African descent to immigrate to America of her own volition.

Meanwhile, it was her *writing* that was the core of her achievement and self-liberation, and we should attend to it. From the beginning, Wheatley's poetry was remarkable for the ways it went beyond what was seen in the eighteenth century as appropriate for women writers, who usually restricted themselves to sentimental styles and domestic subject matter. Her poems take on subjects of public importance — religion, politics, military matters, government officials and their policies. And with incredible audacity, coming from a teenage Black girl in the eighteenth century, she had a habit of addressing her poems directly to prominent male public figures. Listen to some of the people she addressed in her poems, beginning in 1767 when she was fourteen years old: "to the

The frontispiece portrait of Phillis Wheatley from her *Poems on Various Subjects, Religious and Moral,* 1773. (The Gilder Lehrman Institute of American History, GLC06154)

University of Cambridge" (i.e., the faculty and students of Harvard), another "to a clergyman," then "To the Deist," "To the Reverend Thomas Amory," "To Captain H——, of the 65th Regiment," "To a Gentleman of the Navy," "To the Honorable Commodore Hood," "to His Honour the Lieutenant Governor [Andrew Oliver]," "To . . . the Earl of Dartmouth," and topping them all, "To the King's Most Excellent Majesty on His Repealing the American Stamp Act."[7]

What we should also notice is that from early on Wheatley's politics were emerging as staunchly pro-American. She could be diplomatic and politically savvy, as when she praises King George in 1768 for repealing the Stamp Act. What monarch would not succumb to the positive reinforcement of lines like these:

> May George belov'd of all the nations round
> Live and by earth[']s and heaven[']s blessings crown[e]d
> May heaven protect and Guard him from on high
> And at his presence every evil fly
> Thus every clime with equal gladness See
> When kings do Smile it sets their Subjects free.[8]

Wheatley, who was still officially enslaved in 1768, may well have embedded a second, more subliminal message in these lines, because of course King George could also display his benevolence by deciding one day to set other "Subjects" free—his enslaved *Black* subjects—by proclaiming an end to slavery and the slave trade.

For all her discretion and diplomacy in that poem, there are darker themes in the other important political poem she wrote in 1768, the forty-two-line allegorical depiction of "Britannia," the powerful mother figure, in conflict with her newly grown-up son, "Americus," a poem that Wheatley entitled simply "America." Certain lines are very telling. In lines 5–6, for example, Wheatley deftly presents another *double entendre* about tyranny and freedom while also openly presenting herself as an African American:

> Thy Power, O Liberty, makes strong the weak
> And (wond'rous instinct) Ethiopians speak

Thus the prospect of liberty makes not only *colonies* but also enslaved Black people assert their strength, speak out, and seek their freedom. In this little allegory, Wheatley labels the son Americus a "rebel" ("What ails the rebel, great Britannia cried," l.23) who further on in the poem "weeps afresh to feel this iron chain" (l.31) of tyranny. The poem closes with an explicit call for Britain to wake up and treat its unhappy son more kindly: "Turn, O Britannia, claim thy child again." Otherwise, the poet delicately hints, if Britain does not encourage the industry and prosperity of its American colonies, they may be threatened by "distant continents with vulturing eyes"—perhaps taken over or lured away by other European powers? Or worse, become so aggrieved and unhappy as to rebel on their own behalf and claim their independence?

In 1770, the events that Paul Revere taught Americans to remember as "the Boston Massacre" moved Wheatley to write a poem to protest the loss of American life, including that of Crispus Attucks, the first person of color to die in the escalating conflict. She titled the poem "On the Affray in King's Street, on the Evening of the 5th of March," and it was listed in a Boston newspaper ad in 1772, but unfortunately the full text was never published.[9] Modern scholars point to twelve lines published anonymously in 1770, a week after the massacre, as Wheatley's first response to the event, and probably an excerpt from or early version of the lost poem. The lines of lament for these victims of British gunfire close with a patriotic flourish:

> Long as in Freedom's Cause the wise contend
> Dear to your unity shall Fame extend;
> While to the World, the letter'd Stone shall tell,
> How Caldwell, Attucks, Gray, and Mav'rick fell.[10]

Wheatley's modesty in printing these lines anonymously deepens the sense of her serving a purpose larger than herself, what she calls "Freedom's Cause."

In 1772, Wheatley wrote one of her most important political poems, addressed "To the Right Honourable William, Earl of Dartmouth," recently appointed as the British governor of colonial Massachusetts. With the characteristic boldness evident in so many of her poems, directly addressing a powerful white male authority figure, Wheatley welcomes the new governor as an enlightened leader who will hear the colonists' grievances, remedy their wrongs, and restore good government. Whether sincere praise or subtle manipulation, Wheatley's lines develop a parallel between the lawless oppression of the colonies and the enslavement of Africans. In one of the most personally revealing and emotional passages in all of her writings, Wheatley asserts her unique authority as a Black person to speak about freedom and tyranny:

> Should you, my lord, while you peruse my song,
> Wonder from whence my love of *Freedom* sprung,
> Whence flow these wishes for the common good,
> By feeling hearts alone best understood,
> I, young in life, by seeming cruel fate
> Was snatch'd from *Afric's* fancy'd happy seat:
> What pangs excruciating must molest,
> What sorrows labour in my parent's breast?
> Steel'd was that soul and by no misery mov'd
> That from a father seiz'd his babe belov'd:
> Such, such my case. And can I then but pray
> Others may never feel tyrannic sway? (ll.20–31)

Wheatley grounds her love of freedom and her patriotism, paradoxically, in her life experience as an enslaved person.

It is against this background—of Phillis Wheatley as a prominent, explicitly political, increasingly pro-American poet who is confident and assertive enough already by her late teens to address major public figures in print—that we can better understand her return to America to claim her new life as a free woman in late 1773, and her immersion in the events that quickly led up to her producing the poem Washington first held in his hands in December 1775.

Boston Harbor was still blockaded and British troops occupying the city when Wheatley arrived back from England in September 1773. Tensions continued to mount over the next eighteen months, with the familiar sequence of events: the Boston Tea Party in December 1773, the Continental Congress meeting and issuing demands in the fall of 1774, the various petitions and proclamations, tarrings and featherings, clashes in the streets, and musterings of militias, until war broke out at Lexington and Concord on April 19, 1775. Within a few days, Wheatley had joined the massive exodus of people from Boston, taking refuge in Providence along with other members of the Wheatley family. Between 1770 and 1776, the population of Boston dropped from more than 15,000 to less than 3,000.[11] She and her fellow patriot sympathizers followed developments from afar: the Battle of Bunker Hill and the ongoing siege of Boston, and then the arrival of George Washington as commander-in-chief.

When the news of Washington's installation as commander reached Phillis, she was moved to write the poem that is the focus of this essay. She had finished the poem by October 26, and that day she wrote Washington a self-effacing and flowery letter to accompany it, as she sent it off by post:

> SIR,
>
> I Have taken the freedom to address your Excellency in the enclosed poem, and entreat your acceptance, though I am not insensible of its inaccuracies. Your being appointed by the Grand Continental Congress to be Generalissimo of the armies of North America, together with the fame of your virtues, excite sensations not easy to suppress. Your generosity, therefore, I presume, will pardon the attempt. Wishing your Excellency all possible success in the great cause you are so generously engaged in. I am,
>
> Your Excellency's most obedient humble servant, PHILLIS WHEATLEY.[12]

Here it is worth noting two of the political implications of this letter and the accompanying poem. Phillis had become a free woman when she was manumitted in 1773, but at this moment in 1775 she was declaring herself, irrevocably, an *American* and a *patriot*. Her bold declaration of support for General Washington as the commander-in-chief of an army in open rebellion against the British government made her complicitous in that rebellion, an outlaw and an enemy. Even as a woman, her writings put her in danger, whether from capture and prosecution by the British, or from reprisals against her by loyalists. There was bravery here. We have to remember the uncertainty at the time: Who knew how the war would turn out? Who would be the victors, what would they do to the losers? Or as the war went on, at what stage, in what place, at whose hand might those dangers and reprisals befall her? Moreover, as a Black rebel rather than a white one, there was the danger not only of being imprisoned, but being reenslaved and perhaps even shipped off to the West Indies. Wheatley had a lot at stake in backing the American cause, both her life and her liberty.

The other political implication, which Wheatley may not have intended to invoke but Washington and his aides quickly recognized, had to do with race. Racial politics, as recent historiography is demonstrating ever more powerfully, played a major role in the American Revolution from the outset. Enslaved people, for understandable reasons, tended to see the British as potential liberators, or at least as a means to escape their American owners, especially as British commanders throughout the colonies invited enslaved people to escape to their lines and take up arms against their former masters. And at war's end, the British famously took with them as they left New York Harbor some three thousand self-emancipated Black people, while many thousands of others had managed to escape in other ways during the eight years of war.[13] On the other hand, free Blacks like Wheatley, especially in the northern states, were more likely to side with the American cause, not only out of loyalty to their fellow citizens but because they saw new ideas about freedom circulating and the prospect of better opportunities opening up in the new democratic country that was struggling to achieve its independence. To name just two examples: Black people had begun bringing petitions for freedom and the protection of civil rights to Massachusetts courts as early as 1773, and the Pennsylvania Abolition Society (building on the activism in the 1750s and 1760s of Anthony Benezet and others) was founded in 1775. For free Black people, these were hopeful signs.

Some of the political implications might have begun dawning on Washington the first moment that he started reading through her poem and decoding its ornate, highly stylized language. Here it is worth paying close attention to the wording of the poem and the way it sequences its key ideas. The poem begins this way:

[To] His Excellency Gen. Washington.

Celestial choir! enthron'd in realms of light
Columbia's scenes of glorious toils I write.

The use of "Columbia" as a term of address is striking. Wheatley was an early and frequent user of the Latinate nickname for America, "Columbia," which ironically had first been coined in the *Gentleman's Magazine* of London in 1738.[14] This was doubly ironic because the anonymous author behind this coinage was the Tory English writer Samuel Johnson, who would in 1775 denounce the American Revolution in part because of the hypocrisy of white colonists clamoring for freedom while holding enslaved people: "How is it we hear the loudest yelps for liberty among the drivers of Negroes?"[15]

Wheatley's patriotic poem continues in its elevated strain and epic style:

> While freedom's cause her anxious breast alarms,
> She flashes dreadful in refulgent arms.
> See mother earth her offspring's fate bemoan,
> And nations gaze at scenes before unknown!
> See the bright beams of heaven's revolving light
> Involved in sorrows and the veil of night!
>
> The goddess comes, she moves divinely fair,
> Olive and laurel binds her golden hair:
> Wherever shines this native of the skies,
> Unnumber'd charms and recent graces rise.
> Muse! bow propitious while my pen relates
> How pour her armies through a thousand gates:
> As when Eolus heaven's fair face deforms,
> Enwrapp'd in tempest and a night of storms;
> Astonish'd ocean feels the wild uproar,
> The refluent surges beat the sounding shore;
> Or thick as leaves in Autumn's golden reign,
> Such, and so many, moves the warrior's train.

Here Wheatley uses an Homeric image—soldiers as numerous as autumn leaves—that was apparently intended to encourage Washington to believe that troops were flocking to his army to join the fight against the British. It was a kind of morale boost and recruitment pitch all in one.

> In bright array they seek the work of war,
> Where high unfurl'd the ensign waves in air.
> Shall I to Washington their praise recite?
> Enough thou know'st them in the fields of fight.
> Thee, first in place and honours,—we demand

The grace and glory of thy martial band.
Fam'd for thy valour, for thy virtues more,
Hear every tongue thy guardian aid implore!
One century scarce perform'd its destin'd round,
When Gallic powers Columbia's fury found;
And so may you, whoever dares disgrace
The land of freedom's heaven-defended race!
Fix'd are the eyes of nations on the scales,
For in their hopes Columbia's arm prevails.

Here Wheatley proves—in her notion that "the eyes of nations" are "fix'd" on this heroic struggle—that Lin-Manuel Miranda in his hit musical *Hamilton* was not the first to claim for Washington that "History has its eyes on you!"

Anon Britannia droops the pensive head,
While round increase the rising hills of dead.
Ah! cruel blindness to Columbia's state!
Lament thy thirst of boundless power too late.
Proceed, great chief, with virtue on thy side,
Thy ev'ry action let the goddess guide.
A crown, a mansion, and a throne that shine,
With gold unfading, WASHINGTON! be thine.

Reading this, Washington would have been gratified by the personal praise and the political support. But of course he had more urgent matters at hand every day—the siege of Boston, the lack of gunpowder and provisions, troubles manning his army, the constant challenge of outwitting the enemy—and he made no immediate response, though he may have commented orally to some of his staff. But by early 1776, there were new developments that caused Washington to stop and think again about Wheatley's poem and return to it. One was the issue of Black troops in his army. Black men had fought at Lexington and Concord and the Battle of Bunker Hill and were present in the various militias encamped on the Cambridge Common when Washington took command in July 1775. But as Washington knew, there were sensitivities in Congress about enlisting Black soldiers, especially among the southern states. Washington's own prejudices as a Virginian and a lifelong

George Washington, by
Rembrandt Peale, ca.
1852–53. (The Gilder Lehrman Institute of American
History, GLC09119.01)

slaveowner also made him uneasy about arming Blacks and enlisting
them. In October 1775 in a war council, Washington and his generals
voted unanimously "to reject all Slaves, & by a great Majority to reject
Negroes altogether."[16] Still, at the same time there were officers like General John Thomas of Massachusetts who told John Adams, "we have
some Negroes, but I look upon them in general [as] equally serviceable
with other men . . . many of them have proved themselves brave."[17]

By the end of November, however, word reached Washington's headquarters of a proclamation by Lord Dunmore, royal governor of Virginia,
who in desperation to turn the tide of rebellion, had on November 7,
1775, offered freedom to any enslaved person of an American owner
who would come over and fight on the British side. Historians estimate
that within a few weeks, at least one thousand enslaved people did just
that.[18] Dunmore formed them into an "Ethiopian Regiment," and from
November through the summer of 1776, they engaged in a number of
small battles and skirmishes. Ripples of panic spread across Virginia, including Mount Vernon, as rumors of runaway enslaved people and "in-
surrectionist" violence circulated everywhere. Washington was gravely
concerned, writing to Henry Lee that if Dunmore and his regiments

were not "crushed by spring, he will become the most formidable enemy America has."[19] Faced with this threat in the South, and the record of loyal service by Black troops in the North, Washington began to change his mind. In the last week of December 1775, he wrote to John Hancock, then presiding over Congress in Philadelphia, to report that "it has been represented to me that the free Negroes who have served in this army are very much dissatisfied at being discarded. As it is to be apprehended that they may seek employ in the ministerial [British] army, I have presumed to depart from the resolution respecting them and have given license for their being enlisted."[20] In the midst of these mounting pressures, Washington's ideas about Black people were changing, the start of an evolution in his thinking that would continue to the end of his life.

These events help explain why in early February 1776, Washington thought again of the letter and poem from Phillis Wheatley, but not just out of personal gratitude or guilt over failing to write to thank her. Notably, days before he wrote to Wheatley, he sent a copy of the poem along with a letter to his aide Joseph Reed, who until recently had been on his staff in Massachusetts but was now in Philadelphia. On February 10, 1776, in his letter to Reed accompanying the poem, he told him—with perhaps a bit of feigned casualness—that Reed might "be amused by reading a letter and poem addressed to me by Miss Phillis Wheatley. In searching over a parcel of papers the other day, in order to destroy such as were useless, I brought it to light again. At first, with a view of doing justice to her poetical genius, I had a great mind to publish the poem; but not knowing whether it might not be considered as a mark of my own vanity, than a compliment to her, I laid it aside, till I came across it again in the manner just mentioned."[21]

It is worth noting that even in the privacy of this personal letter, Washington treats Wheatley with respect and appreciation. Equally noteworthy, nowhere in his letter does Washington allude to her race or status as a formerly enslaved person, though clearly he and Reed were both fully aware—perhaps from those conversations in Washington's headquarters that went unrecorded back in December, when Reed was on his staff in Cambridge. In any case, Washington had chosen his intermediary deliberately. A skillful political operator, Reed was an opponent of slavery and a few years later, with the war still underway, would support a 1780 gradual emancipation act in Pennsylvania.

Reed immediately saw the same political use that Washington discerned. He arranged to publish Wheatley's poem not in any of the antislavery papers in the North, but in the *Virginia Gazette*, where it appeared on the front page of the March 20, 1776, issue. (Not until a few weeks later, at the end of April, was it reprinted in Thomas Paine's *Pennsylvania Magazine*, a periodical much more inclined to be friendly to Black writers.[22]) It takes a moment for the logic of this brilliant move to sink in: in a period of racial tension and white fear in Virginia—which Jefferson would carry with him to Philadelphia that summer and inscribe in the first draft of the Declaration—Washington and Reed wanted Virginians, and all Americans, to see a prominent, influential African American who was an outspoken supporter of the American cause. Probably they hoped that everyone might calm down: whites might form new ideas about the capacities and loyalties of Black people, and the possibility of including them in the body politic, while Blacks might be moved to see opportunities for themselves as supporters of the American cause.

In the letter that he wrote to Wheatley on February 26, 1776, Washington spoke in ways that he probably had never before used in conversation with a Black woman. He begins with fashionable banter of the kind one might use in a social setting: explaining her letter had not reached his hands until mid-December, he wittily anticipates her response, almost as if they were social equals: "Time enough, you will say, to have given an answer ere this." His opening paragraph is one long apology for not having written sooner:

> Your favor of the 26th of October did not reach my hands, 'till the middle of December. Time enough, you will say, to have given an answer ere this. Granted. But a variety of important occurrences, continually interposing to distract the mind and withdraw the attention, I hope will apologize for the delay, and plead my excuse for the seeming but not real neglect.[23]

Did ever Washington write such a letter, in such a style, to a formerly enslaved person? He goes on to praise in fulsome terms her "great poetical talents" and expresses his view that her poem deserved to be published and he would have done so, were it not for the possible imputation of vanity—an imputation that he further avoids by concealing the fact that he has just arranged to have it published by Joseph Reed:

> I thank you most sincerely for your polite notice of me, in the el-
> egant Lines you enclosed; and however undeserving I may be of
> such encomium and panegyrick, the style and manner exhibit a
> striking proof of your poetical Talents; in honor of which, and as a
> tribute justly due to you, I would have published the Poem, had I
> not been apprehensive, that, while I only meant to give the World
> this new instance of your genius, I might have incurred the impu-
> tation of Vanity. This, and nothing else, determined me not to give
> it place in the public Prints.

Finally, and most astonishingly, Washington invites Wheatley, as an apparent social equal or even guest of honor, to come visit him:

> If you should ever come to Cambridge, or near Head Quarters,
> I shall be happy to see a person so favored by the Muses, and to
> whom Nature has been so liberal and beneficent in her dispen-
> sations. I am, with great Respect, your obedient humble servant.
>
> G. Washington

No proof has yet emerged that she did go meet him in person, though historians have conjectured that if such a meeting took place it would have been in late March 1776, after the British had evacuated Boston and patriot exiles began trickling back into town, or if she was still in Providence, then in the first week of April when Washington passed through Providence and stayed over two nights, en route to his ill-fated deployment in New York.[24] What a treat for the imagination to picture such a meeting! But whether or not it happened, the whole interaction with Wheatley marked a dramatic turning point in Washington's life. In the words of Ron Chernow, "Few incidents in the early days of the war suggest how powerfully Revolutionary ideals were transforming George Washington as his reaction to Phillis Wheatley."[25]

Over the course of the war, beginning with those Black soldiers the General had under his command in Massachusetts and the immediacy with which slavery and race became strategic and political issues, Washington witnessed events and was exposed to ideas that were to bend the arc of his thinking to a moral and political disgust, eventually an expressed opposition, to slavery. Crispus Attucks had died in the Boston Massacre, Black men had fought at Lexington and Concord and

Bunker Hill. In 1775, Massachusetts, Rhode Island, and Connecticut all had Black soldiers serving alongside whites, and later there were some all-Black regiments. Scholars now think that many more than the traditional estimate of five thousand African Americans had served in the American forces before the war had ended.[26] The first man to die at Valley Forge in December 1775, on Christmas Day, was a Black man from a Connecticut regiment.[27] Among Washington's most trusted wartime aides were idealistic young men who opposed slavery vehemently: John Laurens who would propose a Black regiment of formerly enslaved people from South Carolina in 1779, Alexander Hamilton who would support the enlistment of Black troops during the war and afterward co-founded the New York Manumission Society with John Jay in 1785, and the Marquis de Lafayette who would urge Washington to start with him an experimental plantation in 1783 that would educate, train, and manumit enslaved people, and pay them for their labor. Washington admired the project and despaired that there was nothing like it in America. Lafayette pursued the experiment on his own in Cayenne (French Guiana) until 1792, when his property was confiscated by the revolutionary French government and the paid workers on his plantation were sold back into slavery.[28]

The years of the Revolutionary War were to bring dramatic developments in Wheatley's life too. But unlike Washington, who rose from very precarious early circumstances and overcame repeated setbacks, to become by war's end the greatest hero of his age, Wheatley's fate moved the opposite way. She began the war as a transatlantic celebrity and hugely promising literary talent at the top of her game, who by the early 1780s was struggling financially, coping with a difficult marriage, fighting chronic lung disease, and failing, despite multiple efforts, to get a second book of poetry published, even in her own home town. She died in December 1784, still very young, aged thirty-one. She suffered the additional posthumous injury that the full manuscript of her unpublished second book of poems—which many people had seen and admired—disappeared and has never since turned up.[29] (Her lost book of poetry would be one of the greatest literary treasures in American history, should it ever reappear!)

During the years of the war, Wheatley continued to write poems on a wide variety of topics and occasionally published one in a periodical or a pamphlet. More importantly, she continued to write patriotic poems explicitly in support of the war effort. In December 1776, she heard about the capture of General Charles Lee and composed a poem in his honor in which she also included a tribute to Washington. Remarkably, given Lee's rivalry with Washington, which clearly was unknown to Wheatley, in the closing lines she puts in Lee's mouth these words of heroic defiance to the British:

> Yet those brave troops innum'rous as the sands
> One soul inspires, one General Chief commands
> Find in your train of boasted heroes, one
> To match the praise of Godlike Washington.
> Thrice happy Chief! in whom the virtues join,
> And heaven-taught prudence speaks the man divine![30]

She sent the poem off to James Bowdoin, president of the Massachusetts Provincial Congress and a prominent leader in revolutionary America. But Bowdoin, who *was* aware of Lee's erratic behavior and his efforts to undermine Washington, held it back from publication. It was eventually found decades after his death among his papers.[31] Bowdoin may have saved Wheatley from an embarrassing political mistake.

Two years later, her elegy "On the Death of General Wooster" in 1778 rightly celebrated an American war hero who died in battle, while it also served as a personal token of condolence to his widow Mary Wooster whom Phillis knew as a friend and supporter. Mary and her late husband David were also opponents of slavery, which Wheatley acknowledged in the poem by having the spirit of Wooster speak from beyond the grave to criticize America for maintaining slavery while fighting for freedom:

> But how, presumptuous shall we hope to find
> Divine acceptance with th' Almighty mind—
> While yet (O deed ungenerous!) they disgrace
> And hold in bondage Afric's blameless race?
> Let virtue reign—And thou accord our prayers
> Be victory our's, and generous freedom theirs.[32]

Wheatley's struggles after she married in 1778 resulted in less writing, and the disappearance of her unpublished book manuscript after her death has left us a very patchy sense of her last few years. But two of the very last poems she ever wrote were also devoted to the American cause and its heroes. In late December 1783, Wheatley wrote "An Elegy Sacred to the Memory . . . of Dr. Samuel Cooper," a prominent Massachusetts clergyman and patriot. In his Brattle Street Church, Cooper had preached and ministered at various times to John Hancock, Samuel Adams, Joseph Warren, John Adams, and many other American revolutionaries. Shortly before he died, he was one of the inner circle to whom Washington entrusted the editing of the final draft of the Treaty of Paris.

Even more dramatically patriotic is the poem that is probably the last she ever composed, and definitely the last she published. Entitled "Liberty and Peace" and published as a broadside in mid-1784, it is a soaring, hopeful, visionary poem about America after independence and its place in the world. At the close of the poem, she leaves an idealistic prophecy for America and the light the new nation will shine on the world of the future:

> Auspicious Heaven shall fill with fav'ring Gales,
> Where e'er *Columbia* spreads her swelling Sails;
> To every Realm shall *Peace* her Charms display,
> And Heavenly *Freedom* spread her golden Ray.[33]

As she began, so she ended: an American patriot. Wheatley died later that year, on December 6, 1784, her prodigious achievements widely known but her even more enormous potential cruelly foreshortened. The great scholar of African American history and culture, Henry Louis Gates, has called Wheatley "the mother of African American literature."[34] To that well-deserved title, I would like to add another. As the rare American poet who had achieved fame in England and could have pursued her career there, with more acclaim and more financial success than in the colonies, who nonetheless gave all that up to return to America where she risked everything to continue writing some of the most powerful and inspiring poetry of the Revolutionary War period, Phillis Wheatley deserves also to be called the "poet laureate of the American Revolution."

We do not know if Washington ever read anything else by Wheatley, though she was acclaimed enough in the English-speaking world and her work familiar to enough of his contemporaries that some such moment may have occurred—a copy of one of her poems sent to him, or read to him by a visitor, or mentioned in a letter or conversation over dinner or in a meeting at some point in his presidency. We do know that by the mid-1780s Washington was expressing antislavery views in letters to his contemporaries, such as the one of April 12, 1786, to Robert Morris, the financier and businessman in Philadelphia. Although he is writing with reference to a friend's self-emancipated former slave to protest the illegality of someone "stealing" him, Washington is embarrassed enough by the topic to tell Morris:

> I hope it will not be conceived from these observations, that it is my wish to hold the unhappy people who are the subject of this letter, in slavery. I can only say that there is not a man living who wishes more sincerely than I do, to see a plan adopted for the abolition of it—but there is only one proper and effectual mode by which it can be accomplished, & that is by Legislative authority; and this, as far as my suffrage will go, shall never be wanting.[35]

More remarkably, Washington also expressed antislavery views to slaveholders, such as his fellow Virginian John Francis Mercer, whom he wrote in September 1786 that it is "among my first wishes to see some plan adopted, by the legislature by which slavery in this Country may be abolished by slow, sure, & imperceptable degrees."[36] Other markers of his evolving attitude dot his later years. As president in 1789, Washington signed legislation confirming the terms governing the Northwest Territories, which included a permanent ban on slavery. There were no copies of Wheatley's book so far as we know in Washington's library. But we know that over the course of the 1780s and 1790s he acquired several publications by abolitionists, both British and American, calling for an end to slavery. Notably, Washington retained these pamphlets and at one point took the trouble to pull together a collection of them and send them off to his book binder whom he paid to bind them in leather with a label on the spine. That volume, labeled "Tracts on Slavery," still survives and can be seen on the shelves of the Boston Athenæum.[37]

In the quarter-century between Wheatley's poem to Washington in 1775 and Washington's death in 1799, many Americans came to share their belief that slavery was on its way to extinction. One state after another abolished slavery or passed gradual emancipation acts, beginning with Vermont in 1777, Pennsylvania in 1780, Massachusetts (by court decisions) in 1781–83, Connecticut and Rhode Island in 1784, and New York in 1799, as would New Jersey in 1804. Meanwhile, as noted, Congress had banned slavery in the Northwest Territories in 1787 (from which five free states would eventually emerge in the nineteenth century). And in 1794, the first national conference of regional abolition societies met in the capital, Philadelphia, and would meet annually until 1806, in pursuit of its agenda to abolish slavery throughout the United States.[38]

It is in this context that we should turn to Washington's final expression of antislavery thinking, which features prominently in his last will and testament. For Washington, who knew his will would be widely published after his death and closely read by thousands, eventually millions of Americans, this was a final message to the American people almost as important as his "Farewell Address" three years earlier. Unlike that famous speech, which has become canonical and reached a transcendent level of importance to all generations through its magnificent rendering in the musical *Hamilton*, the text of his will has slipped from our collective memory. But we can see in it Washington's hopes that other Americans would follow his lead and free their enslaved people, pay to educate and train them to be self-sufficient, and support with decency and care the young, the elderly, and those too ill to care for themselves. In its details, we can see a final intersection with the story of Phillis Wheatley. It is in his emphasis on education and his implied view of the capacities of Black people. He specifies that in the lead-up to being freed, the young among his enslaved people "be taught to read & write, and be brought up to some useful occupation." He goes on to block *anyone* from evading this stipulation, saying "I do hereby expressly forbid the Sale or transportation out of the Commonwealth of any slave I may die possessed of, under any pretense whatsoever."[39] Through the lawyer language, we can see the depth of his feeling on this topic, even stressing that this is the single most important section of his will: "I do moreover, most pointedly and most solemnly enjoin it upon my executors hereafter named, or the survivors of them, to see that *this* [his emphasis] clause respecting slaves, and every part thereof, be religiously fulfilled at the Epoch at which it is directed to take place, without evasion, neglect, or delay." As he here signaled his belief in the capacity of Black people to be educated and to become free, self-sufficient, productive members of society, could Washington have been drawing on his memory of *any* example more powerful or more impactful on the country they both helped to found, than Phillis Wheatley?

Appendix

From George Washington's Last Will and Testament (July 9, 1799)

‹Ite›m Upon the decease ‹of› my wife, it is my Will & desire th‹at› all the Slaves which I hold in ‹my› *own right*, shall receive their free‹dom›. To emancipate them during ‹her› life, would, tho' earnestly wish‹ed by› me, be attended with such insu‹pera›ble difficulties on account of thei‹r interm›ixture by Marriages with the ‹dow›er Negroes, as to excite the most pa‹in›ful sensations, if not disagreeabl‹e c›onsequences from the latter, while ‹both› descriptions are in the occupancy ‹of› the same Proprietor; it not being ‹in› my power, under the tenure by which ‹th›e Dower Negroes are held, to man‹umi›t them. And whereas among ‹thos›e who will recieve freedom ac‹cor›ding to this devise, there may b‹e so›me, who from old age or bodily infi‹rm›ities, and others who on account of ‹the›ir infancy, that will be unable to ‹su›pport themselves; it is m‹y Will and de›sire that all who ‹come under the first› & second descrip‹tion shall be comfor›tably cloathed & ‹fed by my heirs while› they live; and that such of the latter description as have no parents living, or if living are unable, or unwilling to provide for them, shall be bound by the Court until they shall arrive at the ag‹e› of twenty five years; and in cases where no record can be produced, whereby their ages can be ascertained, the judgment of the Court, upon its own view of the subject, shall be adequate and final. The Negros thus bound, are (by their Masters or Mistresses) to be taught to read & write; and to be brought up to some useful occupation, agreeably to the Laws of the Commonwealth of Virginia, providing for the support of Orphan and other poor Children. and I do hereby expressly forbid the Sale, or transportation out of the said Commonwealth, of any Slave I may die possessed of, under any pretence whatsoever. And I do moreover most pointedly, and most solemnly enjoin it upon my Executors hereafter named, or the Survivors of them, to see that th‹is cla›use respecting Slaves, and every part thereof be religiously fulfilled at the Epoch at which it is directed to take place; without evasion, neglect or delay, after the Crops which may then be on the ground are harvested, particularly as it respects the aged and infirm; seeing that a regular and permanent fund be established for their support so long as there are subjects requiring it; not trusting to the ‹u›ncertain provision to be made by individuals. And to my Mulatto man William (calling himself William Lee) I give immediate freedom; or if he should prefer it (on account of the accidents which ha‹v›e befallen him, and which have rendered him incapable of walking or of any active employment) to remain in the situation he now is, it shall be optional in him to do so: In either case however, I allow him an annuity of thirty dollars during his natural life, whic‹h› shall be independent of the victuals and cloaths he has been accustomed to receive, if he chuses the last alternative; but in full, with his freedom, if he prefers the first; & this I give him as a test‹im›ony of my sense of his attachment to me, and for his faithful services during the Revolutionary War.

Notes

Thanks are due to the staff of the Gilder Lehrman Collection, particularly Laura Hapke and Sandra Trenholm; to Dr. Nicole Seary, Senior Editor at the Gilder Lehrman Institute, for her invaluable help with copyediting; and to Lewis Lehrman and the late Richard Gilder, Cofounders of the Gilder Lehrman Institute of American History.

1. Vincent Carretta, *Phillis Wheatley: Biography of a Genius in Bondage* (Athens: University of Georgia Press, 2011), 6–14. All biographical details are from Carretta unless otherwise noted.
2. Carretta, *Phillis Wheatley*, 14.
3. Carretta, *Phillis Wheatley*, 46.
4. *Critical Review* 36 (September 1773): 232, and *London Magazine* 42 (September 1773): 456.
5. Mukhtar Ali Isani, "The Contemporaneous Reception of Phillis Wheatley: Newspaper and Magazine Notices during the Years of Fame, 1765–1774," *The Journal of Negro History* 85, no. 4 (fall 2000): 266–72.
6. See *Virginia Gazette,* 27 August 1772, and *Boston Gazette,* 21 September 1772, and the discussion of colonial awareness of the *Somerset* decision in Carretta, 128–30.
7. See all these and more in Vincent Carretta, ed., *Phillis Wheatley: Complete Writings* (New York: Penguin, 2001).

8. "To the King's Most Excellent Majesty on His Repealing the American Stamp Act," in *Wheatley: Complete Writings*, 106. Five years later, when Wheatley included this poem in her volume *Poems on Various Subjects* (London, 1773), she shortened the title to read "To the King's Most Excellent Majesty" and modified the text slightly to avoid insulting the king and his supporters. See *Wheatley: Complete Writings*, 12–13.

9. Carretta, *Phillis Wheatley*, 72, 213n41.

10. *Boston Evening Post*, 12 March 1770, 4. The twelve untitled lines are attributed to Wheatley by Antonio T. Bly, "Wheatley's 'On the Affray in King Street,'" *Explicator* 56, no. 4 (summer 1998): 177–80, and William H. Robinson, *Phillis Wheatley and Her Writings* (New York: Garland, 1984), 455.

11. Carretta, *Phillis Wheatley*, 153.

12. Wheatley to George Washington, 26 October 1775, in *Wheatley: Complete Writings*, 160.

13. Maya Jasanoff, *Liberty's Exiles: American Loyalists in the Revolutionary World* (New York: Knopf, 2011), 358. See also Robert G. Parkinson, *The Common Cause: Creating Race and Nation in the American Revolution* (Chapel Hill: University of North Carolina Press, 2016), 98–184.

14. *Gentleman's Magazine* 8 (June 1738): 285.

15. Samuel Johnson, *Taxation No Tyranny* (London, 1775), 89.

16. "Council of War, 8 October 1775," *Founders Online*, National Archives, https://founders.archives.gov/documents/Washington/03-02-02-0115.

17. Ron Chernow, *Washington: A Life* (New York: Penguin, 2010), 212.

18. Woody Holton, *Forced Founders: Indians, Debtors, Slaves, and the Making of the American Revolution in Virginia* (Chapel Hill: University of North Carolina Press, 1999), 156.

19. Chernow, *Washington*, 212.

20. Chernow, 213.

21. Carretta, *Phillis Wheatley*, 156–57.

22. *Pennsylvania Magazine* 2 (April 1776): 193.

23. Carretta, *Phillis Wheatley*, 156.

24. Carretta, *Phillis Wheatley*, 157.

25. Chernow, *Washington*, 220.

26. Per Henry Louis Gates, "Gates Inducted to Sons of the American Revolution," *Harvard Gazette*, 20 July 2006, https://news.harvard.edu/gazette/story/2006/07/gates-inducted-to-sons-of-the-american-revolution/.

27. Bob Drury and Tom Clavin, *Valley Forge* (New York: Simon and Schuster, 2018), 129.

28. Henry Wiencek, *An Imperfect God: George Washington, His Slaves, and the Creation of America* (New York: Farrar, Straus and Giroux, 2003), 262–64.

29. Carretta, *Phillis Wheatley*, 189–90.

30. *Wheatley: Complete Writings*, 92.

31. *Wheatley: Complete Writings*, 188. The manuscript is now at the Bowdoin College Library.

32. *Wheatley: Complete Writings*, 93.

33. *Wheatley: Complete Writings*, 102.

34. Henry Louis Gates Jr., *The Trials of Phillis Wheatley: America's First Black Poet and Her Encounters with the Founding Fathers* (New York: Basic Civitas Books, 2003), 30.

35. Washington to Robert Morris, 12 April 1786, *Founders Online*, National Archives, https://founders.archives.gov/documents/Washington/04-04 -02-0019.

36. Washington to John Francis Mercer, 9 September 1786, Gilder Lehrman Institute, GLC03705.

37. Appleton P. C. Griffin, *A Catalogue of the Washington Collection in the Boston Athenaeum* (Boston, 1897), entry for George Buchanan, "An Oration upon the Moral and Political Evil of Slavery" (1791), 35–36.

38. James Basker, *American Antislavery Writings: Colonial Beginnings to Emancipation* (New York: Library of America, 2012), xxxiv.

39. George Washington, "Last Will and Testament," 9 July 1799, *Founders Online*, National Archives, https://founders.archives.gov/documents /Washington/06-04-02-0404-0001. For the whole passage providing for his enslaved people, see Appendix A, below. On the other hand, where Washington freed his own enslaved people, he was at pains to prevent Martha's dower slaves from gaining their freedom, which might have left him legally and financially liable. See Erica Armstrong Dunbar's award-winning book *Never Caught: The Washingtons' Relentless Pursuit of Their Runaway Slave, Ona Judge* (New York: 37Ink/Atria Books, 2017).

ABIGAIL ADAMS AND THE PRESIDENT'S PORTRAIT

SARA GEORGINI

She admired him as a general, but Abigail Adams knew George Washington best as a politician. Acting as her husband John's one-woman cabinet, Abigail sent strong advice in early 1796 about the consequences of Washington's impending exit: "As to holding the office of V P, there I will give my opinion. Resign retire. I would be Second under no Man but Washington."[1] When Abigail stepped into the national spotlight, serving as First Lady during her husband's embattled administration from 1797 to 1801, she looked to the Washingtons for political cues. Abigail approached her new role — an unpaid and undefined position — with trepidation, asking Martha privately for advice. While the title of "First Lady" did not exist until the mid-nineteenth century, Abigail often conducted political work and cultural initiatives well within the nation's view, earning criticism and praise. A lifelong student of government, Abigail assessed George's honor, intellect, and religious faith with her customary candor and insight. Not quite an apprentice, and not yet able to serve as an elected official, Abigail used Washington's life to explore presidential power.[2] The commander-in-chief's role, even when carved out by a decorated general like George, was not her goal. Abigail sought to define her power within the federal realm. What she learned and adapted, from their first face-to-face meeting in July 1775 to her curation of the national mourning of his death in 1799, forms the narrative of this essay.

Washington's struggles to exercise federal power held up a mirror for Abigail's review. The steady pulse of war news primed her to keep monitoring his career, yielding a quarter-century's worth of candid missives in which she lauded George, excoriated George, and tried to see what he stood for in the eyes of her colleagues who could vote. Throughout the revolution, plenty of generals and congressmen peaked in Abigail's correspondence, then slipped away from her letters. Washington remained a running thread, and a bright symbol in bleak times. When the Continental army stumbled badly on the battlefield, Abigail used Washington to explain it away. Invoking one of her favorite writers, Edward Young, she told Mercy Otis Warren that the conflict's grisly turn in early 1777 signified that "our late misfortunes have called out the hidden Excellencies of our Commander in chief— 'affliction is the good mans shining time.' The critical state of our affairs has shown him to great advantage."[3]

Washington's surge into the presidency comforted Abigail's hopes that the new nation would get off to a strong start. Her daughter Abigail 2d (Nabby) was quick to tip the first election results long before polls opened, alerting her father in the summer of 1788 that "the general voice has assigned the presidentship to General Washington."[4] It was an event that the Adams family, newly reunited after a scattering of years in Europe, welcomed. Washington's inauguration cemented independence, and he seemed (at first) to operate above party politics. Abigail lamented his death in 1799 and helped to lead the nation in mourning. But she was troubled by the hero worship that encircled him and what it meant for the future of federalism. Like many First Ladies, Abigail took up the task of cultural memory with mixed feelings. "He deserved all the gratitude and affection which a gratefull people can bestow," she wrote in December 1800. "But at the very period when they are voting to raise trophies to his Memory, they are placing those very Men in the seat, which he occupied with so Much dignity to himself, & benifit to his Country who they know, will pull down the Edifice which he and his Successor, have laboured to preserve."[5] Washington changed in front of Abigail, even as she grew from fan to critic. Her letters offer us a look at how the presidency was fashioned, in real time. And she offers a glimpse of how women approached the new government: with the same excitement and expectation that their male counterparts voiced in Congress and the press.

The presidency belonged to Abigail as much as it did any other American citizen. Minus a vote, she exerted serious power of her own.

Abigail's analysis of Washington's service shows us how women toggled between blurry public and private spheres, relying on personal ties to cultivate influence. Early American women like Abigail have shifted in our modern imagination, evolving from patriot wives and republican mothers to rights bearers and female politicians who guided national virtue and votes.[6] Regional case studies have exposed the intellectual and cultural currents that steered their household work and civic participation.[7] How we approach the mood of the founding era has also changed. New scholarship on the nature of Enlightenment-era friendships, the Washingtons' deep family history, and the personal strains of state-building, bring us closer to understanding the first president's mindset.[8] Washington needed women citizens like Abigail to stabilize the government, and he knew it. Over time, he found her to be a stalwart ally for Martha, a swift interpreter of New England mores, a gifted Second Lady, and a fellow theatre fan. Her cultural power extended beyond the ballot box, evident in her deep New England roots and correspondence networks with male and female politicians on both sides of the Atlantic. How did Abigail's vision of federal progress reach fruition under Washington's leadership, and when did he fail? In order to understand her political thought, and to see how he embedded the presidency in popular culture, we must revisit their relationship.

For Abigail Adams and George Washington, the president's portrait was a joint effort, a chance to etch an American leader's image into history and into the souls of the people he served. The legitimacy of the revolution depended on it. Prominent politicians like the Adamses and the Washingtons were eager to show the world that America was a viable republic. Every detail mattered, from Washington's use of the Constitution's broad powers to the mud-spattered boots that he donned on his daily strolls with constituents in downtown New York. Replacing royal pageantry with presidential decorum presented a challenge that the Adamses and the Washingtons were uniquely equipped to undertake. They fundamentally understood the importance of visual culture and public image. Both Abigail and George sat for hours on end, stiffly enduring a nonstop parade of painters who trimmed them in heavy gilt and icy lace. Both Abigail and George weathered the wounds of ugly character attacks in the press. Both knew that the president's portrait evolved constantly in public imagination and that they had the power to curate it. The executive branch required a sturdy partner in the second slot—"a Man without intrigue, without party Spirit, with an honest mind and a judicious Head, with an unspotted Character"—and a president ready to face "the whips and Scorpions, the Thorns without Roses, the Dangers anxieties and weight of Empire," Abigail wrote of her vision for the nation's highest office, adding: "This is the bright and desireable light of the picture."[9]

Producing the presidency for the people became their next common cause. The odd couple of Abigail Adams and George Washington often shared the national stage, bound together by social obligations. Abigail, a Yankee diplomat's wife who navigated British and French courts, was acutely aware of how America's first elected ruler interacted with constituents. In Washington, she surmised lessons for future leaders, which she passed along to son John Quincy. In her private letters, the second First Lady sized up Washington as a man, politician, and leader. She found him exemplary as a public official, and polite to the point of inscrutability. Washington's model manners may have marked him out as a Virginia gentleman, but Abigail never discounted his political motives.

Abigail Adams, who sat for many artists throughout her life, always favored this work by Gilbert Stuart. (Courtesy of the National Gallery of Art, Washington; gift of Mrs. Robert Homans, 1954.7.2)

"If he was not really one of the best intentiond Men in the world he might be a very dangerous one," she wrote.[10] It is worth exploring further the Washington whom Abigail Adams knew, and the worlds she opened up to his view. This is not the story of a woman who built her political knowledge solely around the choices of a powerful man. Rather, it is a study of how elite women and men, like Abigail and George, collaborated to create the presidency in the minds and hearts of a people made weary by revolution.

Abigail met Washington on the page long before they sat down for coffee in Braintree. Prior to that afternoon in July 1775, her information came mainly from John's reports. His frustratingly short six-line missives from Philadelphia emphasized war talk. He seldom communicated the "sentimental Effusions of the Heart" that she longed to hear.[11] Like the contemporary caricaturists who skewered political personalities in public thought, Adams painted his peers in the Continental Congress with acid glee. He tagged them, variously, as learned or laborious, ingenious or petty. From the outset, he found Washington harder to evaluate, summing him up as a southern veteran and a silent, steely tactician. Their first exchanges were little more than formal committee business, trading routine memoranda on aspects of colonial politics and military support. Yet some level of early trust bonded the Massachusetts delegate with the Virginia general. In mid-June 1775, eager to shed the congressional "scuffle" of appointing officers, Adams crowded along with the rest of Philadelphia to watch Washington review the troops. He marveled at the two thousand uniformed soldiers who, "created out of nothing so suddenly," now followed Washington's intricate orders to wheel, fire, and hold. The battalions moved with "great Exactness," Adams reported proudly to friend James Warren. Then he packed up his letters, likely enclosing several missives to Abigail. He asked his new friend, the "sage, brave, and amiable General Washington," to deliver them when he reached Boston.[12]

Ever a flinty judge of character, Abigail was not easily impressed. And, within New England, Abigail's opinion mattered. Her political power gathered force in the 1770s as she nurtured a network of revolutionaries. Her local reportage influenced John's actions. Neighbors relied on her for accurate news from the Continental Congress. Abigail also cared for four small children, managed the family farm, and pocketed a hefty profit by reselling European luxury goods. By contrast, Washington was far from his family, he depended on the enslaved labor at Mount Vernon to carry on his estate, and speculated heavily in western lands. Washington's celebrity failed to stir Abigail, who claimed ties to several prominent Massachusetts colonels and clans. Their political educations varied widely. Even as John's respect grew for the General's talents, Abigail protested that elite southern slaveholders like Washington would not commit wholly to the American cause. In the same March 31, 1776, letter where Abigail advised John to "Remember the Ladies," she doubted if Virginia's "savage" riflemen and their commanders could be trusted: "I have sometimes been ready to think that the passion for Liberty cannot be Eaquelly Strong in the Breasts of those who have been accustomed to deprive their fellow Creatures of theirs."[13] Abigail's reticence faded only once she met Washington in person.

On July 16 Washington made the half-day's ride from his Cambridge headquarters out to Braintree at Abigail's invitation. Two more guests, Mercy Otis Warren and son Winslow, sent their regrets at the last minute. Prepared for disappointment, Abigail was pleasantly "struck" by the General, writing that he embodied "dignity with ease, and complacency, the Gentleman and Soldier look agreably blended in him. Modesty marks every line and feture of his face." His overall air and the gravity of his speech prompted Abigail to quote poet John Dryden, likening Washington to "a temple Sacred by birth, and built by hands divine."[14] Interestingly, Abigail flipped the lines' intended gender to praise the General. Dryden's original paean in the 1689 play *Don Sebastian* referred to a *woman* of model character. What did Washington make of Abigail? No clear mention survives of his first impression. His diary fell silent in June, and lapsed until early 1780. His extant letters for that eventful summer show that his acclimation to northern life was a feat of necessity, mainly stray notes on weather and a battery of general orders to the army-in-progress.

If the war hero left few clues at this turn in the saga, here is a hinge to remember: George was a dozen years older, but he and Abigail were of an age. They shared some experiences of British imperial disappointment, outright mismanagement, and cruelty. To Abigail's generation, the language of revolution must have seemed both old (English liberties to uphold) and new (popular sovereignty replacing monarchical rule). As momentum grew for American freedom, women and men like Abigail and George sharpened their political arguments. Abigail believed that Britain governed America by will and not by law. Like many, she thought that imperial overreach and an abusive Parliament threatened personal liberties. To her friend Mercy Otis Warren, Abigail wrote that the next step would be war, and she was ready for it: "I think upon the Maturest deliberation I can say, dreadful as the day would be I had rather see the Sword drawn."[15] George Washington's arrival signified a fine omen for success.

So what did the revolution sound like in Boston that summer, in that hive of action that drowned out George's journal? Abigail offered a dramatic account of the reading of the Declaration of Independence at the Old Statehouse: "When Col. Crafts read from the Belcona of the State House the Proclamation, great attention was given to every word. As soon as he ended, the cry from the Belcona, was God Save our American States and then 3 cheers which rended the air, the Bells rang, the privateers fired, the forts and Batteries, the cannon were discharged, the platoons followed and every face appeard joyfull . . . After dinner the kings arms were taken down from the State House and every vestage of him from every place in which it appeard and burnt in King Street. Thus ends royall Authority in this State, and all the people shall say Amen."[16] Ripping down a king, Abigail quickly learned, also meant quashing the moblike scrum of would-be successors. She wondered if Washington was among them.

Abigail and John scrutinized Washington throughout the conflict, calling out episodes where his dignity and modesty soared or plummeted in the public eye. At times, they fretted that too much was made of his genius, thereby eclipsing the contributions of others. Nor did Abigail think that he was above replacement on the battlefield. With British General William Howe lunging toward Philadelphia, Abigail eyed Washington's troop movements with the helpless fury of an armchair general with intelligence trickling in. "If How should get possession of that city it would immediately negotiate a peace," she wrote to John in late September 1777. "I could not help warmly replying, that I did not believe it even tho that should be the case and the General with his whole Army should be cut of. I hoped then that an Army of women would oppose him. Was it not the Sarassens who turnd their Backs upon the Enemy and were slain by their women who were placed behind them for that purpose?"[17]

At other turning points in the war, the Adamses saw that the pressure of popularity doomed Washington to an impossible historical burden. When the Continental Congress proclaimed a day of thanksgiving in late 1777 to mark "the Glory of turning the Tide of Arms" in Americans' favor, John felt relief for Washington's plight. "Now We can allow a certain Citizen to be wise, virtuous, and good, without thinking him a Deity or a saviour," he told Abigail.[18] She had raised the question of Washington's patriotism early on. John resumed it when news of treasons and defectors leapt across the Atlantic. He doubled down on Washington's long history as a southern advocate of independence. He pointed to Benedict Arnold and his ilk as deplorable exceptions. Washington, as John reassured his influential friends in Europe, would not yield to British bribery. "Is it possible that So fair a Fame as Washingtons should be exchanged for Gold or for Crowns? A Character so false so cruel, so blood thirsty, so detestible as that of Monk might betray a Trust," Adams wrote in autumn 1780 from The Hague. "But a Character so just, so humane, so fair, so open honourable and amiable as Washingtons, never can be stained with so foul a Reproach."[19]

As Washington's army fought over many months, Abigail watched the war unfold and coalesce into an uneasy peace in 1783. She was eager to mold the new government through the production of moral leadership. America, Abigail believed, needed a firm federalist at the helm. Washington was one of several possible presidents in contention—as was her husband, newly returned from a decade of diplomatic service in Europe. Abigail approved of the final poll results in 1789. She tracked Washington's speeches and public attitudes toward his leadership. In the weeks following his inauguration, as newspaper editors marveled at the war hero turned president, Abigail took stock of his morality. Despite the waves of popular adulation, Washington seemed able to separate his fame from his duty. She detected that Washington's inner religion, bolstered by years of combat, was the key. "He appears to be most sensibly affected with the supreme and over Ruling providence which has calld him to Rule over this great people rather to feel Humble than Elated, & to be overpowerd with the weight & Magnitude of his Trust," she observed to Vice President John Adams on May 7, 1789, as the nation paused for a fast day.

Abigail was equally impressed by First Lady Martha. "She received me with great ease & politeness, she is plain in her dress, but that plainness is the best of every article," she recounted when they first met that June in New York City, adding: "Her manners are modest and unassuming, dignified and femenine, not the Tincture of ha'ture about her."[20] That skill, to serve the public while keeping Protestant values intact, was one of Abigail's favorite lessons to her growing family. Cultivating Christianity and practicing good citizenship were joint skills in nation-building, she believed. "A patriot without religion in my estimation is as great a paradox, as an honest Man without the fear of God," Abigail reminded Mercy Otis Warren in late 1775.[21] Now she saw George and Martha putting that theory into practice before a nation of spectators.

The Washingtons and the Adamses, thrown together by electors, began to forge a lasting friendship. Under the hot glare of a newly national press, all the traits that Abigail surmised at that first encounter with Washington magnified as they settled into New York City. United at the polls, the two families were nearly torn apart by gossip as Washington's administration stirred to life. Would northern and southern backgrounds divide them? Would the hazy powers of the president and vice president provoke jealousy? Could the machinery of the federal government survive if their personal alliance did not? Would social rivalry force Martha and Abigail to separate camps in the emerging republican court? This kind of talk, underlined by debates over executive etiquette and the perks of patronage, laced through Abigail's private letters during George Washington's first term. Back in their native Boston, emotions ran especially high. "I know not but that the distinction of Southern & Northern may have an Influence even upon the greatest Man, But I cannot believe it," Abigail's nephew William Cranch reported in fall 1789. "The people of the new England States are crazy. They are divided among themselves. They can not see their own Interest—blind as Beetles—."[22] Part of that confusion arose from a partisan press that encouraged dissent to roil the executive branch, as Abigail learned.

In reply, she and Martha joined forces to present a united front. They hosted weekly levees, entertained foreign dignitaries, and completed marathon circuits of private visits. When George nearly died, twice, during his first year in office, Abigail rushed to check in. She concluded that the "August Pressident is a singular example of modesty and diffidence. he has a dignity which forbids Familiarity mixed with an easy affibility which creates Love and Reverence." Beset by the agonies of Washington's illness and a host of other family afflictions, Abigail found that the "unaffected" Martha easily outshone the crowned heads of Europe. She was "one of those unassuming Characters which Creat Love & Esteem," Abigail confided to her sister Mary Smith Cranch.[23] Perhaps so, though Martha did not always agree. Her route from Mount Vernon had been thronged by well-wishers, catapulting Martha into her unpaid role as First Lady on the road. Once in New York, she made a rough transition to the presidential mansion and the fishbowl of federal activity. Early American women leave us rich political history in their private letters to female relatives, and Martha was no exception. To her niece Fanny, Martha confessed: "I lead a very dull life here, and know nothing that passes in the town. I never goe to any publick place, — indeed I think I am more like a state prisoner than anything else, there is certain bounds set for me which I must not depart from — and as I cannot do as I like I am obstinate and stay at home a great deal."[24]

Abigail recorded how the presidency changed the Washingtons' marriage dynamics, realizing that a successful President and First Lady must operate as a social team. She also perceived the challenge inherent in "creating" the people's love and respect, which hinged on the First Lady's curation of her husband's public image. And Abigail saw the value in cultivating Martha. Just a few years into their acquaintance, Abigail was careful to close letters to her husband with a plea to "present me affectionatly to mrs washington who I respect and Love."[25] This was more than just a soft-focus sentiment of female friendship; both women relied on trading respects to keep their husbands in conversation, and in power.

Founding-era figures can be fixed points in our minds, but they were rarely home. Constantly on the road throughout the 1790s, the Adamses and the Washingtons were always the most famous strangers in town. New York City, and then Philadelphia, constituted a whirlwind for Abigail and George. There, at the first seats of government, a political friendship born of circumstance evolved into a permanent social alliance. Abigail commanded Martha's right-hand seat at most public dinners. When other women tried to usurp her prime spot, the president intervened and shuffled them down the table. Abigail savored the special attention, but she never forgot that Washington's reasons were political at heart. "He is polite with dignity, affable without familiarity, distant without Haughtyness, Grave without Austerity, Modest, Wise, & Good these are traits in his Character which peculiarly fit him for the exalted station he holds—and God Grant that he may Hold it with the same applause & universal Satisfaction for many many years," she wrote.[26] Washington's savvy in fostering useful friends in a select circle proved fruitful. He organized day trips and tours for his Cabinet members and their wives. Poignantly, they spent congressional recesses visiting the sites of his wins and losses up and down the length of New York City. Abigail and George shared public toasts, hard-to-find theatre tickets, and even a dancing instructor for their small grandchildren. Yet he kept a fairly low profile. "He is Perfectly averse to all marks of distinction," Abigail complained. She was swift in recommending, to her family, that he sharpen the optics. George's flashes of grandeur were too brief to dazzle the world, she thought, and young America sorely needed good press. One early example stood out.

An ailing Washington spent the Fourth of July propped up in his doorway, honoring members of the Society of Cincinnati as they saluted and marched by. In a rare display, he wore a regimental uniform that glittered with diamond-flecked eagle buttons. Sensitive to the power of political dress, Abigail approved his choice but wanted more. "I think he ought to have still more state, & time will convince our Country of the necessity, of it," she observed to her sister in 1789.[27] Adams's time with kings and queens had taught her something about the visual impact that a leader needed to make, and she was a well-read student of history. Empires might fall in revolution, but the danger of demagogues remained live. When senators first debated erecting an equestrian statue to Washington and striking U.S. currency with his profile, Abigail followed the monument and memorial processes closely. Both ideas foundered by the spring of 1792, prompting Abigail to comment on Congress: "Now the coin is not permitted to wear the stamp of the President because it would savor too much of Royalty. so inconsistant are Men—and the same Men—."[28]

Against the noise and heat of party politics, Abigail's Washington stood resolute as a sentinel. Beneath that calm exterior, George maneuvered to shore up support in the Adamses' base of power. Four days after his cameo at the 1789 parade, Washington wrote to thank the Massachusetts legislature for its congratulations on his election. "In executing the duties of my present important station I can promise nothing but purity of intentions," he wrote, adding a "most ardent wish that we may all, by rectitude of conduct and a perfect reliance on his beneficience, draw the smiles of Heaven on ourselves and posterity to the latest generation."[29] The letter went through several drafts, evincing Washington's efforts to express his commitment to a union that melded northern and southern sensibilities. Ever a surveyor, he made use of what he saw on his regional tours. His desire to use humble, holy language over showy sentiment played well. New England farmers, merchants, and lawmakers turned out en masse to welcome Washington on his autumn tour. A young orator, John Quincy Adams, hastened to give a public address in which he greeted Washington as "the friend, the benefactor, the father of his Country."[30]

Above all, in his manners and his actions, the first president could not look like a king. Abigail and Washington were in consensus on that point. But as he segued into his second term, she inched toward interrogating his policies and decisions with some care. Perhaps as practice for her husband, now the "heir apparent," Abigail turned often to free discussion of his nominations, his suppression of domestic insurgencies like the Whiskey Rebellion, and his handling of an increasingly unruly and overly ambitious Cabinet. Abigail deployed her criticism privately but hesitated to undermine the president's status and thereby destabilize the federal interest. She stood by him on questions of Anglo-American foreign policy and U.S. neutrality, especially if they coincided with John's views. When the release of papers related to the Jay Treaty mired Washington in bad press, Abigail claimed victory for the aging General, who simply could "not be taken by surprize" every time that sly editors laid "a snare to entangle him."[31] When Cabinet members like Edmund Randolph dabbled in overly bold maneuvers, Abigail pointed out that "he represents the President as in leading strings, and between ourselves, I cannot but think, that he had gaind too great an assendency over the mind of the President."[32]

She mixed strict censure for those who mocked the office with robust personal concern for the president's health. Yet she did not shun the chance to dissent. When accusations of executive privilege bedeviled his patronage choices, Abigail sided against him, quietly. "Genll W——n used some times to give a man an office of whom he was afraid . . . It was Gen'll W—n wish to make Friend's of foes, and he aimd at converting over those who were lukewarm," she wrote of Washington's preferences for appointment, adding: " A different conduct is now observed and wisdom taught by experience."[33] The first presidency, to a politician like Abigail, offered a valuable example to vet and thus refine. Over the course of eight formative years, Abigail studied George Washington's handiwork to see how an Adams administration might correct flaws in the federal marble.

To Abigail's mind, Washington's management of the country was wise, tempered by his providentialist Christianity and bolstered by a set of advisers who engineered their own interests within those of the nation. She watched George and Martha age, and grow frail. The physical and intellectual labor of leading a nation took a grave toll. Amid the whirl of legislative wrangling, social obligations, and all-out rejoicing that accompanied his second term, George looked ready to retire. His experience had quashed some of John's appetite for succession, too. "But the Man the most to be pitied is the President," John remarked to Abigail in 1794, warning her to keep his comments private. "With his Exertions, Anxieties Responsibilities for twenty Years without fee or reward or Children to enjoy his Renown to be the Butt of the Insolence of Genets and Clubbs is a Tryal too great for human Nature to be exposed to— Like The Starling he cant get out of his Cage but Knox says and I believe it, he is Sick very sick in it."[34] Washington was, as Thomas Jefferson claimed him to be, a president who hoped for one term's labor and never managed to "conquer his longing for retirement."[35] Abigail glimpsed the weight of his decision to leave public life, and she supported his willingness to step down from power. "With a modesty, I could almost say, peculiar to himself, with a Heart and mind Duly imprest with Religious Sentiments and an affectionate attachment to his Countrymen, he resigns the important trusts Committed to him," she wrote to son Thomas Boylston in September 1796, declaring it a moment of "solemn pause."[36] Washington had endured the partisan struggle with stoicism, and now neither of them knew what might come next. For the first time since the revolution, Abigail's letters took on an extra tinge of concern as Washington's exit loomed. "I feel anxious for the Fate of My Country," she wrote.[37]

When Washington's farewell address appeared in the Boston newspapers, Abigail joined the chorus of eulogies for his leadership and wove in praise for Martha's steady tenure. "If any people on earth are to be envyd they are the ones: not for what they have been in power and Authority, but for their transit," she reminded John.[38] On the cusp of her husband's ascent to the presidency, Abigail labored to interpret Washington's legacy. What did he mean to her, and to the American people? What did they owe him? She drafted, revised, and polished her September 1796 letter on the subject to Ruth Hooper Dalton, the wealthy and well-connected wife of Tristram, a former U.S. senator. Abigail's manuscript edits are fascinating to read. She shifts from mention of George Washington's departure as "the Event You notice" to "the expected Event," indicating her confidential knowledge of his plans. She reflects on the glory of his "Whole Li[fe]," and changes that line to a blanket consideration of his "former actions." Finally, Abigail speaks of Washington in a quasi-past tense, honoring the "Death of the Greatest Character that America ever produced," at the great finale of his political life. As soon as he left the capital, Abigail suggests, Washington was enfolded in history, which "will cover him with unfadeing Lawrels . . . untill Time shall be no more."[39] For the Adamses, he proved a wildly difficult act to follow. Never a king, not quite a god: this was the man whom Abigail Adams last saw making a grateful — and graceful — exit to Mount Vernon.

Then he was gone. Word of Washington's death reached the new First Lady in Philadelphia. Again, she turned to a beloved poet, John Macgowan, to mark the scene: "Death, thou art no Respecter of Persons; Washington is no More! a Great Man has fallen, and his End is peace," Abigail wrote to sister Mary on December 18, 1799.[40] She continued to eulogize him in her family letters, weighting her assessment toward praise but offering some subtle critiques meant to blunt the outpouring of rhapsodic sermons, artworks, addresses, and biographies that reshaped Washington's memory for the masses. "He never grew giddy; but ever mantaind a Modest diffidence of his own talents; and if that was an error, it was of the amiable and engageing kind, tho it might lead Sometimes to a want of decisions in some great Emergencys," she observed.[41] Abigail sent her condolences to Martha, urging her to seek solace in her faith and the "Sympathetic Sorrow of a Nation."[42] As the two women watched, the world cracked open in grief.

The tragic chore of designing and implementing the custom of the country, when it came to mourning a president, fell largely to John and Abigail Adams. Decisions about how to pay respects, when to host events, and where the role of religion fit into the memorialization of public officials complicated the continuance of colonial practices.[43] Meanwhile, the First Lady transitioned to mourning wear. Abigail hosted gatherings of bereaved women who wore white crepe dresses decked with black silk fringed epaulets, ready to honor the fallen Washington. Deathbed scenes splayed out across memorial handkerchiefs, with the great man's last moments engraved in brown transfer print on Glasgow cotton. For ten days, Paris street flags fluttered in mute signals of black crepe. London newspapers let Washington's memory rest in praise, honoring his military skill. At home, American soldiers donned special armbands, and the second president ordered flags to fly at half-staff. A public funeral united citizens grappling with the news; many, like Abigail and John, had lost both a figurehead and a friend.[44] Within the next year, personal and political tragedies mingled bitterly for the Adamses. Their young son Charles died, and John's reelection hopes steadily evaporated. Loss amplified loss.

A winter's trip to Mount Vernon in late 1800 reconnected Abigail with the Washingtons. Accepting Martha's invitation to venture beyond the wilderness of a Washington, D.C., under construction, Abigail set out to see George's haven. The rooms she found "small & low," and the "greatest ornament" to the visitor's eye, Abigail decided, was a long piazza that blended together the Potomac with lush green lawn. Signs of decay, she wrote, now threatened parts of the plantation's beauty. Abigail's summit with her old friend and colleague is worth a ponder. What did the two First Ladies discuss? We know one topic for certain: slaves. Specifically, Abigail wrote to Mary Smith Cranch on December 21, 1800, the deepening anxiety that Martha, "with all her fortune finds it difficult to support her family, which consists of three Hundred souls." With 150 members of the enslaved community on the brink of emancipation, Abigail wrote

Many Americans purchased elaborate mourning handkerchiefs, like this one, to grieve the loss of the first president. (Collection of the Massachusetts Historical Society)

that Martha was "distrest" for the fate of "Men with Wives & Young children who have never Seen an acre, beyond the farm, are now about to quit it, and go adrift into the world without house Home or Friend."[45] A lifelong opponent of slavery, Abigail hurried home to relate her experiences. "If any person wishes to see the banefull effects of slavery. as it creates a torpor and an indolence and a Spirit of domination," Abigail wrote, "let them come and take a view of the cultivation of this part of the United States. I shall have reason to Say. that my Lot hath fallen to me in a pleasant place. and that verily I have a goodly Heritage."[46] As always, the personal and the political blurred in retelling. "The Sight of an old Friend, and the cordial reception I met With from every branch of the family, served to Sooth my Heart," she added. Abigail's visit with Martha reveals how the women of George Washington's world moved on, marking out new avenues of revolution and reform to explore.

Colonists-turned-citizens like the Adamses and the Washingtons discovered that their founding-era ideals were hard to sustain in an America dominated by partisan rivalry and an ambitious press. As she went about her duties as First Lady, the collision of those forces complicated Abigail's goals. The tug of duty and the call of history often compelled her to persevere, but Abigail never really enjoyed, as George did, the perks of being a "publick character" in the new republic. By January 1800, her patience was thin: "I must sit down to day to a table of Antis, the members of this state and N york," she wrote to her cousin, Hannah Carter Smith, "but as I am you know the Servant of these good people, I must endeavour to discharge my Duty to them."[47] To Abigail's mind, the formation of political parties and the rise of campaigning undermined the old patriot cause. She urged Americans to maintain the union at all costs, writing to daughter Nabby that, "the Spirit of party has become so Rancorous that a civil war will break out, unless some method can be devised to subdue the base passions of envy, jealousy, and moderate the contending factions."[48] For Abigail, the political and the personal were one. It was a truth she knew from reading history, and she suffered through it during her husband's administration. She wrote: "I challenge either party, in their hour of calmness to produce a single instance, or one action where the honour independence and safety of the Country has not been the ultimate object of every member of the family where personal safety has not been hazarded, personal property Sacrificed and the Whole long Life of its most ancient Member Solely devoted to the public interest."[49] Achieving independence, Abigail believed, had strengthened her commitment to republican ideals. Both the Adamses and the Washingtons had made great sacrifices for the nation's progress. Naturally, the question of how people framed a pantheon of "the Founders" drew her interest. Washington had no son, no sequel. What America might an Adams inherit?

Years before her husband started to sketch his 1807 summary of Washington's "ten talents," Abigail considered the thorny path that politicians, North and South, faced next.[50] A former friend and new rival, Jefferson, occupied her most recent home in the new wilderness of

Washington, D.C. Settling back into life at Peacefield, Abigail wrote: "My sincere Wish and desire is, that the Country may enjoy an equal degree of prosperity and happiness under the new administration, as it has possesst under the two former; but if it should prove that the people have ungratefully, and Wantonly abused the blessing which they possesst, and have cast them from them; they only have been the instruments of their own overthrow."[51] In the sun-glazed second-floor study of their family farm, John sketched out his autobiography, drafting reminiscences for a Boston newspaper. Abigail focused her thinking on how to frame the presidency for the public, and for history. From her earliest days as First Lady, Abigail had shrewdly knit together the popular General's administration with her husband's less-loved endeavors in the same role. "The task of the President is very arduous, very perplexing and very hazardous. I do not wonder Washington wishd to retire from it, or rejoiced at seeing and old oak in his place," she observed.[52] In Washington, Abigail found a sturdy leader who articulated federalist principles without resorting openly to party intrigues. He boasted charisma, patience, and a charming lack of self-interest. He fostered national growth without overly profiting from it and managed to "combine all Hearts in his favour, and every voice in unison," Abigail wrote.[53]

Washington's solid emphasis on American union and neutrality sparked the imagination of rising citizens like John Quincy Adams, who made those tenets his political creed for a half-century. Now that Abigail knew what to look for, she detected the raw skills of a president in her eldest son. Washington, who launched John Quincy into diplomatic life, thought highly of the next Adams generation's talents as well. "I know with what delight your truly maternal heart has received every testimonial of his favourable voice, and it is among the most precious gratifications of my life to reflect upon the pleasure which my conduct has given to my Parents.—The terms indeed, in which such a character as Washington has repeatedly expressed himself concerning me, could have left me nothing to wish, if they did not alarm me, by their very strength," John Quincy wrote to his mother in late June 1797, oscillating between anxiety and pride.[54] For the Adamses, the Washingtons had always been another living link between revolution and republic. Posted at The Hague with his father during the war's height, fifteen-year-old John Quincy mulled what to pin up on his bedroom wall. A fledgling practitioner of Abigail's politics, he chose a gilt-edged portrait of George Washington.[55]

Notes

Tracing the lives of Abigail Adams and George Washington is a delightful archival adventure: I had the chance to roam, onscreen and off, through some very famous early Americans' private letters and lush estates, then travel back to the writing desk to tell a new story. I'm very grateful to my fellow Adams Papers editors and Massachusetts Historical Society colleagues for sharing resources, reading drafts, and helping me think through the pivotal role of women in political history. In addition, I wish to thank the generous scholars, archivists, and curators at the Fred W. Smith Library at George Washington's Mount Vernon, the Library of Congress, the National Archives, and the Boston Athenaeum, who nurtured this project with manuscripts, ideas, and more.

1. Abigail Adams to John Adams, Jan. 21 [1796], in Hobson Woodward, Sara Martin et al., eds., *Adams Family Correspondence*, 14 vols. (Cambridge: The Belknap Press of Harvard University Press, 1954–), 11:143. Hereafter cited as *Adams Family Correspondence.*

2. Scholars have assessed Abigail Adams's political education and public career from multiple perspectives. Major studies include Phyllis Lee Levin, *Abigail Adams: A Biography* (New York: St. Martin's, 1987); Edith B. Gelles, *Portia: The World of Abigail Adams* (Bloomington: Indiana University Press, 1992); Woody Holton, *Abigail Adams* (New York: Free Press, 2009); G. J. Barker-Benfield, *John and Abigail Adams: The Americanization of Sensibility* (Chicago: The University of Chicago Press, 2010); Joseph J. Ellis, *First Family: Abigail and John* (New York: Knopf, 2010); and Jeanne E. Abrams, *First Ladies of the Republic: Martha Washington, Abigail Adams, Dolley Madison, and the Creation of an Iconic American Role* (New York: New York University Press, 2018).

3. Abigail Adams to Mercy Otis Warren, [Jan. 1777?] in *Adams Family Correspondence*, 2:151. Adams quoted Young, *The Complaint; or, Night-Thoughts on Life, Death, and Immortality* (London, 1742–1745).

4. Abigail Adams to John Adams, July 27, 1788, in *Adams Family Correspondence*, 8:282.

5. Abigail Adams to Thomas Boylston Adams, Dec. 25, 1800, in *Adams Family Correspondence*, 14:499.

6. On the shifting interpretations of early American women's political lives, see Linda K. Kerber, *Women of the Republic: Intellect and Ideology in Revo-*

lutionary America (Chapel Hill: University of North Carolina Press, 1980); Rosemarie Zagarri, *Revolutionary Backlash: Women and Politics in the Early American Republic* (Philadelphia: University of Pennsylvania Press, 2007); and Catherine Allgor, *Parlor Politics: In Which the Ladies of Washington Help Build a City and a Government* (Charlottesville: University Press of Virginia, 2000).

7. The power of place and domestic labor factors into these surveys of women across the emerging nation: Nancy F. Cott, *The Bonds of Womanhood: "Woman's Sphere" in New England, 1780–1835* (New Haven: Yale University Press, 1977); Jeanne Boydston, *Home and Work: Housework, Wages, and the Ideology of Labor in the Early Republic* (New York: Oxford University Press, 1990); and Cynthia A. Kierner, *Beyond the Household: Women's Place in the Early South, 1700–1835* (Ithaca: Cornell University Press, 1998).

8. Cassandra A. Good, *Founding Friendships: Friendships between Men and Women in the Early American Republic* (New York: Oxford University Press, 2015); Alexis Coe, *You Never Forget Your First: A Biography of George Washington* (New York: Viking, 2020); Lindsay M. Chervinsky, *The Cabinet: George Washington and the Creation of an American Institution* (Cambridge: The Belknap Press of Harvard University Press, 2020).

9. Abigail Adams to John Adams, Feb. 20, 1796, in *Adams Family Correspondence,* 11:179–81.

10. Abigail Adams to Mary Smith Cranch, Jan. 5, 1790, in *Adams Family Correspondence,* 9:1.

11. Abigail Adams to John Adams, July 16, 1775, in *Adams Family Correspondence,* 1:246–47.

12. John Adams to James Warren, June 20, 1775, in Sara Georgini, Sara Martin et al., eds., *The Papers of John Adams,* 20 vols. (Cambridge: The Belknap Press of Harvard University Press, 1977–), 3:34. Hereafter cited as *Papers of John Adams.*

13. Abigail Adams to John Adams, March 31, 1776, in *Adams Family Correspondence,* 1:370–71.

14. Abigail Adams to John Adams, July 16, 1775, in *Adams Family Correspondence,* 1:246–47.

15. Abigail Adams to Mercy Otis Warren, [Feb. 3?], 1775, in *Adams Family Correspondence,* 1:183–84.

16. Abigail Adams to John Adams, July 21, 1776, in *Adams Family Correspondence,* 2:56–57.

17. Abigail Adams to John Adams, Sept. 21, 1777, in *Adams Family Correspondence,* 2:346–49.

18. John Adams to Abigail Adams, Oct. 26, 1777, in *Adams Family Correspondence*, 2:361. On the controversies generated by the fast and thanksgiving day practices, see David Waldstreicher, *In the Midst of Perpetual Fetes: The Making of American Nationalism, 1776–1820* (Chapel Hill: Published for the Omohundro Institute of Early American History and Culture, by the University of North Carolina Press, 1997); Benjamin H. Irvin, *Clothed in Robes of Sovereignty: The Continental Congress and the People Out of Doors* (New York: Oxford University Press, 2011); and Spencer W. McBride, *Pulpit and Nation: Clergymen and the Politics of Revolutionary America* (Charlottesville: University of Virginia Press, 2016).

19. John Adams to Hendrik Calkoen, Oct. 10, 1780, in *Papers of John Adams*, 10:219.

20. Abigail Adams to John Adams, May 7, 1789, in *Adams Family Correspondence*, 8:349.

21. Abigail Adams to Mercy Otis Warren, Nov. [ca. 5], 1775, in *Adams Family Correspondence*, 1:323. On the nexus of Abigail's political and religious views, see Sara Georgini, *Household Gods: The Religious Lives of the Adams Family* (New York: Oxford University Press, 2019).

22. William Cranch to John Quincy Adams, Oct. 1, 1789, in *Adams Family Correspondence*, 8:412.

23. Abigail Adams to Mary Smith Cranch, July 12, 1789, in *Adams Family Correspondence*, 8:388–89.

24. Martha Washington to Fanny Bassett Washington, Oct. 23, 1789, in David R. Hoth et al., eds., *The Papers of George Washington, Presidential Series*, 26 vols. (Charlottesville: University Press of Virginia, 1987–), 2:204–6. Hereafter cited as *Washington Papers, Presidential Series*.

25. Abigail Adams to John Adams, Dec. 21, 1793, in *Adams Family Correspondence*, 9:494–96.

26. Abigail Adams to Mary Smith Cranch, Jan. 5, 1790, in *Adams Family Correspondence*, 9:1–2.

27. Abigail Adams to Mary Smith Cranch, Aug. 9, 1789, in *Adams Family Correspondence*, 8:399–400.

28. Abigail Adams to Mary Smith Cranch, March 25–29, 1792, in *Adams Family Correspondence*, 9:273–74.

29. George Washington to the Massachusetts General Court, July 9, 1789, in *Washington Papers, Presidential Series*, 3:165–66.

30. For Washington's highly successful tour of New England from Oct. 15 to Nov. 13, 1789, see *Washington Papers, Presidential Series*, 4:200–201, and *Papers of John Adams*, 20:179.

31. Abigail Adams to John Adams, Mar. 25, 1796, *Adams Family Correspondence,* 11:227.

32. Abigail Adams to John Adams, Jan. 10, 1796, in *Adams Family Correspondence,* 11:134–37.

33. Abigail Adams to Mary Smith Cranch, June 8, 1798, *Adams Family Correspondence,* 13:94–95.

34. John Adams to Abigail Adams, Dec. 30, 1794, in *Adams Family Correspondence,* 10:329.

35. Thomas Jefferson's Conversation with George Washington, July 10, 1792, *Washington Papers, Presidential Series,* 10:535–37.

36. Abigail Adams to Thomas Boylston Adams. Sept. 25, 1796, in *Adams Family Correspondence,* 11:382.

37. Abigail Adams to Thomas Boylston Adams, Nov. 8, 1796, in *Adams Family Correspondence,* 11:395.

38. Abigail Adams to John Adams, Nov. 27, 1796, in *Adams Family Correspondence,* 11:418.

39. Abigail Adams to Ruth Hooper Dalton, [ca. Sept. 14, 1796], in *Adams Family Correspondence,* 11:379.

40. Abigail Adams to Mary Smith Cranch, Dec. 18, 1799, in *Adams Family Correspondence,* 14:77. She quoted Part III of Macgowan's "Death, A Vision; or, the Solemn Departure of Saints and Sinners."

41. Abigail Adams to Mary Smith Cranch, Dec. 22, 1799, in *Adams Family Correspondence,* 14:78–79.

42. Abigail Adams to Martha Washington, Dec. 25, 1799, and Martha Washington to Abigail Adams, Jan. 1, 1800, in *Adams Family Correspondence,* 14:82, 96.

43. For a sense of mourning practices in early America, see Gary Laderman, *The Sacred Remains: American Attitudes toward Death, 1799–1883* (New Haven: Yale University Press, 1996); and Max Cavitch, *American Elegy: The Poetry of Mourning from the Puritans to Whitman* (Minneapolis: University of Minnesota Press, 2007).

44. On the cultural and political significance of memorializing Washington, see Matthew R. Costello, *The Property of the Nation: George Washington's Tomb, Mount Vernon, and the Memory of the First President* (Lawrence: University Press of Kansas, 2019).

45. Abigail Adams to Mary Smith Cranch, Dec. 21, 1800, in *Adams Family Correspondence,* 14:492–95.

46. Abigail Adams to Mary Smith Cranch, Dec. 21, 1800, in *Adams Family Correspondence,* 14:492–95.

47. Abigail Adams to Hannah Carter Smith, Jan. 17, 1800, in *Adams Family Correspondence*, 14:107.

48. Abigail Adams to Abigail Adams Smith, DeWindt Family Papers, Massachusetts Historical Society.

49. Abigail Adams to Abigail Adams 2d, DeWindt Family Papers, Massachusetts Historical Society.

50. John Adams to Benjamin Rush, Nov. 11, 1807, Letterbook Copy, Adams Family Papers, Massachusetts Historical Society, APM Reel 118.

51. Abigail Adams to Cotton Tufts, Dec. 15, 1800, in *Adams Family Correspondence*, 14:483.

52. Abigail Adams to Mary Smith Cranch, June 23, 1797, in *Adams Family Correspondence*, 12:172.

53. Abigail Adams to Elbridge Gerry, Dec. 31, 1796, in *Adams Family Correspondence*, 11:475.

54. John Quincy Adams to Abigail Adams, June 26, 1797, in *Adams Family Correspondence*, 12:173–76.

55. Marie Dumas' Inventory of Household Furnishings, [June 22, 1784], in *Papers of John Adams*, 13:40–44.

"YOU ARE WELCOME TO EAT AT HER TABLE"

Elizabeth Willing Powel's World of Philadelphia

SAMANTHA SNYDER

In her portrait, Elizabeth Powel's blue eyes hold the stories of a life well lived. She is around fifty, in the zenith of her presence in the elite society of Philadelphia. The artist painted her in the latest fashion of the era. She likely wore dresses such as this for her many parties, the candles burning, the music echoing throughout her ballroom. The portrait is unfinished, but her face is clear, rosy cheeked, with a slight smile. The spark is there, and one can easily imagine her as a woman who was "sufficiently open & friendly to convince you that you are welcome to eat at her table & drink from her Glass."[1]

A number of the most powerful people in the transatlantic world ate at Elizabeth Powel's table, including George Washington. In the world of the Philadelphia elite, Elizabeth was an extraordinarily well-connected political power player, who for decades in her home on Third Street debated the merits of the new government, pondered the meaning of republican virtue and education, and performed rituals of sociability with the nation's leading politicians. She implemented some of the first European-style salons in the United States and confidently embodied the role of a female politician as she orchestrated these intellectual gatherings. In the context of her robust network of connections, her relationship with and influence on George Washington illustrates the crucial place she occupied in Philadelphia and in the development of American politics throughout her lifetime. Her formative presence for nearly ninety years in all facets of Philadelphia society forever shaped the social and intellectual lives of the most significant people in the early years of the United States.

Elizabeth Willing Powel was born to Philadelphians Charles Willing and Anne Shippen on February 10, 1742–43. Her father was a high-power merchant, the owner of one of the largest merchant houses in the mid-Atlantic. His firm, Willing and Son, was one of the last that actively participated in the transatlantic slave trade.[2] Her mother was a third-generation Philadelphian, rooted in the social and political community, specifically through her grandfather Edward Shippen, the first mayor of Philadelphia. The Willings, among other prominent families, built their townhouse, which future observers called "Castle Willing," on South Third Street in a neighborhood known as Society Hill. Their home was one of the first built in the budding area, highlighting the family's leading place in society. Elizabeth's father served in numerous city organizations, including as a member of the Common Council, Vestryman at Christ Church, and two terms as mayor of Philadelphia.[3]

From her "Castle," Elizabeth watched the city of Philadelphia develop

Elizabeth Willing Powel, attributed to Joseph Wright, ca. 1793. This portrait likely is a commission, given as a gift in celebration of Elizabeth Powel's fiftieth birthday. It remains unfinished, as the attributed artist died of yellow fever during the 1793 yellow fever epidemic in Philadelphia, just prior to Samuel Powel's passing. (Courtesy of the Mount Vernon Ladies' Association)

as "buildings, mercantile establishments, and domestic structures stretched out in a long thin line along the Delaware River."[4] This brought flocks of people to the upper-class neighborhood that bordered the packed waterfront. Elizabeth lived on the same block of South Third Street for nearly fifty-seven years. When her father died just before her twelfth birthday in 1754, the family experienced little change to their level of financial comfort. Elizabeth's oldest brother Thomas, at the age of twenty-three, took on the responsibility of handling the family finances and the welfare of his nine younger siblings.[5] In 1818, Elizabeth's grandniece wrote about the tense dynamic between Thomas and his siblings, explaining how "all feared him & few loved him."[6] Though Thomas did not fill the emotional role of a father, he made the right connections for his family by stepping into the positions of power his father had held in Philadelphia.

Through these beneficial choices made by her brother, Elizabeth established her early position as a leader in the social life of the city. She and her two older sisters, as three of the most desirable women in Philadelphia, navigated the burgeoning social scene with ease. During the Seven Years' War, one captain referred to them as the "three Goddesses."[7] Another soldier described arriving to the family's "Castle" in 1761 to find the "tea table filled with 16 Ladies, and yesterday 22," who "form'd a beautiful Circle."[8] By hosting such events, attending assemblies, and going on leisure trips with a number of friends and soldiers quartered in Philadelphia, they developed valuable social and political relationships.

As a member of the most "agreeable and Genteel family" in Philadelphia, Elizabeth had access to a number of educational disciplines, many of which were not common for women, such as geography and philosophy.[9] She also learned ornamental arts, including French and dancing. The combination of these disciplines made her into a woman of status and gave her a platform to promote her social accomplishments. She also took advantage of her access to a large library and developed an avid love of reading. Family and friends frequently solicited her advice and opinions on a variety of texts for themselves and their children.

Elizabeth applied her comprehensive education and asserted her intellectual influence through her conversations and epistolary exchanges with members of her extensive social network.[10] She developed a prestigious reputation among the men who advocated for women's education in the new republic. Dr. Benjamin Rush, a preeminent physician and promoter of women's education, dedicated the publication of his seminal speech, "Thoughts Upon Female Education," to her. This speech, originally given at the first board meeting of the Young Ladies' Academy in Philadelphia in 1787, argued that women should be educated not only in ornamental skills but also in the principles of liberty and government. He believed these skills were necessary to teach future generations, as "the first impressions upon the minds of children are generally derived from women."[11] His dedication stated that in order to publish ideas so "contrary to general prejudice and fashion," he wanted the protection and patronage of "Mrs. Elizabeth Powel, a respectable and popular female name."[12] Elizabeth agreed with Rush's ideas, and "dispersed the work with avidity" to her many connections.[13]

Amongst the elite circles of Philadelphia, Elizabeth's clever mind and social graces made her one of the most advantageous matches in the city. "The charming Miss Willing" attracted a crowd of suitors but settled for nothing less than an equal companion, even as her sisters married and had children.[14] In October 1763, a friend wrote inquiring why she still had not married, because "shure[ly] So many Charms were never intended to be kept alone." They knew she was a "valuable prise" but hoped she would make a "good choice and be completely happy."[15] She took her time finding a husband who met her high standards as an intellectual and societal equal. Six years later, she made her choice: a wealthy and learned politician named Samuel Powel.

Samuel, born on October 28, 1738, was the oldest surviving son of a Quaker merchant family. As a young man, he had attended the Academy of Philadelphia and received the finest education available in the city.[16] At nineteen, after his mother died, he gained unlimited access to his large inheritance. He used this new fortune to travel on a grand tour of Europe. He stayed abroad for seven years, socializing with Enlightenment thinkers, politicians, and religious figures in both continental Europe and the British Isles. This included dinners with the philosopher Voltaire, being presented to King George III, and visiting with Pope Clement XIII at the Vatican. Upon his return in November 1767, Samuel constructed his reputation as a refined gentleman using his experiences and knowledge gained during his time abroad. He became vice president of "the American Society" and began attendance at Christ Church, the oldest Anglican Church in the city, where generations of the first families attended. He used these new networks to rise within the ranks of society.[17]

Samuel's worldly experiences and superior place in Elizabeth's circles caught her eye, and she knew he was the ideal match to her own sophisticated mind and celebrated reputation. Sentiments expressed by Elizabeth in private documents show that Samuel met her high expectations for a husband, and she frequently referred to him as her best friend.[18] "From the moment of their union" on August 7, 1769, Samuel considered her "happiness as the dearest Object of his Life."[19] Throughout their twenty-four years of marriage, he would "always anticipate every wish of [Elizabeth's] heart, and mitigate her sorrows."[20] Their friends also acknowledged their intimate relationship and described them as a couple who was "difficult to separate from one another . . . and lived in the sweetest union: as two friends, singularly matched in spirit, tastes & knowledge."[21]

Shortly after their marriage, the Powels moved into a fashionable townhouse which stood just south of Elizabeth's childhood home on South Third Street.[22] They decorated their home with a number of luxury goods, both locally made and imported from England. By acquiring these material goods, they set up their home to be the prime location for Philadelphia's social scene and publicly established their class status and political identities.[23] They also used many items Samuel purchased during his time abroad, including covering the walls with the "beautiful prints and very good copies of the best paintings" that he acquired in Rome.[24] They purchased a coach from the Clarke Brothers, one of the finest Philadelphia carriage makers of the late eighteenth century. This opulent vehicle broadcasted their social power as they rode through the streets of Philadelphia, occasionally with their friends George and Martha Washington.

The Powels successfully established their powerful network and accumulated immense wealth, but these worldly achievements did not shield them from personal tragedy. Within their first five years of marriage, they lost four infants—the first three only months apart. Elizabeth's despair over her losses is apparent in her response to a letter written by her friend Ann Fitzhugh in late 1783. Ann, who had recently celebrated the successful birth of her first child, expressed her desire for Elizabeth to have another. On Christmas Eve 1783, Elizabeth wrote a heartbreaking response. While she appreciated that her "dear friend . . . wished her to be again a Mother" she "knew not what she wished." She said her "mind, habituated to Mortification & Disappointment, is become weaker; & unfortunately, [her] Sensibilities stronger. A thousand Circumstances that formerly were Sources of Pleasure have now lost their charm." She feared that she was "doomed never to be happy in this World." Her "fine spirits," which she believed "would never be broken," had instead "yielded to the severe Trials of life."[25]

As Elizabeth mourned the loss of her infants, she watched her siblings repeatedly enjoy successful pregnancies throughout the 1770s, providing Elizabeth with a growing number of children in her life. By 1783, she had thirty nieces and nephews, all of whom lived to adulthood. To avoid dwelling on the juxtaposition of her losses and her siblings' happiness, she refocused her maternal instincts on the next generation of the Willing family. She chose her favorites out of the thirty young charges, with whom she played the role of a surrogate mother, encouraging their education and elevating their standing within society.

Elizabeth established her political authority primarily in her role as "female politician," though she also acted as a surrogate republican mother.[26] Her sister described this dichotomy of roles in a letter where she explained how Elizabeth, "with no children to chear or animate her[,] . . . god instead blessed her with a commanding talent for society."[27] Elizabeth exercised her political power in organizing public French-style salons and was one of the earliest women in the United States to implement these intellectual gatherings into American society. She cultivated an impressive network of politicians and other elites in the city of Philadelphia. As a salonnière, she chose the topics for conversation, facilitated the discussion, and provided the space in which these intellectual exchanges unfolded. Attendees at these salons discussed "cultural and intellectual pursuits." Women led salon culture, but guests included Enlightenment thinkers of both sexes.[28]

One attendee of these salons was the French military officer and member of the Académie française, the Marquis de Chastellux, who travelled to Philadelphia in the winter of 1780. The French Ambassador Chevalier de la Luzerne hosted a dinner with politicians and military officials, which Samuel Powel attended. The next day, the Chevalier took the marquis around the city to visit with women and experience the social scenes Philadelphia had to offer. His final visit of the day was with Elizabeth. The marquis, who kept a travel journal during his visit, usually commented on the appearance and social graces of the women he met, but his passages on his time with Elizabeth focused solely on her intellect. He wrote that the she was "head of the household," contrary to the American custom of a male-dominated home. With her "taste for conversation and her truly European use that she knows how to make of her understanding and information," Chastellux felt as though he were back in Paris. Elizabeth, in Chastellux's mind, was the only traditional salonnière he had met during his time abroad.[29] George Washington, a good friend of the marquis, likely also attended these salons.

Just prior to moving next door in 1781, the Washingtons attended a Twelfth-Night ball given by the Powels, which included a host of notable guests. Elizabeth used her power as a political agent by orchestrating the spirited event in order to reunite influential individuals, encouraging them to set their partisan differences aside for an evening. Attendee Sarah Bache, in a letter to her father Benjamin Franklin, highlighted the feel of the evening: "There never was so much dressing and pleasure going on; old friends meeting again, the Whigs in high spirits and strangers of distinction among us."[30]

While Elizabeth's privilege and reputation facilitated initial connections with a variety of powerful figures, her intellect and charm is what developed many of these relationships into genuine friendships. These interactions elevated her place in society, but her close relationship with George Washington represented the pinnacle of her social position. In 1781, when the Washingtons rented the house next door to the Powels, they developed a fast friendship. Through them, the Washingtons gained entrance into the world of Philadelphia's cultural and economic elites. As the Washingtons did not often frequent city-centers for long periods during the Revolutionary War, the Powels helped them maneuver the latest fashions and practices of sociability.

Upon hearing of George Washington's resignation as commander of the Continental army, Elizabeth wrote a long commentary to her friend Ann Fitzhugh, the day after he resigned his commission. In this letter, she publicized her advantageous relationship with the General with her interpretation on his emotional state. She demonstrated how she used her own cultivated wisdom to develop such a personal connection with a powerful figure. She explained that the public speeches acknowledging his resignation "were too strong for him to digest without such a shock to his Feelings." She also proclaimed that George would be much happier returning home to Virginia, a state she described as "having the exclusive Honor of giving birth & Education to a greater Hero than ancient or modern Times can boast."[31]

When George's nephew Bushrod Washington came to Philadelphia to study law just prior to George's resignation as commander, George immediately introduced him to the Powels. He knew this beneficial introduction would provide the young, up-and-coming law student with instant access to the best circles in Philadelphia. The Powels developed an immediate fondness for Bushrod, who wrote of spending "the most happy hours" at their home, where he "found both Instruction and entertainment." Elizabeth, with no children of her own, adopted the twenty-year-old as a surrogate son. Bushrod reciprocated this relationship and told his mother "that his friendship increased for her every day, and he did not know when it would end." Elizabeth gave him lessons in how a proper gentleman should carry himself, dress, and converse. Bushrod thought of these lessons as Elizabeth affectionately pointing out "his every foible." The Powels helped Bushrod choose a portrait artist during his time in the city because he believed their opinion on an artist carried "the most weight." He returned to Virginia the following year, and continued his correspondence with Elizabeth, in which her habit of "admonishing" him, as she called it, "still prevailed . . . though she made no apology for it."[32] She kept up this witty correspondence with Bushrod throughout the late eighteenth and early nineteenth centuries.[33]

In politically charged periods such as the Constitutional Convention in 1787, Elizabeth capitalized on the conversations with the delegates, including the president of the convention, George Washington. Elizabeth later reflected on this period in Philadelphia in a letter to her niece in 1814. She wrote how she "well remembered to have frequently associated with the most respectable, influential Members of the Convention that framed the Constitution, and that the all-important Subject was frequently discussed at our House."[34] During George's time in Philadelphia for the convention, he visited with the Powels twelve times, more

Bushrod Washington, by Henry Benbridge, 1783. Elizabeth Powel influenced Bushrod Washington in choosing the artist and style of this portrait. He spent several months in Philadelphia, where he became close friends with Elizabeth and Samuel Powel. (Courtesy of the Mount Vernon Ladies' Association)

than any other family in the city. These visits likely included discussions of the changing government. Elizabeth's knowledge of the framing of the Constitution, and her fluent French, even led George to entrust her to translate at least one letter to him from the French ambassador Chevalier de La Luzerne during the convention.[35]

The Washingtons returned to Mount Vernon after the convention ended in September 1787 but maintained their friendship with the Powels. After the Washingtons returned to their plantation, the Powels visited Elizabeth's sister Mary Byrd at Westover Plantation in southern Virginia. On their journey southward, they stayed at Mount Vernon for four days in early October 1787. George used this visit as a way to connect on a more personal level with the Powels. He took them to see the ruins of Belvoir Plantation, once the home of George William and Sally Fairfax. George rarely shared these private pieces of his early life. As a young man, the Fairfaxes had been George's closest connections outside of his own family and he credited them with his introduction to the gentry class—not unlike the role the Powels played in bringing the Washingtons into Philadelphia society. To visit this sentimental place with the Powels showed the comfort George felt with them.

After their stay at Mount Vernon, the Powels had another glimpse into his private life. They stopped in Fredericksburg for an evening with George's mother and sister, Mary Washington and Betty Lewis. On the way back from Westover, they stayed once more with the Washingtons at Mount Vernon. After the Powels returned to Philadelphia, Elizabeth paid her respects to Martha for the "sense of the elegant Hospitality exercised at Mount Vernon . . . a most delightful residence." These two visits in 1787 were the only times the Powels stayed at Mount Vernon, though the Washingtons extended many additional invitations.[36]

Within two years after the Powels' visit, George was elected as the first president of the United States. When Philadelphia became the temporary seat of the federal government in 1790, the city again became the center of the nation's political activities. Elizabeth had the easily accessible Washington family to socialize with, and the ear of the president to voice her own opinions regarding governmental affairs. Throughout the first term, the Powels—especially Elizabeth—were trusted confidants, respites for entertainment, and political sounding boards for the president.

Six months after the Washingtons moved to Philadelphia, the stresses of public life began to wear on them, and reached a breaking point at the end of 1792, near the close of the president's first term. On Thursday, November 1, 1792, George and Elizabeth privately discussed his hesitation to serve another term as president. This was not the first time they discussed his anxieties, so, after their latest conversation, Elizabeth decided the best way to convey her feelings and impart her advice was to write him a letter. She docketed the letter with, "To The President of the United States on the Subject of His Resignation," and filled it with strongly worded "sentiments that would be inconsistent to their friendship to withhold."[37] It is the only surviving document written by a woman, and non-cabinet member, on the subject of his resignation.

Elizabeth knew this letter could be a turning point in the nation's future and did not write it solely as private advice to her friend. This was a deliberate political act. She prepared for this letter in a way not seen amongst her other correspondence. Her first draft has minor grammatical edits from Samuel, which shows she consulted him after she initially wrote the letter, but she did the methodical work of constructing the letter, as well as the emotional work of appealing to Washington's patriotic sensibilities.

Before Elizabeth began her draft, she read a European political treatise written by the Comte de Mirabeau, entitled *The Secret History of the Court of Berlin*. Mirabeau wrote this text based on his observations as an "unofficial observer" to the fragile Prussian government in the 1780s.[38] In a separate nine-page document, she embarked on the painstakingly detailed process of choosing relevant passages within the text and proceeded to rework them into her own ideas. She then strategically inserted some of these phrases into her own letter, intertwining her words with Mirabeau's to construct her compelling argument and sound political advice for the president, who valued her as a political actor, regardless of her gender.[39]

After detailing the effects that George's resignation would have on the nation's fledgling government, Elizabeth skillfully deployed her emotional connection with Washington to attain her political goals. She insisted that, in writing this letter, she did not mean to "give him Pain by wounding [his] feelings." She cared about Washington, but she cared more about protecting the "welfare of their Common Country." As a Federalist, if the president stepped down, the government she supported would "crumble and decay." She believed Washington "could not and would not" watch the "Antifederalist[s] . . . exalt in its ruins." Though she understood how much he longed for private life, she urged him not to "yield to a Love of Ease, Retirement, rural Pursuits, or a false Diffidence of Abilities which those that best know [him] so justly appreciate." At the end of her "train of reflections," she borrowed from the end of Mirabeau's letter, and wrote that she hoped the president, until he was in the "extremist of old age," would have nothing but happiness in his choice of serving another term.[40]

A month after she sent her letter, George was unanimously reelected as president of the United States. He accepted the position, though he continued to have doubts. In January 1793, he wrote to a friend that as his "particular, & confidential friends well know," the decision to serve a second term was decided only after "a long and painful conflict in [his] own breast."[41] Elizabeth was one of those friends, and among the most trusted ones. The beginning of his second term rapidly filled with political conflict and changes in the capital city. As the president's term unfolded, partisan rancor consumed the nation. Throughout these tumultuous years, he continued to rely on the advice and trusting companionship of his friend Elizabeth.

In February 1793, Elizabeth celebrated her fiftieth birthday with a grand ball hosted in her honor at her home. The Washingtons could not attend, as they were back at Mount Vernon because of a death in the family. Taking inspiration from Elizabeth's gift of a poem the previous year for his sixtieth birthday, George sent a poem written for Elizabeth by the poet Elizabeth Graeme Fergusson.[42] The author inserted Elizabeth into the poem, comparing her to a Greek goddess called Mira, which means "wonderful" and the name of the "brightest star in the constellation." The poem discussed how Elizabeth (as Mira), had aged gracefully, and continued to emit a youthful beauty, with a "fascinating" gift of speech. Washington made sure to note his praise of the poem for its "just sentiments."[43]

Though the year started with a celebration, the summer brought drastic changes for both the cosmopolitan city and the Powels. Yellow fever overtook Philadelphia that August, when Congress was on a scheduled recess. The executive branch still met in the city, but as the disease spread, the seat of government temporarily moved out of Philadelphia.[44] George and Martha left for Mount Vernon at the beginning of September and extended a verbal invitation to the Powels to join them. The Powels were the only people they asked to travel with them, clearly wanting to spare their friends. In a letter to "her dear Friend and very dear Madam," Elizabeth explained that "at this awfull Moment," she and Samuel decided to stay in Philadelphia. Though Samuel desired Elizabeth make her own decision, as the matter could "affect her Life and his happiness," the thought of him contracting the disease and being "deprived of her Consolation and Aid," was too much for Elizabeth to bear.[45] Within a week of writing the letter to the Washingtons, the disease ravaged the city. Elizabeth fled to her brother's country residence, regretfully leaving her husband behind.[46]

Samuel spent the majority of his time in Philadelphia, feeling a civic duty to stay involved in governmental affairs. While he was visiting Elizabeth, his free Black valet Philip Roedel became ill with the fever back in the city. Samuel returned and attended to him for a brief period, until he also contracted the fever and removed to his farmhouse, Powelton, across the Schuylkill River.[47] Samuel was in good spirits and tried to make light of the situation. After a session of bleeding and purging, he wrote to Dr. Benjamin Rush that he "certainly wasn't feeling any worse."[48] Unfortunately, Samuel's good humor could not keep the disease at bay. Over the course of his illness, Rush visited Samuel five times, performing his controversial medical procedures, which would eventually play a part in Samuel's death. As his condition worsened, Elizabeth, following Rush's advice to "keep at a distance from infected persons & places," could not tend to Samuel at Powelton.[49] She sent multiple notes per day to Rush, inquiring about Samuel's prognosis and comfort. In Samuel's final hours, an "inexperienced young doctor" was his only attendant. The doctor did not follow Rush's directions to bleed Samuel a fourth time in a final effort to ease his suffering. Instead, the doctor called for Rush to come to the house, but when Rush arrived, he could not save the dying man.[50] Samuel died just after six o'clock in the morning on September 29, 1793. On his own request, he was buried in Christ Church Burial Ground that day, alongside the Powels' four children.[51]

Two days later, Oliver Wolcott Jr., comptroller of the treasury, alerted the president of Samuel's death as part of his regular updates about the progress of the disease. The comptroller acknowledged Samuel's death specifically and wrote, "he mentioned Mr. Samuel Powel's death with the more sincere regret."[52] By early December 1793, at the end of the epidemic, most residents of Philadelphia had lost someone to the fever, which claimed a tenth of the city's 50,000 residents within the four-month period. Elizabeth returned to Philadelphia in mid-November and continued to mourn her "most true, tender, and constant friend."[53] While no condolence letter to Elizabeth survives from either George or Martha, they would have been one of the many visitors to her residence to express their sympathies.

Elizabeth, though "very much distresed" at the loss of her husband, continued to move in Philadelphia's social circles.[54] She invited Vice President John Adams to a dinner for her family in mid-January 1795 to signal that her political influence was undiminished as she transitioned back into public life. John's wife, Abigail, was not in the city and John wrote to her afterward that Elizabeth was disappointed she could not attend, as she found her so "congenial to her own Disposition & Taste."

Elizabeth told John that she admired Abigail's "well-informed Mind" and thought her "an honour to her sex. &c. &c. &c."[55]

After the death of her husband, Elizabeth maintained her close friendship with George. At a private dinner in early June 1796, George entrusted her with the information that he was going to step down as president. The next day, she wrote him a response reflecting on their conversation. Her description suggested that the conversation was unproductive and ultimately unresolved. She wrote that she had reassessed her previous reaction, after "feeling incapable of nourishing an implacable Resentment" and a "mature reflection" on what he told her. She felt, as did many of her fellow citizens of the nation, that losing him would irreparably damage the new United States. On a personal level, he had been an unfailing presence in Elizabeth's life for twenty years, and though she knew he longed for retirement, she did not want him to leave. However, in consideration of his feelings and their friendship, she scheduled another dinner with him "to meet his ideas with fortitude."[56]

When George's presidency ended, Elizabeth found a way to honor her friend and keep a piece of him with her in Philadelphia. Before the Washingtons left in late March 1797, the new administration sold the excess furniture and sundries from the President's Mansion. Elizabeth purchased George's presidential desk.[57] When the desk arrived to her home, Elizabeth found a bundle of letters from Martha to her husband left inside a drawer. Elizabeth immediately wrote to George, who had already left the city. This exchange, with its humorous and trusting tone, shows that their friendship eclipsed politics and societal gain. She teased him that she had found "Love letters of a Lady addressed to you under the most solemn Sanction." Since "he had never blundered as President," she posited that he was "determined to try its Delights as a private Gentleman." She wrapped up the letters with "three seals of her blessed friend's arms."[58] Elizabeth noted that if he did not want Martha to know what had transpired (as she would recognize the Powel seal), he should remove the outer package. George wrote a light-hearted reply. He said that "he had no love letters to lose" and the correspondence in Elizabeth's possession was filled with sentiments of friendship. He disclosed that the letters would only be of the warmth of the "romantic order, if they were committed to the flames."[59]

Elizabeth and George fell into their old routine of dining, tea, and conversation during George's final trip to Philadelphia in the wake of the Quasi-War in late 1798. Just before he left Philadelphia, Elizabeth wrote her last surviving letter to him, in which she expressed that, because he was leaving, her heart was "so sincerely afflicted, and Idea's so confused," that she wished that he may be "happy here and in the hereafter."[60] George replied with kind sentiments and stopped once more to see her before leaving Philadelphia for the last time.[61] Some historians hypothesize this exchange may allude to a finally acted on "forbidden action or feeling" or a "misunderstanding of the nature of their long friendship," but a less sordid explanation is more likely.[62] Elizabeth came to the realization how, with George's advanced age and clear desire for retirement, she likely would not see him again unless she traveled to Mount Vernon. In the style of many of her letters, she expressed her feelings with a dramatic turn of phrase. Platonic friendships, such as Elizabeth and George's, were often deeply emotional, but there is no indication that they had any type of falling out over an affair or another matter.[63] No subsequent letters between George and Elizabeth survive after his return to Mount Vernon, but they likely continued to write to one another, as Elizabeth still corresponded with Martha and Bushrod throughout the following year.

George's death in December 1799 signified the closing of a long chapter in Elizabeth's life. She wrote a condolence letter to Martha on December 24, expressing her own grief, but focusing more on Martha herself. The two women shared the common bond of outliving both their husbands and children. In this letter, Elizabeth brought up the idea of a visit to Mount Vernon, but, likely reflecting on the death of her own husband, knew "that no Consolation can be effected by human Agency." Elizabeth summed up her own feelings on George's death in one sentence: "I have lost a much valued friend."[64]

On Christmas Day, Elizabeth hosted a dinner for family and close friends. One attendee observed that "the Dowager" was "really aflicted at the death of her old friend the General." He poked fun at the situation and wrote that she "thinks it necessary to appear more so than she is in fact, and that she is called upon in decency to shed tears whenever his name is mentioned."[65] This visitor, however, had not been a witness to the private moments of friendship between Elizabeth and George. He therefore likely did not understand the level of grief Elizabeth experienced, having so recently lost two pillars of support in her life: her husband and one of her best friends. The day after Christmas, the national funeral procession held in honor of President Washington proceeded near Elizabeth's residence. The sounds of cannons firing, church bells tolling, and the muffled drums of the New Theater band filled the city. These sounds became the background noise to Elizabeth's mourning as she grieved the loss of her friend.

By that point, Elizabeth had recently sold her Third Street residence to her nephew, another symbol that she had moved into a new period of life. With the inheritance left by her husband, she focused on her future and constructed a new townhouse on Chestnut Street. As the city expanded toward the Schuylkill River, this neighborhood became the social epicenter of nineteenth-century Philadelphia.[66] Her new home, a block west of Independence Hall, gave her a fresh perspective on life in her city, leaving the memories of the past to her old home. Though Philadelphia was no longer the seat of the federal government, Elizabeth still kept an interest in political affairs. She subscribed to various national newspapers and joined a host of philanthropic organizations to retain her place in public society.[67] Even as Elizabeth's health gradually deteriorated throughout the 1810s, she continued to hold court in her home with members of the younger generation. During the Marquis de Lafayette's tour of America in 1824, for example, he spent the evening at her home with a "select circle of ladies and gentlemen" after attending a concert at the Chestnut Street Theater.[68]

Even late in life, Elizabeth's desire to educate the younger members of society never faltered. Letters from her younger relatives and the children and grandchildren of her earliest friends frequently mention her many anecdotes and pieces of advice. In a lasting connection to the Washingtons, she kept up correspondence with their grandchildren. She was particularly close with Eleanor Parke Custis Lewis, who lived with the Washingtons during George's presidency. Elizabeth represented the sophisticated woman Eleanor desired to become. However, as a young woman, Eleanor was quite spirited, and Elizabeth often teased her about her appearance. Elizabeth frequently told her that "her clothes looked as if they were thrown on with a *Pitch-fork!*"[69] Elizabeth's admonishments, as they had on Bushrod so many years prior, had a lasting effect on Eleanor. As an adult, she always asked after Elizabeth and included updates on her life for her in letters back to a close connection in Philadelphia. These milestones included the birth of her first grandchild, of which she wrote that Elizabeth's *"little Nelly* would soon become *grandmother!"*[70] After Elizabeth's death, Eleanor recalled how she "always received me with such affectionate fondness, has always been so partial to me, & was so superior in mind, so delightful in conversation, that in my youngest & gayest days I loved to pass many hours in her company."[71]

Elizabeth also stayed in touch with her friend Bushrod Washington. Bushrod became an associate supreme court justice in 1798, and when riding the circuit, he ate dinner with Elizabeth every Sunday during his time in Philadelphia. Elizabeth's great-nephew Samuel later wrote about attending these weekly dinners alongside his father, John Hare Powel, Elizabeth's adopted nephew and closest friend. He said that his father "delighted to tease" Elizabeth about the portrait of George Washington she owned by the artist Joseph Wright.[72] He repeatedly told her it "was badly painted." Bushrod, however, always "entertained her in asserting it was an admirable likeness."[73] Even in his advanced age, Bushrod still respected Elizabeth and her ideals, especially in relation to his uncle.

The Washington and Custis descendants were not the only relatives of the revolutionary generation that expressed kind sentiments toward Elizabeth. Louisa Adams, wife of John Quincy Adams, wrote that she considered "her friend Mrs. Powell" as "first in rank" in an 1822 letter to her father-in-law, John Adams. She said that Elizabeth's "mind was as vigorous as ever and she loved to talk over times past." Louisa noted her "active memory" that "retraced pleasures long gone by and filled her still vivid fancy with actors and scenes in which she shone a brilliant constellation" and filled her "conversation . . . full of anecdotes." Louisa wished that she could see John and Elizabeth, two of the remaining members of the "old school," together, as their "reminisces would be delightful."[74] He replied that if he were to visit Philadelphia again, he would visit "Mrs. Powel above all else . . . as she was a Lady of as Masterly an understanding as ever [he] knew."[75]

When Elizabeth died on January 17, 1830, the *National Gazette* published a detailed obituary. It painted a clear picture of a highly respected figure and only regretted that Philadelphia had lost a woman whose "mind was cast in an unusual mold of strength and proportion" and associated her with the "greatest men of the Revolutionary age." The discussions with these men gave her an "elevated direction to her conversations and reflections." In these conversations, she "continued to impart a philosophical tone to her consideration of every question, and gave dignity and depth to her opinions, as well as to her mode of expressing them, which very few possessed."[76] Many years prior, she had used these skills to influence and advise one of her "best friends and favorites," George Washington.[77]

Elizabeth Willing Powel represents the power that women held as political actors in the early republic, when viewed both through the lens of her relationship with George Washington, in which he considered her both a peer and advisor, and in her invaluable political, social, and philanthropic positions in Philadelphia. In looking at her long life, it is clear she was a fundamental presence in the story of Philadelphia and the founding of the United States. The epitaph on her tombstone in Christ Church Burial Ground summarizes her life in only a few words. Elizabeth, the vibrant presence in the evolution of Philadelphia, was "distinguished by her good sense, and good works."[78]

Notes

Thank you to my friends Krysten Blackstone, Lydia Brandt, and Rachel Walker for your helpful and humorous comments on my drafts. Also, a heartfelt thank you to my dear friend Kayla Anthony for our many entertaining phone calls about the Powels.

1. Roger Griswold to Fanny Griswold, 9 May 1796, Roger Griswold Papers (MS 256), Manuscripts and Archives, Yale University Library.

2. Thomas M. Doerflinger, *A Vigorous Spirit of Enterprise: Merchants and Economic Development in Revolutionary Philadelphia* (Chapel Hill: University of North Carolina Press, 1986) provides a detailed overview of the economic structure of transatlantic trade. More information on Charles Willing's participation in the transatlantic trade can be found in Marc Egnal, "The Changing Structure of Philadelphia's Trade with the British West Indies, 1750–1775," *The Pennsylvania Magazine of History and Biography* 99, no. 2 (1975): 156–79.

3. Stephen Hague, *The Gentleman's House in the British Atlantic World 1680–1780* (London: Palgrave Macmillan, 2015) looks at how the elite built their lives around British culture; Alexander Lunan to Colonel Henry Bouquet,

16 July 1760, in *Papers of Henry Bouquet,* ed. S. K. Stevens et al. (Harrisburg: The Pennsylvania Historical and Museum Commission, 1984), 119 (hereafter cited as *PHB*); see Mary M. Schweitzer's article, "The Spatial Organization of Federalist Philadelphia, 1790," *The Journal of Interdisciplinary History* 24, no. 1 (1993), for information on the development of the Society Hill neighborhood.

4. Nancy E. Richards, "The City Home of Benjamin Chew, Sr., and His Family: A Case Study of the Textures of Life" (unpublished manuscript, Clivden of the National Trust, 1996), 3.

5. Thomas Willing was a well-known merchant, politician, and financier in the eighteenth and early nineteenth centuries. He was the first president of the Bank of the United States and served a number of other political positions. See Robert E. Wright, "Thomas Willing (1731–1821): Philadelphia Financier and Forgotten Founding Father," *Pennsylvania History: A Journal of Mid-Atlantic Studies* 63, no. 4 (1996): 525–60.

6. Elizabeth Gibbs Willing Alleyne to Ann Willing Morris, 18 May 1818, Ann W. Morris Letters, William L. Clements Library, The University of Michigan.

7. Lewis Ourry to Henry Bouquet, 14 September 1760, in *PHB*, 4:36.

8. Lewis Ourry to Henry Bouquet, 11 February 1761, in *PHB*, 5:288–89.

9. Alexander Lunan to Henry Bouquet, 16 July 1760, in *PHB*, 4:639; Lucia McMahon's *Mere Equals: The Paradox of Educated Women in the Early Republic* (Ithaca: Cornell University Press, 2012) and Mary Kelley's *Learning to Stand and to Speak: Women, Education, and Public Life in America's Republic* (Chapel Hill: University of North Carolina Press, 2006) provide an overview of the impact of young women's education in the eighteenth century.

10. Lindsay O'Neill, "Networking in the Epistolary World," in *The Opened Letter: Networking in the Early Modern British World* (Philadelphia: University of Pennsylvania Press, 2015), specifically 108–12 for information on women and networking in the eighteenth century.

11. Benjamin Rush, *Essays, Literary, Moral, and Philosophical* (Philadelphia, 1798), 6–7. Rush's passage echoes an idea written by Elizabeth Powel in a letter dated July 1786: *"certain it is that the Groundwork of Education with both Sexes rests on the Mother. She gives the first & most lasting Impressions,"* Historic Manuscripts Collection (hereafter cited as HMC), George Washington National Library (hereafter cited as GWNL).

12. Benjamin Rush, *Thoughts Upon Female Education Accommodated to the Present State of Society &c.,* (Philadelphia: Prichard & Hall, 1787), 3.

13. Elizabeth Powel to Benjamin Rush, 24 January 1795, Rush family papers, 1748–1876, Library Company of Philadelphia (hereafter cited as LCP).

14. George Mercer to Henry Bouquet, 9 January 1763, in *PHB*, 12:11–12.

15. Rudolph Bentinck to Henry Bouquet, 24 October 1763, in *PHB*, 12:107.

16. "Book of Accounts Belonging to the Academy in Philadelphia, January 7, 1751–July 26, 1757," Matriculation and Class Records, Archives of the University of Pennsylvania.

17. For more information on Samuel Powel's grand tour, see Sarah Jackson, *Journal of Samuel Powel in Rome, 1764* (Firenze: SPES, 2001). See Daniel Kilbride, *Being American in Europe, 1750–1860* (Baltimore: Johns Hopkins University Press, 2013), and Caroline Winterer, *American Enlightenments: Pursuing Happiness in an Age of Reason* (New Haven: Yale University Press, 2016), for more scholarship on Grand Tours and the Enlightenment. "The American Society held at Philadelphia for promoting Useful Knowledge" was a short-lived learned society that combined with the American Philosophical Society in 1769. See the editorial essay within "[Charles Thomson] to Benjamin Franklin, 6 November 1768," in *The Papers of Benjamin Franklin*, ed. William B. Willcox (New Haven: Yale University Press, 1972), 15:259–62 for more information.

18. Sarah M. S. Pearsall, *Atlantic Families: Lives and Letters in the Later Eighteenth Century* (New York: Oxford University Press, 2008) and Susan Klepp, *Revolutionary Conceptions: Women, Fertility, and Family Limitation in America, 1760–1820* (Chapel Hill: University of North Carolina Press, 2009) provide scholarship on the evolution of marriage during the early republic.

19. "Notebook pertaining to the Shippen Family, 1887," Powel Family Papers (1582) (hereafter cited as PFP [1582]), Historical Society of Pennsylvania (hereafter cited as HSP).

20. Elizabeth Powel to Martha Hare, 20 November 1810, PFP (1582), HSP.

21. François Jean Marquis de Chastellux, *Travels in North-America in the Years 1780, 1781, and 1782* (London: Printed for G. G. J. and J. Robinsons, 1787), 203.

22. Financial Ledger: 1760–1793, Powel Family Papers (LCP.in.HSP91), LCP.

23. Kariann Akemi Yokota, "A Culture of Insecurity: Americans in a Transatlantic World of Goods," in *Unbecoming British: How Revolutionary America Became a Postcolonial Nation* (New York: Oxford University Press, Incorporated, 2011), 86–94, explains the difficultly in shifting from British to American goods. The Powels also solicited goods from a number of the finest Philadelphian artisans, including silversmith Joseph Richardson, car-

penter William Savery, and ironmonger Daniel King. See Financial Ledger: 1760–1793, Powel Family Papers (LCP.in.HSP91), LCP. Historian Robert J. Gough completed a detailed study of the financial records of Philadelphia from 1775–1800. He categorized the top of the elite class as the "2.5%," and placed Samuel Powel at the top. See his work, "The Significance of the Demographic Characteristics of Wealthy Philadelphians at the End of the Eighteenth Century," *Proceedings of the American Philosophical Society* 133, no. 2 (1989): 307, for more information on the elite population of Philadelphia.

24. Chastellux, *Travels in North-America*, 203–4.

25. Elizabeth Powel to Ann Randolph Fitzhugh, 24 December 1783, HMC, GWNL.

26. Rosemarie Zagarri, "Female Politicians," in *Revolutionary Backlash: Women and Politics in the Early American Republic* (Philadelphia: University of Pennsylvania Press, 2007), 46–82, provides scholarship on elite women's participation in the political world of the United States. See Linda Kerber's *Women of the Republic: Intellect and Ideology in Revolutionary America* (Chapel Hill: University of North Carolina Press, 1980) and Mary Beth Norton's *Liberty's Daughters: The Revolutionary Experience of American Women, 1750–1800* (Ithaca: Cornell University Press, 1980), for the foundational scholarship on "republican mothers."

27. Anne Willing Francis to Charles Stirling, 6 October 1805, ms38526, Papers of Stirling of Cadder family, University of St. Andrews.

28. Susan Branson, *The Fiery Frenchified Dames: Women and Political Culture in Early National Philadelphia* (Philadelphia: University of Pennsylvania Press, 2001), 126–27; Lucia McMahon's *Mere Equals*, 80–84, focuses on the importance of the conversations between the guests at the salon.

29. François Jean Marquis de Chastellux, *Voyage de Newport à Philadelphie* (Newport: l'imprimerie royale de l'escadre, 1781), 80–81; Charlene M. Boyer Lewis, *Elizabeth Patterson Bonaparte: An American Aristocrat in the Early Republic* (Philadelphia: University of Pennsylvania Press, 2012), 158–64, shows the experience of an American at a public French salon in Paris, highlighting the roles of women among the European and American attendees.

30. Sarah Bache to Benjamin Franklin, 17 January 1779, in *The Papers of Benjamin Franklin*, ed. Barbara B. Oberg (New Haven: Yale University Press, 1990), 28:390–92.

31. Elizabeth Powel to Ann Randolph Fitzhugh, 24 December 1783, HMC, GWNL.

32. Elizabeth Powel to Bushrod Washington, 22 June 1785, HMC, GWNL.

33. Bushrod Washington's series of letters to his mother Hannah Washington (dated 12 April 1783, 7 June 1783, and 1 July 1783) describe his affectionate feelings for Elizabeth. These letters are located at the Louis A. Watres Library, George Washington Masonic National Memorial. For more on the Henry Benbridge portrait of Bushrod Washington, see Stephen E. Patrick's, "'I Have at Length Determined to Have My Picture Taken': An Eighteenth-Century Young Man's Thoughts about His Portrait by Henry Benbridge," *The American Art Journal* 22, no. 4 (winter 1990): 68–81.

34. Elizabeth Powel to Martha Hare, 25 May 1814, PFP (1582), HSP.

35. Anne-César de La Luzerne to George Washington, April 1787, in *The Papers of George Washington, Confederation Series,* ed. W. W. Abbot (Charlottesville: University Press of Virginia, 1997), 5:161–63 (hereafter cited as *PGW*).

36. Samuel Powel Travel Journal, October 1787, Genealogical Society of Pennsylvania Collection, HSP; Diary: 9 October 1787, in *PGW*, 5:192; Elizabeth Powel to Martha Washington, 30 November 1787, Martha Washington Collection (hereafter cited as MWC), GWNL. Ami Pflugrad-Jackisch's essay, "'What Am I but an American': Mary Willing Byrd and Westover Plantation during the American Revolution," in *Women of the American Revolution: Gender, Politics, and the Domestic World,* ed. Barbara Oberg (Charlottesville: University of Virginia Press, 2019), tells the story of Mary Byrd, a powerful plantation owner in southern Virginia.

37. Elizabeth Willing Powel to George Washington, 4 November 1792, George Washington Collection (hereafter cited GWC), GWNL.

38. R. M. Johnston, "Mirabeau's Secret Mission to Berlin," *The American Historical Review* 6, no. 2 (1901): 253.

39. Powel's draft and final copy use direct quotes from the book authored by Honoré-Gabriel de Riquette comte de Mirabeau, *The Secret History of the Court of Berlin &c* (London: S. Bladon, 1789), 321–24, 391. Elizabeth took the most inspiration from Mirabeau's letter to Frederick William II, in which he tried to give the new king the confidence he needed to begin his reign. The nine-page document is located within the PFP (1582), HSP; Abigail Adams, in her 31 March 1776 letter to John Adams, borrows from several texts, as discussed by historian Elaine Forman Crane in her article "Abigail Adams, Gender Politics and *The History of Emily Montague*: A Post Script," *The William & Mary Quarterly* 64, no. 4 (October 2007): 839–44.

40. Elizabeth Willing Powel to George Washington, 4 November 1792, GWC, GWNL.

41. George Washington to Henry Lee, 20 January 1793, in *PGW*, 12:30–31.

42. Stanzas on the President's Birthday, 22 February 1792, GWC, GWNL.

43. George Washington to Elizabeth Powel, February 1793, GWC, GWNL.

44. See Simon Finger, "Those Friendly Reciprocations: Panic and Participation in the Yellow Fever," in *The Contagious City: The Politics of Public Health in Early Philadelphia* (Ithaca: Cornell University Press, 2012), 120–34, for more on the yellow fever epidemic.

45. Elizabeth Powel to George Washington, 9 September 1793, in *PGW*, 14:54–55.

46. Anne Willing Francis to son, 16 September 1793, Joshua Francis Fisher Papers (1858), HSP.

47. "Notebook pertaining to the Shippen Family, 1887," PFP (1582), HSP; "Memorandum to my Children, 1851," *Hare-Powel Kindred Families* (New York, 1907).

48. Samuel Powel to Benjamin Rush, ca. 17 September 1793, Rush family papers, 1748–1876, LCP. Elizabeth blamed the "ignorance of the physicians" for causing the death of her husband, as written in "Notebook pertaining to the Shippen Family, 1887," PFP (1582), HSP.

49. Samuel Powel to Benjamin Rush, 1 September 1793, Rush Family Papers, 1748–1876, LCP. This advice is written on the back of this letter in Rush's hand.

50. Benjamin Rush to Julia Stockton Rush, 29 September 1793, Letters 1777–1824, Benjamin and Julia Stockton Rush Papers, Duke University.

51. Burial: Samuel Powel, Christ Church Register 1785–1900, Christ Church Parish Records. Elizabeth Powel paid Absalom Jones and Richard Allen for the removal of the bodies of both Samuel Powel and Philip Roedel and for the cleaning of the rooms they died in, as shown in check stubs located in "Materials removed from volume 41," Powel Family Papers, LCP. Jones and Allen, leaders of the free Black community in Philadelphia, were seminal in the operations of the city during the epidemic. See Phillip Lapsansky's essay, "'Abigail a Negress': The Role and Legacy of African Americans in the Yellow Fever Epidemic," in *A Melancholy Scene of Devastation: The Public Response to the 1793 Philadelphia Yellow Fever Epidemic*, ed. J. Worth Estes and Billy G. Smith (Philadelphia: College of Physicians of Philadelphia, 1997), 61–78, for more information.

52. Oliver Wolcott Jr. to George Washington, 1 October 1793, in *PGW*, 14:156–57.

53. Elizabeth Powel to Margaret Willing Hare, 3 January 1796, Society Collection, HSP.

54. Mary Smith Gray Otis to Abigail Adams, 23 February 1794, in *The Adams Papers, Adams Family Correspondence,* ed. Margaret A. Hogan et. al (Cambridge: Harvard University Press, 2011), 10:88–89 (hereafter cited as *PJA*).
55. John Adams to Abigail Adams, 12 January 1795, in *PJA*, 10:346–47.
56. Elizabeth Powel to George Washington, 5 June 1796, GWC, GWNL.
57. Tobias Lear to Elizabeth Powel, 9 March 1797, Society Collection, HSP.
58. Elizabeth Powel to George Washington, 11–13 March 1797, GWC, GWNL.
59. George Washington to Elizabeth Powel, 26 March 1797, GWC, GWNL. According to a descendant of the Custis family, Martha Washington burned their personal correspondence after George's death, as seen in an undated enclosure in the letter, George Washington to Martha Washington, 23 June 1775, GWC, GWNL.
60. Elizabeth Powel to George Washington, 7 December 1798, in *PGW*, 3:246.
61. George Washington to Elizabeth Powel, 9 December 1798, in *PGW*, 3:247–48.
62. Flora Fraser, *The Washingtons: George and Martha, "Join'd by Friendship, Crown'd by Love"* (New York: Knopf, 2015), 374–75. Fraser also interprets Washington's signoff in one of his last surviving letters to Powel to be a sign of romance. In a letter to Elizabeth dated 4 December 1798 (GWC, GWNL), he signs off with "I am always yours." Though affectionate, he uses this signoff at least sixty times in both political and private correspondence beginning in 1789.
63. See Cassandra A. Good, *Founding Friendships: Friendships between Men and Women in the Early American Republic* (New York: Oxford University Press, 2015) for more information on friendship in the early republic.
64. Elizabeth Powel to Martha Washington, 24 December 1799, MWC, GWNL.
65. Harrison Gray Otis to Sophia Otis, 26 December 1799, Harrison Gray Otis papers, Massachusetts Historical Society (hereafter cited as MHS).
66. Gary Nash, *First City: Philadelphia and the Forging of Historical Memory* (Philadelphia: University of Pennsylvania Press, 2006), 144–45.
67. Philadelphia Society for the Preservation of Landmarks acquired several previously unrecorded account books in late 2016, owned by Elizabeth Powel, from ca. 1810–1828. These accounts highlight her subscriptions to philanthropic societies, including the Female Society for the Relief and Employment of the Poor, the Hospitable Society, and the Abolition Society.
68. "Lafayette," *The National Gazette* (Philadelphia), 2 October 1824.
69. Eleanor Parke Custis Lewis to Elizabeth Bordley Gibson, 29 January 1833, Elizabeth Bordley Gibson Collection (hereafter cited as EBGC), GWNL.

70. Eleanor Parke Custis Lewis to Elizabeth Bordley Gibson, 1 December 1826, EBGC, GWNL.

71. Eleanor Parke Custis Lewis to Elizabeth Bordley Gibson, 30 January 1830, EBGC, GWNL.

72. See Nicholas Wainwright, "The Powel Portrait of Washington by Joseph Wright," *The Pennsylvania Magazine of History and Biography* 96, no. 4 (1972) for more information on the specific copy of the portrait once owned by the Powels.

73. Samuel Powel Jr. note, July 1876, written on the back of Elizabeth Powel to Hannah Bushrod Washington, 17 April 1783, HMC, GWNL.

74. Louisa Adams to John Adams, 1 August 1822, Adams Family Papers, MHS.

75. John Adams to Louisa Adams, 8 August 1822, Adams Family Papers, MHS.

76. "Obituary, Mrs. Elizabeth Powel," *The National Gazette* (Philadelphia), 23 February 1830.

77. Elizabeth Powel to Ann Fitzhugh, July 1786, HMC, GWNL.

78. Edward L. Clark, *A Record of Descriptions on the Tablets and Grave-stones in the Burial-Grounds of Christ Church, Philadelphia,* (Philadelphia: Collins, 1864), 129.

"I HAD FRIENDS AMONG THE COLORED PEOPLE OF THE TOWN"

The Enslaved Women of the President's Household and Philadelphia's African American Community

GEORGE W. BOUDREAU

On the rainy afternoon of Saturday, May 18, 1796, a lone figure stepped out of the door of 190 High Street in Philadelphia. She probably left quietly, working hard to attract little attention, but people who shared her rank were used to being expected to move silently and not being noticed. Just yards away, the master of the house, the president of the United States of America and his wife, were enjoying their dinner, likely the regular impressive fare skillfully crafted by Hercules, the enslaved chef who was one of the best known cooks and most colorful characters in the nation's capital. Ona Judge certainly bade no good-byes to the people gathered around the fine table that afternoon. As she stepped out the doorway, she was doing the unimaginable: escaping. The house's stone steps and brick façade were elegant indicators of the power of the people who lived inside number 190, and previous residents had used it as a seat of power under Penn family rule, during the War for Independence, and finally in the new nation. For six years, the Georgian townhouse had been Ona Judge's residence, but what she felt about this "home" we can only imagine. She had arrived there in 1790 with no free will about her move from New York City or her native Virginia; she had been the body servant of a wealthy, prominent woman, seen to her needs and whims, cared for her clothes and her grandchildren. Now, Ona Judge declared her own independence.[1]

Leaving 190, we can surmise that she first turned left, away from the busiest part of Philadelphia toward Sixth Street, still considered the edge of town just a few years ago, but rising populations and new fashions were leading to new developments beyond that former boundary. She likely turned left at Sixth, walking the one block to Chestnut, passing the building where twenty years earlier another Virginian's admonition that "all men are created equal" had been used to free a new nation. She also passed the building where, just three years before, the Congress of that new nation had voted in the Fugitive Slave Law, tightening the chains of slavery tighter around the bodies of those who were enslaved. Any American magistrate could be drawn in to help capture an enslaved person who tried to flee slavery.

Now, Ona Judge was a runaway.

The image of Ona Judge, alone, in danger, on the run has grown in recent years to be one of the most widely known and carefully studied in the new nation. Where a quarter-century ago few outside a small coterie of specialized historians knew her name, she has now become perhaps the most famous enslaved woman in early American history. Her story, her decision to run, her ability to avoid the most powerful people in America, and the story of the remainder of her life and death as a free woman have all become part of the United States' founding narrative.[2]

Yet while her biography has undergone profound research and widespread distribution, part of her life has received less scrutiny. From 1789 to 1796, Ona Judge left the plantation on which she was born and she lived in two northern cities, associated with their free and enslaved populations, and absorbed changing messages about slavery and freedom. That experience would shape her mental world and lead her to the decision that she would no longer be led. Ona Judge's narrative is remarkable for so many reasons: she ran away and remained free for the rest of her life; unlike most other enslaved persons who escaped, she was a woman; she was found living in freedom but avoided return to the South and to reenslavement; and she leaves us narratives—arguably the earliest narratives—in which an American describes her journey from slavery to freedom. In those two interviews, published decades later, she gives critical clues to her life in slavery, to the master and mistress she served from birth until her early twenties, to the decision she made to run, and to the causes that shaped that escape. All this played out in Philadelphia, one of the largest cities in the United States. Ona Judge made her decision in a city that had a large population of African Americans. Still a teenager when she arrived, now a woman, she had grown up in the middle of a Black community that included enslaved and free people who were still being held in the Anglo-American institution of human chattel slavery and others who were now free and in the midst of creating one of the country's first free Black communities with institutions and connections to support and aid one another. When interviewed as an old woman in 1845, Ona Judge Staines left us clues about the importance of that community to her escape and her freedom: "Whilst they were packing up to go to Virginia, I was packing to go, I didn't know where; for I knew that if I went back to Virginia, I should never get my liberty. I had friends among the colored people of Philadelphia, had my things carried there beforehand, and left Washington's house while they were eating dinner." Those friends and that story shape this narrative.[3]

Ona Judge's Philadelphia story, her life at 190 High Street and among the free and enslaved Black people of the city, began in November 1790, when she was about sixteen years old. Born at Mount Vernon in 1774 or 1775, she had become a "favorite" of the plantation's mistress while still a girl, was chosen to serve in the main house, working for the comfort and personal needs of Martha Dandridge Custis Washington and her offspring, rather than in the fields, farm outbuildings, or in the host of workshops making clothing or other stuffs that were necessary to the plantation, which functioned almost like a somewhat self-sufficient small town. Why Mrs. Washington had chosen Ona Judge to care for her hair, clothing, and other needs we cannot know. Perhaps it was because of Ona's personality, perhaps because of perceived skills, perhaps because of her appearance. The child of Betty, an enslaved woman of African descent, and Andrew Judge, an indentured white man who had come to Mount Vernon to work as a tailor, she had inherited both a light complexion and a greater rarity: a last name, something denied to almost all people who lived in bondage in the era.

Ona was born at a critical moment in the history of her owners, her native colony, and the world. George Washington had been born into a landed family but also in the unenviable position of being a younger son, not slated to inherit. Washington had risen to fame for his military service. After inadvertently starting what became the first true world war, the Seven Years' or French and Indian War, he gained fame and a rising status in the colonies. Those factors as well as an impressive physique likely helped draw the interest of Martha Custis, recently widowed and now responsible for raising her children and caring for the estate left to the family by her late husband, Daniel Parke Custis. The Washingtons' marriage in 1759 had brought new security to both. From the beginning, this new family unit was surrounded by enslaved workers, his and hers, who would do the backbreaking labor of sowing fields, bringing in crops, processing what they grew into items for local consumption and use or for export to factors in London, and building and rebuilding the structures and landscape of Mount Vernon. Working and living together, dower and Washington–enslaved people created families and communities that spanned generations. They were living in a world that later decisions and age-old inheritance practices would transform in the years to come.[4]

When Ona Judge was born, George Washington was already embroiled in the trans-colonial conflict that would become the American Revolution. About the time she began taking her first steps, Washington would be assuming the role of general of the new army established by the Continental Congress. Enslaved workers like Ona's mother and her children were living on a plantation where their master was absent, where their mistress lived in a strange middle ground between marriage and separation, and where overseers of varying levels of skill were a constant concern. Some members of this enslaved community took up Lord Dunmore's offer of freedom for service in the British Army; others simply took the opportunity to run when it presented itself. The enslaved community of Mount Vernon lived in a world that turned upside-down, over and over again. Washington's eventual return, on Christmas Eve 1783, may have signaled relief for some. They might have perceived his safe return as a sign that their families would stay together, that some small amount of postwar prosperity might trickle down to keep them alive and safe, and that the constant threat to enslaved people—sale that led to separation—might be avoided. Within a few short years, their world would again be changed, as George Washington reentered politics, helped create the United States Constitution, and was called to serve as the first president under it.[5]

Washington's election would change Ona Judge's life, and the lives of every member of the presidential household, profoundly. For her, the years in the nation's first two capitals would lead to a radical departure from what she might have expected had she remained in Virginia. She accompanied George and Martha Washington to Philadelphia in the fall of 1790, coming to a leased townhouse that would be the center of America's executive branch. That household would include a large, diverse "family" consisting of the presidential couple, Martha's grandchildren, an entourage of eight enslaved servants (a ninth would join them later), hired white domestics, and employees who would see to the president's domestic as well as official needs. Each of these people would have to adjust to their new home, but the enslaved workers who served the Washingtons would experience something in the temporary capital unlike anything they had seen before. For six years, this urban setting would play host to a transplanted Virginia household with assumptions about work, status, and place that did not readily take root in a state that was undergoing rapid and profound transformations in beliefs about human bondage.[6]

George Washington knew the importance of place, and from his early years onward, carefully planned his residences, their furnishings, and their staff. His relocation to Philadelphia had come as something of a surprise, but like earlier moves and renovations, he gave it careful scrutiny. That the Washingtons and their enslaved workers became part of Philadelphia's citizenry was the result of a series of political upheavals and changes to the nature of the new nation. The city where the United States was born had lost its role as nation's capital in 1783, when a group of rowdy, disenchanted, and likely hungry militiamen had surrounded the Pennsylvania State House on Chestnut Street demanding back pay. The Confederation Congress had simply slipped away that day, never to return. The young country's capital had eventually settled in New York. Almost by inertia, the government had remained there. Philadelphia's boosters wanted the government to return, but there seemed little likelihood of it happening. That changed, of course, when one of the new government's first major compromises placed the government in Philadelphia for ten years, then to a permanent spot, which Washington would select.[7]

With just weeks to prepare, Philadelphia's leaders scrambled to find space for all three branches of the federal government, and the home for the president required particular care. The Washingtons were used to spacious and grandly appointed residences. Housing had been a central aspect of their combined efforts since they married in 1759, as the groom sent detailed instructions for food, cleaning, and decoration back to Mount Vernon, the still modest Virginia plantation house. Upon his marriage, Washington assumed responsibility for not just his wife, but also the children she had borne to her first husband, Daniel Parke Custis. But wife and stepchildren were not the only change in Washington's life at the time of his marriage. He had also acquired a vast number of enslaved laborers, women and men who grew his crops, cleaned his house, built his structures, increased his wealth, and gave him the leisure time to practice politics, wage war, and head a government.[8]

All of these experiences informed George Washington's perspective as he prepared to move to the newly chosen capital. Washington visited Philadelphia in September 1790, en route to Mount Vernon for an extended holiday with his wife and family. The family moved into America's newly designated capital just as the dust of revolution was settling. They arrived in the American seaport where fundamental changes were taking place related to slavery and freedom, where century-long expectations about race and enslavement were undergoing new scrutiny.[9]

With a surveyor's careful eye and a landholder's grasp of the importance of a dwelling house and its contents, he studied 190 High Street. His assessment was not entirely positive. Writing to his secretary Tobias Lear, the president observed "The House of Mr R. Morris had, previous to my arrival, been taken by the Corporation for my residence. It is the best they could get. It is, I believe, the best single House in the City; yet, without additions it is inadequate to the commodious accomodation of my family. These, I believe, will be made."[10]

Now in the second year of his presidency, Washington continued to attempt the delicate balancing act of being the leader of a modern republic, the squire of a Virginia plantation, and the holder of a social status that had been less elevated in his youth. He knew that his reputation and his power required a display of his status, and his home, family, and servants had to reflect that. Planning the use of his presidential house—mansion might be too grand a term for the Georgian-style building—he anticipated what and who would go where: "The first floor contains only two public Rooms (except one for the upper Servants). The second floor

William Breton print of 190 High Street, where Moll, Ona Judge, and the extended Washington official family lived. (Courtesy of the Library Company of Philadelphia)

will have two public (drawing) Rooms, & with the aid of one room with the partition in it in the back building will be Sufficient for the accomodation of Mrs Washington & the Children, & their Maids—besides affording me a small place for a private Study & dressing Room," the president wrote.

The "maids" George Washington wrote of were in constant, intimate contact with the family. Ona Judge and Moll were both of mixed race, both "dower slaves," a peculiar terminology that was related to Virginia's peculiar institution and the complex patterns of family and inheritance that perpetuated the enslaved-master relationship over generations. Twenty-one years older than his wife Martha, Daniel Parke Custis had died in 1757, intestate. He left a twenty-six-year-old widow of considerable means with two surviving young children and a sizable estate to manage. Because of his lack of a will, the estate would be managed and carefully documented until his heirs could come of age, with his widow having one-third of the funds and the rest being held in trust and managed for the Custis children. Into this complex legal and emotional story rode George Washington—handsome, famous, ambitious, and single— and the young war hero soon began courting the pretty widow. Their relationship would last forty years, until his death in 1799. But Custis's estate would be part of that marriage every day of those four decades. In addition to real estate and cash, the estate contained almost two hundred enslaved workers, eighty-five of whom were the "dower slaves"— Martha Washington's share. These men and women's work could benefit the Washingtons and their household, but their ownership remained in the hands of Custis's heirs. When Washington took his bride and her children to Mount Vernon he initiated a process of blending the enslaved community that he himself had inherited or purchased with the people who accompanied is wife.[11] A plantation was like a collection of small farms, a place where privacy was limited, distances created loneliness, coworking and living in community produced comradery. From the beginning, the people in these two cohorts—Washington slaves and dower ones—were thrust together. The resulting friendships and relationships created a complex web in the decades that followed that would have profound ramifications.[12]

This complicated labor system shaped the Washington family as they departed for New York after Washington's election in 1788. Martha Washington was not immediately delighted with her new role as the president's spouse. Celebrated and feted along her journey to New York, the city did not seem to have known what to do with her, and she did not know what to make of the crowded, noisy town crammed into the southern tip of Manhattan, a vast difference from her native Virginia farms or the quiet colonial capital of Williamsburg, where she had lived as a young bride. "Lady Washington"—the term some took to calling her—could feel left out. Writing to her niece Fanny Bassett Washington from New York in October 1789, she noted, "I live a very dull life hear and know nothing that passes in the town—I never goe to the publick place—indeed I think I am more like a state prisoner than anything else—and as I can not do as I like I am obstinate and stay at home a great deal." The *Federal Gazette* noted that upon the Washingtons' departure on August 30, 1790, "Mrs. Washington, alas, seemed hurt at the idea of bidding adieu." Perhaps the president's wife had changed her mind over time. Perhaps she was a good actor, skilled at hiding her feelings.[13]

Far from comfortable in her new locale, Martha Washington brought enslaved workers to perpetuate the work and life routines from Virginia.[14] The senior member of this staff was Moll, who had a longstanding role as caregiver for the Custis children. Born around 1740, Moll was among the enslaved workers owned by the estate of Martha Washington's first husband and had come to Mount Vernon when the Washingtons married in 1759. After raising Martha's children, Moll eventually served the children of her son, John Parke Custis. Eliza Custis, one of his four surviving children, recalled that after her father's death from a fever which he caught while visiting George Washington in camp after the surrender at Yorktown, her grandmother had brought her two younger siblings, Wash and Nelly Custis, to Mount Vernon and brought Moll to care for them. Constantly required, Moll likely slept on an unrolled pallet bed on the floors of their childhood bedrooms.[15] The oldest of the enslaved workers in the presidential household, "Mammy Molly"—as the Custis children called her—likely had a position of respect as well as authority in the servant's hall at 190 High Street, but no record has been found of her own personal life and experience. Moll would be the only one of the nine enslaved workers the Washingtons brought to Philadelphia who remained with them for the entire term of his presidency.[16]

Ona Judge was a generation younger than Moll but was already placed in a position of responsibility and status within the household by the time George Washington became president. Skilled at caring for clothing and doing needlework, a skill she may have learned from her parents, Mrs. Washington prized "Oney" for her companionship and the work she did. Yet the president's wife saw no inconsistency in the affection she felt and the fact that she also saw Ona as a possession, something to be used, gifted, sold, or relocated with no more thought than if she were giving away an old dress, a piece of furniture, or a farm animal.

Six enslaved males joined Ona and Moll at 190 High Street: Austin, Ona's older half-brother who was a waiter and messenger, had come as a dower slave to Mount Vernon as an infant, when Martha Washington brought Betty, their mother, in 1759; Paris, a postillion and stable boy born in 1780; Giles, another worker in the stable who rode postillion and whose ill health resulted in his being returned to Virginia in April 1791; Hercules, the Washingtons' skilled cook, and his son Richmond, who worked under his father as scullion; and Christopher Sheels, born around 1775 and who was being trained to succeed longtime-valet William Lee after Lee injured his knees. A ninth worker, Joe, came with the family in October 1795, but may not have stayed long in Philadelphia.[17] This plantation cohort was now transplanted to Philadelphia, the thriving port city on the Delaware River. Seaport cities were places of innovation and communication, and northern cities were the locales of dialogs about changing or ending slavery. It is intriguing to imagine how each member of the presidential household perceived life in these urban centers. For the enslaved workers, city life offered new opportunities to connect, imagine, and plan.[18]

As laws and the status of slavery changed after the American Revolution, so too did some slaveowners. The decade before his presidency had seen George Washington begin to reexamine his beliefs about slavery and labor. He had seen many enslaved people escape during the war, including seventeen who took the opportunity to depart with the British warship *Savage* in April 1781. Later in the 1780s, he had come to question the continued expansion and existence of slavery in the United States. While working with an associate's heir to settle debts the departed had owed to him, Washington declined to accept enslaved people as payment. "I never mean (unless some particular circumstances should compel me to it) to possess another slave by purchase; it being among my first wishes to see some plan adopted, by the legislature by which slavery in this Country may be abolished by slow, sure, & imperceptable degrees," he wrote. But his financial world and social status as a Virginian was based on the enslaved laborers who met his every need and represented the wealth that he and his wife combined. Now the newly elected president, taking up residency in Manhattan in April 1789, had little to fear from his new home's laws or culture for his expectations of the role of slavery in his fortune, status, family, or daily life. The relocation of the capital less than eighteen months later would give him a disquieting challenge to all of these things.[19]

The presidential household moved into a very different city in November 1790. Slavery had been a part of Pennsylvania's society and economy almost from the very moment of its founding, but during the revolution and immediately thereafter, a growing number of people had begun to question it. By 1780, the state's government began a series of changes to established slave labor laws. The decade that followed brought changes to Philadelphia's African American community.[20]

In 1780, Pennsylvania's state assembly passed a gradual abolition act—America's first—which set time limits on the service of people born into slavery, and slowly, surely, began the institution of slavery's death knell in the Commonwealth of Pennsylvania. One provision—almost an oversight really—stated that slavery would no longer grow through importation. Some families, like that of Benjamin Chew on whose front lawn George Washington had lost the Battle of Germantown in 1777, had married into wealthy slaveholding families from other colonies. That was over now. Any slaveholder who brought human possessions into Pennsylvania now had six months to send them elsewhere, or they were free. While migration from colony to colony was not unheard of, it is likely that most of the state legislators did not see that provision as having much effect on the state or its citizens.

Then, the national government decided to move to the capital of Pennsylvania.

Clearly, no government leader took much notice of the Gradual Abolition Act of 1780 when they passed the Residency Act of 1790. Clearly, some thought they were exempt from this state law; that assumption quickly proved false. Soon after her move to Philadelphia, as Martha Washington's husband embarked on a goodwill tour of southern states, Attorney General Edmund Randolph arrived at 190 High Street to share some disturbing news: he and his fellow southern slaveholders would be required to free any enslaved people they brought to the capital after six months in residence. Randolph and other Virginians who did not share the fervor for abolition held by some of their new neighbors could perceive an assault on their private property and thus had to start making plans. For the Washingtons, this was doubly problematic: the enslaved workers they had brought were dower slaves, owned by the Custis heirs. Should any be free by the provisions of the Act, George Washington could be held accountable and would owe reimbursement to his step-grandchildren.[21]

The Washingtons' solution, well known now but avoided or ignored by historians for centuries, was creative if legally sketchy: they would circulate Moll, Ona Judge, and their other enslaved workers in and out of Pennsylvania, sometimes sending or taking them home to Mount Vernon, sometimes just on short jaunts. No Custis-Washington enslaved person was ever freed by Pennsylvania's gradual abolition act. It was in this milieu that Ona Judge lived and worked in the six years that led to her escape from the Washingtons and slavery.[22]

Standing at the corner of Sixth and Market Streets in Philadelphia now, where industrialization and urban renewal have obliterated almost every sign of the physical world where the presidential family lived, it is challenging to envision the world in which Ona Judge, Moll, and the other Washington slaves lived. But a glimpse through a variety of surviving documents offers some clues. The women and men serving the presidential household were living in a growing, changing, challenging urban center during those years. A look around offered glimpses into worlds that had been unimaginable at Mount Vernon.[23]

On a daily basis, the Washingtons' slaves would have come into contact with freed men and freed women who had begun to establish themselves in new roles in the community. Washington's surviving second term financial accounts relate one such important contact. On March 14, 1793, George Washington paid "R'd. Allen for sweeping chimneys per bill."[24] Richard Allen, sweep, was already a rising leader among the city's Black population. Born enslaved to Pennsylvania chief justice Benjamin Chew in Maryland, and sold to another farmer, Allen had acquired his freedom, moved to Philadelphia, and become active in the rising Methodist movement. He and his wife, Flora, also formerly enslaved, were married on October 19, 1790, just before Ona and the Washingtons settled at 190 High Street. Their home on Dock Street near Second became a center of Philadelphia's Black community, and in the decade that followed, both became integral citizens. Both Allens and their fellow African American Philadelphians carried out heroic work in the yellow fever epidemic of 1793. Both were critical to the Establishment of the African Methodist Episcopal Church. Flora Allen, a woman born into slavery but now free, legally married, property holding, and serving respected roles in church and society, must have made a lasting impression on Ona Judge and other enslaved women in the nation's capital.[25]

In this city of slavery and freedom, ascertaining how these new developments included those who were still enslaved is a complex question. How much freedom did enslaved women and men have to move about the capital in the 1790s? Were they sent to run errands? Were free hours—scant though they likely were—time when they could leave

190 High Street and walk out into the city? In this urban space, what confines did they experience?[26]

As Ona Judge contemplated her decision to escape from slavery, the city and people she had come to know over the previous six years undoubtedly shaped her perspectives. Now twenty-one or twenty-two years old in the spring of 1796, she resided in a world that was vastly different from the Virginia in which she was born. Plantations were busy places of production and labor with a select few living in luxury at the center, and many more surrounding them working for their happiness. Should Ona have had any experience of a town before departing for New York in 1789, it would have been Alexandria, the riverside seaport a few miles upriver from the farm on which she was born. Much of life in Virginia was rural. The Old Dominion's parishes still did not build bell towers in this era; there was no community close enough to hear them. A crowd might be a few dozen people gathered for a political or economic event.[27]

Now, Ona lived in a walkable city full of people and places to know and contemplate as she pondered her future.[28] Surviving records reveal that, upon leaving the residence, she would have encountered a bustling, busy neighborhood in which many people who shared her status as enslaved worked, lived, and toiled. The records relate slaveowners' names and professions and the number of enslaved workers at their residences, but their stories are lost to history. Robert Morris, the English-born merchant who had leased his residence to house the new president and moved into smaller quarters next door, was listed in the Federal Census of 1790 as owning four Black workers. Turning east toward the bustling market where farmers sold their produce on Wednesdays and Saturdays, Ona would have passed Abraham Kintzing, wagon maker, who had two enslaved workers; further up the street Mary House at Number 170 had four enslaved people, likely serving in a boarding house she ran there. Nearby, Dr. Casper Wister owned one enslaved person, as did shopkeeper Jacob Cox and attorney William Barton, Esq., who dwelt at Number 112, near where Fourth Street crossed High. As we imagine this walk on a busy market day, it is easy to conjure the sights, sounds, and smells of a large town fully awake and aware of bargains and bartering. The buildings facing the market shambles included the shops of ironmongers, grocers, booksellers, hatters, tailors, a tea merchant, a goldsmith, and shopkeepers whose wares fulfilled the desires of the Washingtons and similar status-conscious men and women.[29]

At Second Street, where the market's two-story headhouse sat, Ona would have encountered a bustling city scene perhaps unlike anything she had seen before. Vendors jockeyed for space with drivers of large wagons, all come to town that day to sell late fall produce or other goods. Physical representations of African Americans in late eighteenth-century America are exceedingly rare, but the British printmaker and painter William Birch, attempting to capture the daily life of the nation's capital in the last years of the century, reveals many of these Philadelphians at work. His "Second Street North from Market St. with Christ Church, Philadelphia," published in 1799, shows a busy market day complete with a racially diverse population of sellers and buyers. A young Black boy encounters a horseback rider and his dog at the center of the print, while just north on Second a Conestoga wagon, the creation of nearby Germantown, heads toward the market, laden with farm produce to sell. In the shadow of the townhouse and the shambles below, a group of Philadelphians sit in conversation, filling the types of "indoor" seating later prized by antique collectors. But for those seeking to understand the racial history of the capital, it is two women, just to the left of the arched opening, who give us a glimpse of African American life. One appears to balance a large basket of goods atop her wrapped hair. Continuing a custom brought from West Africa and used generations after the experience of the slave ship, these women's identities remain a mystery, but their existence carefully recorded by Birch provides clues into continuing African cultural customs in a changing Federal America.

So prevalent was this image of basket-bearing Black women that William Breton included a similar image in his engraving of "The London Coffee House." In this engraving, a Black woman walks west through the intersection of Front and High streets, just one block away from the market house. Perhaps Breton sought to show the exotic; perhaps his placement of a Black woman in this geographical location had more poignant, racial meaning. Just feet in front of the pedestrian, a group of Black women and children are standing atop a platform constructed of boards and two hogshead barrels. One of these women is holding a baby. Each wears a simple white garment that may represent that they

William Birch's view of the Philadelphia townhouse and market. Note the inter-racial crowd sitting in the shade of the market façade at left, including women using traditional West African means of carrying produce and goods. (Courtesy of the Library Company of Philadelphia)

are newly arrived for auction, either from an African or another English port. Under the cool shade of the coffeehouse's awning stand a group of men who appear to be wearing the broad-brimmed hats that signified membership in the Society of Friends. An auctioneer's arm is raised, conducting the sale. African Americans had been integral to Pennsylvania's economy for generations.[30]

For Ona Judge, the sight of so many large houses of worship for the diverse Philadelphia population must have been remarkable. Just west of Second was the Presbyterian Church, newly reconstructed with a neoclassical flair that showed the expanded wealth and power that the congregation had achieved during the American Revolution. A few steps east was the "Friends Great Meeting House." So simple in design that it might have been confused for a townhouse in 1796, the brick structure was the center of the life of worship for members of the Society of Friends. But for a young enslaved woman that building and what it would come to mean had relevance.

From the start, Quakers were slaveholders. Led by William Penn, they saw no violation in the owning of other people and the profit it could involve. Penn owned slaves, and saw their purchase as a thrifty, practical way to clear lands, grow crops, manage households, and build the settlement. As the eighteenth century progressed, slave labor was a critical aspect of Philadelphia's rise. Philadelphia grew rich, and rich Philadelphians, whether members of the Society of Friends or of the other religious groups who settled there—members of the Church of England, Presbyterians, Lutherans, and others—signaled that wealth by purchasing enslaved Africans. Blacks labored in fields, cleaned houses, cooked meals both in homes and the number of inns that lined Pennsylvania's roads, drove cattle, loaded ships, dug foundations and formed bricks from the native red clay that lay below, and at the same time formed families, lived, died, were buried. Slavery was as much a part of Pennsylvania's past as it was Virginia's.[31]

True, some members of the Friends on both sides of the Atlantic grew unhappy about slavery and began to speak out against it, but "weighty Friends" dismissed their words and tried to ignore their actions, if possible. Benjamin Lay was one of the first Friends to publicly and dramatically protest slavery, going so far as to kidnap a white child temporarily to show its parents how Black families must feel when a loved one was sold away, and in 1738, presenting a dramatic antislavery speech before the Philadelphia Yearly Meeting in Burlington, New Jersey, which he concluded by plunging a dagger into a Bible which contained a bladder of pokeberry juice. His splattered fellow sectarians were not amused. At the time of his death in 1759, the number of fellow Quaker abolitionists remained small. In the years that followed, that changed. Friends began to adopt abolitionist beliefs, freed or sold their enslaved people, and took actions in meeting in 1776 to ban slaveholders from their community. By the end of the revolution, the sect had come to be associated with antislavery. Quakers were often silent, but not shy about expressing their abolitionist beliefs to anyone, including the president of the United States.[32]

The bustle and noise of the market in the spring of 1796 was an obvious draw for any young person, and Ona Judge could surely see that she was not the sole woman of African heritage in the crowd packing the market sheds, glimpsing poultry and cheeses, early vegetables, and whatever other goods had made their way into the city from the hinterlands that day. Perhaps her walk would have been diverted from the market by a sound unlike anything she or her fellow Virginians had ever heard that morning, had Christ Church's ringers been playing their octave of bells. The tallest building in the United States of America, this elegant Georgian Anglican church was one of the founding spaces of Episcopalianism in the new nation, presided over by the venerable William White, who was recently appointed Pennsylvania's first bishop.

Blacks had attended Philadelphia's three Anglican churches for years, and the Church of England had led the way in educating, marrying, and baptizing free and enslaved Africans in the prewar period. One of Christ Church's most noteworthy congregants was a woman named Alice, sometimes known as "Black Alice," whose memory stretched back to the days of William Penn and Pennsylvania's founding. She was likely the child of two of Pennsylvania's first enslaved immigrants, arriving around 1684. In memoirs dictated when she was over one hundred years old, Alice could recall galloping to attend services at her church, long before the large brick structure replaced a small, squat structure on what was then the edge of town in the early eighteenth century.[33]

In her own life story, written a half-century later, Ona Judge related that she had received no lessons in religion and no encouragement to practice while in the Washington household. Could encounters with Alice or other Black members of Christ Church have sparked this desire?

Bishop White's support for the free and enslaved communities became well known in this era, and he made a decision that shocked some of his co-religionists when he ordained Absalom Jones, a freed man, as an Episcopal deacon. The devout Jones had crowdsourced funds needed so that he could purchase his wife Mary's freedom, so that the baby they expected could be born free. Only later did he scrimp to save enough to purchase his own emancipation. Philadelphia's 1796 directory lists "Rev. Absalom Jones (an African) rector" of the church on the west side of Fifth, below Walnut.[34]

Continuing her walk east, Ona Judge would have discovered the steep grade of High Street in the blocks from Front Street to the Delaware River, the equivalent of a block or so. Every enslaved person at

Mount Vernon was a person of the river, and to fully understand Mount Vernon—and indeed why anyone would call it a "mount" at all, requires seeing it from the Potomac. Washington's older brother had positioned his farmhouse to have a commanding presence over that body of water, and the changes and expansions George Washington made, decade after decade, had secured that position's majesty and beauty. The experience of the Delaware was something different. Philadelphians had quickly ignored their founder's admonition to remain a "greene countrie towne," and instead recreated an English port town, as much as they could. By the 1790s, this busy port was crammed with docks and warehouses, and the two- and three-story brick homes of leading merchants lined Front and Water streets. There, Ona would have seen many Black laborers hard at work on this market day: loading ships, carting materials to and from vessels, and peddling food and other goods. William Birch's views of activity along the docks show these men and women of African descent hard at work. To a young enslaved person, the sight of free Blacks working for wages in all of these aspects of capitalism must have made a striking impression.[35]

The din of the docks and the bustle of the crowds might have encouraged Ona Judge to duck into a quieter area along her walk. Where she turned was a precarious decision, and perhaps one of the Black women like those portrayed in Birch's engraving of the Arch Street Ferry helped guide her choice. Just north of that location along the river was an area called "Helltown," noted for its illegal bars, frequent crime, and prostitution. Sexual molestation and exploitation of women of color was a constant if horrifying aspect of human chattel slavery. We have no idea how or when Ona learned of this reality, no idea if she knew a woman "receiving visits" from a white overseer or visitor to Mount Vernon. Extensive research has found no evidence that George Washington took advantage of any of the women he or his wife's heirs owned, as did so many plantation masters. But Ona Judge must have known instances of sexual molestation. In Philadelphia, to be a light-skinned enslaved woman had ramifications, as some observers associated them with prostitution. In 1779, Charles Lee wrote to General Gates, "love as usual to Miss Gates, Bob, and to that excellent young Man, Major Armstrong—whose father, the General, I am sorry to say it, I saw the other night with a mullata girl in the streets."[36] The streets lining the seaport continued the reputation of being the Quaker City's red light district. French visitor Moreau de St. Mery recorded in 1798, "Americans will not rent houses to colored prostitutes. In Philadelphia they are lodged for the most part on the outskirts of town or in alleys or small side streets."[37]

Perhaps Ona turned from the riverfront in a narrow lane called Gilbert's Alley, sometime still referred to by the name of the blacksmith Jeremia Elfreth, who had cut the street through in 1702. No record exists that this was one of the alleys that housed Philadelphia's mixed-race prostitutes. Instead, in close proximity to white neighbors lived Phoebe Douglas, a freed woman and her husband, Cuff. Cuff Douglas's testimony to the newborn Pennsylvania Abolition Society on October 19, 1787, recorded their family's rise from slavery to freedom. Now in his seventieth year, he stated that his last master had "left him free on conditions of serving four years, at which time he was allow'd the liberty of going out to work, in order to redeem this last mentioned time, which was valu'd at Thirty pounds." Douglas had carefully planned his family's emancipation. He "hired out at twenty pounds per annum, and by living close, and hard, he took up none of his wages, by which means, and his exertions at every leasure time in the tayloring business . . . he was enabled, in about fifteen or sixteen months, to raise that sum, with which he paid for his own freedom; he then sett up his business of tayloring, and in about three years made up the sum of Ninety pounds, which he paid for the redemtion of his Wife and two younger children, who were till then held in slavery, soon after which he paid Forty five pounds for the enlargement of his son Cuff, having thus extricated himself and family from the iron hand of oppression." Phoebe and Cuff now lived in a small brick house, along with her disabled father and their family. Cuff had assumed leadership roles in the emerging free Black community and related a strong commitment to the Christian religion. In Philadelphia, this story was possible, a young enslaved woman like Ona Judge could see.[38]

Returning to the president's house, Ona would have walked west along Mulberry or "Arch" Street, a wide street lined with the brick homes that characterized the world of Philadelphia's middling sort. Visitors' accounts rarely talk about it, but this street was also notable in relating Philadelphia's early religious diversity. Block after block along Arch were burial grounds—Baptist, Quaker, Anglican, Presbyterian—where congregations could bury their dead, sure that no one with religious beliefs radically different from their own was interred nearby. Would Ona Judge have known that burials were racially segregated in Philadelphia? Statistically speaking, she would have known many Blacks—free and enslaved—who had died during her years in the city. The Free African Society had petitioned the state to allow them to erect a fence around the African burial ground at Southeast Square, just a few blocks from the front door of 190 High Street, to permanently mark the burial spots of friends and family who had died. The state had denied the request, instead seeing the profits available for allowing cattle to graze on their potters' field, and then reimagining what a later generation would name Washington Square as a pleasant landscaped park.[39]

But in the years that Ona Judge lived in Philadelphia, the square remained a burial ground for African Americans who died, enslaved and free. Years later, antiquarian John Fanning Watson would interview an elderly resident who recalled, "It was the custom for the slave blacks, at the time of fairs and other great holidays, to go there to the number of one thousand, of both sexes, and hold their dances, dancing after the manner of their several nations in Africa, and speaking and singing in their native dialects, thus cheerily amusing themselves over the sleeping dust below! An aged lady, Mrs. H. S., has told me she has often seen the Guinea negroes, in the days of her youth, going to the graves of their friends early in the morning, and there leaving them victuals and rum!"[40] Africa may have been a long time ago for Black people living in 1790s Philadelphia, but African customs of commemoration, celebration, and mourning remained, in the form of grave goods, musical tributes, and commemorations at solemn or festive moments.

Ona Judge's walk through Philadelphia is conjectural, but the people we encounter on this walk were very real. The City of Brotherly Love was no utopia in the 1790s. Racism persisted, economic inequality was rampant, crowded conditions and premodern medicine were no match for epidemic disease. Yet the city was still a small village by comparison to modern standards, and for a young enslaved woman it offered rich examples of possibility: of freedom, family, a life of her choosing. As George Washington chose not to seek a third term and Martha planned to will Ona Judge to her granddaughter, as later generations might leave an antique piece of silver or a favorite item of furniture, Ona could build her decision on the people she encountered on the streets of Philadelphia. Craftspersons and laundresses, artisans and clergymen, "the coloured people of the town" offered examples of worlds that would never be available if she returned to Virginia and followed the pattern of Moll, or her mother Betty, or the other women of Mount Vernon and other plantations. Instead, she chose a path to freedom. Relying on both her own determination and the people she had come to call friends during the previous six years, Ona stepped out of 190 High Street and into a new world, pursued but free forever.[41]

Notes

I am deeply grateful to the staff of Independence National Historical Park, who allowed me to use their extensive library and archives during the COVID-19 spring and summer of 2020. My sincere thanks to Karie Diethorn, Anna Coxe Toogood, Mary Jenkins, Jed Levin, and Deborah Miller. Early ideas on this topic were shaped by INHP staff members Frances Kolb Delmar and Karen Stevens, now both deceased, who helped in innumerable ways. Judy Van Buskirk and Mary Thompson shared insights as well as editorial skills. My interest in presidential households and the people who work in them goes back many years. I am deeply grateful to the late Lillian Rogers Parks, who encouraged me as a budding historian. The story of Ona Judge and Moll was the beginning of a narrative about African American women that weaves into the story of what Maggie Rogers dreamed of writing after working for six presidents, and that her daughter completed when she retired during the Eisenhower administration. See Lillian Rogers Parks, *My Thirty Years Backstairs at the White House* (New York: Fleet Publishing, 1961).

1. Throughout this essay, I use the name she chose, Ona, rather than the "Oney" that Washington letters and plantation records called her from childhood until after she ran away. Like many of the neighbors she knew and witnessed in Philadelphia, Ona Judge likely used her choice of a name as an indicator of her new personal power and freedom. Absalom Jones, Richard Allen, James Dexter, and others had done so.

   On Hercules's prowess in the kitchen, see Adrian Miller, *The President's Kitchen Cabinet: The Story of African Americans Who Have Fed Our First Families* (Chapel Hill: University of North Carolina Press, 2017), chap. 3; Mary V. Thompson, "Hercules the Cook," in *Dining With the Washingtons:*

Historic Recipes, Entertaining, and Hospitality from Mount Vernon, ed. Stephen A. McLeod (Chapel Hill: University of North Carolina Press, 2018), 25–26.

2. See Edward Lawler Jr., "The President's House in Philadelphia: The Rediscovery of a Lost Landmark," *Pennsylvania Magazine of History and Biography* 86, no. 1 (January 2002): 5–96; Henry Weincek, *An Imperfect God: George Washington, His Slaves, and the Creation of America* (New York: Farrar, Straus, and Giroux, 2003); Erica Armstrong Dunbar, "'I Knew That If I Went Back to Virginia, I Should Never Get My Liberty': Ona Judge Staines, the President's Runaway Slave," in *Women in Early America*, ed. Thomas A. Foster (New York: New York University Press, 2005); and Dunbar's masterful *Never Caught: The Washingtons' Relentless Pursuit of Their Runaway Slave, Ona Judge* (New York: 37Ink/Atria Books, 2017). All of us who seek Ona Judge's story owe a profound debt of gratitude to Evelyn B. Gerson, whose "A Thirst for Complete Freedom: Why Fugitive Slave Ona Judge Staines Never Returned to Her Master, President George Washington" (master's thesis, Harvard, 2000) relates pathbreaking material on her life and freedom.

3. "Washington's Runaway Slave," The Granite Freeman, Concord, NH (May 22, 1845). On escaping slavery in Pennsylvania, see David Waldstreicher, "Reading the Runaways: Self-Fashioning, Print Culture, and Confidence in Slavery in the Eighteenth-Century Mid-Atlantic," *William & Mary Quarterly* 56, no. 2 (1999): 243; Richard Newman, "'Lucky to Be Born in Pennsylvania': Free Soil, Fugitive Slaves and the Making of Pennsylvania's Anti-Slavery Borderland," *Slavery & Abolition* 32, no. 3 (2011): 413–43.

4. See Fred Anderson, *Crucible of War: The Seven Years' War and the Fate of Empire in British North America, 1754–1766* (New York: Knopf, 2000), 159–204; Wiencek, *Imperfect God*, chaps. 2 and 3; Patricia Brady, *Martha Washington: An American Life* (New York: Penguin Books, 2006).

5. On the war and the enslaved in Virginia, see Alan Taylor, *The Internal Enemy: Slavery and War in Virginia, 1772–1832* (New York: W.W. Norton, 2013).

6. George and Martha Washington's ownership of African Americans has undergone a profound historiographical transformation. Most recently, Mary V. Thompson's *"The Only Unavoidable Subject of Regret": George Washington, Slavery, and the Enslaved Community at Mount Vernon* (Charlottesville: University of Virginia Press, 2019) has provided a critical reinterpretation. Thompson and other members of Mount Vernon's professional staff also curated a pathbreaking show that grew into the book *Lives*

Bound Together: Slavery at George Washington's Mount Vernon, ed. Susan Schoelwer (Mount Vernon, VA: Mount Vernon Ladies' Association, 2016).

7. I explore the government's departure in George W. Boudreau, *Independence: A Guide to Historic Philadelphia* (Yardley, PA: Westholme Publishing, 2012), 282–287.

8. George Washington to John Alton, 5 April 1759, *Founders Online*, National Archives, https://founders.archives.gov/documents/Washington/02-06 -02-0163. My thanks to Mount Vernon's Interpreter One, Annet Ahrens, for walking me through the spaces and revealing how the house would have looked and felt in 1759.

9. On slavery and freedom in Philadelphia, see Gary B. Nash, *Forging Freedom: The Formation of Philadelphia's Black Community, 1720–1840* (Cambridge: Harvard University Press, 1988); Gary B. Nash and Jean R. Soderlund, *Freedom by Degrees: Emancipation in Pennsylvania and Its Aftermath* (Oxford: Oxford University Press, 1991).

10. George Washington to Tobias Lear, 5 September 1790, *Founders Online*, National Archives, https://founders.archives.gov/documents/Washington /05-06-02-0190.

11. Rhys Isaac, *The Transformation of Virginia: 1740–1790* (Chapel Hill: University of North Carolina Press, 1982); Darrett B. Rutman and Anita H. Rutman, *A Place in Time: Middlesex County, Virginia, 1650–1750* (New York: Norton, 1984); Martha Saxton, *The Widow Washington: The Life of Mary Washington* (New York: Farrar, Straus and Giroux, 2019).

12. Thompson, "*The Only Unavoidable Subject of Regret*," chap. 1; Dennis J. Pogue, "Interpreting the Dimensions of Daily Life for the Slaves Living at the President's House and at Mount Vernon," *Pennsylvania Magazine of History and Biography* 129, no. 4 (October 2005): 433–44. For details of the dower inheritance, see "Account of Land and Acreage, Estate of Daniel Parke Custis," in Martha Washington, *Worthy Partner: The Papers of Martha Washington*, comp. Joseph E. Fields (Westport, CT: Praeger, 1994), 103–4.

13. Martha Washington, *Worthy Partner*, 219–20; "Fanny Bassett," *The Digital Encyclopedia of George Washington*, https://www.mountvernon.org/library /digitalhistory/digital-encyclopedia/article/fanny-bassett/. The quotation is found in Dunbar, *Never Caught*, 21.

14. Recent scholarship has shaped my perceptions of the mistress-enslaved relationship in this essay, particularly Stephanie E. Jones-Rogers, *They Were Her Property: White Women as Slave Owners in the American South* (New Haven: Yale University Press, 2019); Cynthia A. Kierner, *Beyond the Household: Women's Place in the Early South, 1700–1835* (Ithaca: Cornell

University Press, 1998); and Cynthia M. Kennedy, *Braided Relations, Entwined Lives: The Women of Charleston's Urban Slave Society* (Bloomington: Indiana University Press, 2005).

15. Y. K. Atkinson, "Mammy, How I Love Ya, How I Love Ya: The Mammy Figure in American History, Literature, and Popular Culture" (PhD diss., UC-Riverside, 2001); Tony Horwitz, "The Mammy Washington Almost Had," *The Atlantic*, 31 May 2013.

16. William D. Hoyt Jr., "Self-Portrait: Eliza Custis, 1808," *The Virginia Magazine of History and Biography* 53, no. 2 (April 1945): 89–100. "Moll," in Anna Coxe Toogood Papers, Independence National Historical Park Archives. See also "Appendix C. List of Artisans and Household Slaves in the Estate, c.1759," *Founders Online*, National Archives, https://founders .archives.gov/documents/Washington/02-06-02-0164-0025.

17. On their arrival, see Jacob Cox Parsons, ed., *Extracts from the Diary of Jacob Hiltzheimer of Philadelphia, 1765–1798* (Philadelphia: Fell and Co., 1893), 165. On the workers, see Anna Coxe Toogood, "Enslaved Men and Women at President's House, 1790–1797," Independence National Historical Park Archives, 190 High Street Files. Lawler, "The President's House in Philadelphia," 5–97; Edward Lawler Jr., "The President's House Revisited," *Pennsylvania Magazine of History and Biography* 129, no. 4 (October 2005): 371–411. This issue also includes essays by Damie Stillman, Dennis J. Pogue, Doris Devine Fanelli, Michael Coard, and Sharon Ann Holt. See also Gary B. Nash, "For Whom Will the Liberty Bell Toll? From Controversy to Cooperation," in *Slavery and Public History: The Tough Stuff of American Memory*, ed. James Oliver Horton and Lois E. Horton (New York: The New Press, 2006), 75–102.

18. See Gary B. Nash, *The Urban Crucible: Social Change, Political Consciousness, and the Origins of the American Revolution* (Cambridge: Harvard University Press, 1979); and Benjamin Carp, *Rebels Rising: Cities and the American Revolution* (New York: Oxford University Press, 2009).

19. George Washington to John Francis Mercer, 9 September 1786, *Founders Online*, National Archives, https://founders.archives.gov/documents /Washington/04-04-02-0232.

20. See Nash, *Forging Freedom*, chaps. 3 and 4.

21. Tobias Lear to George Washington, 5 April 1791, *Founders Online*, National Archives, https://founders.archives.gov/documents/Washington/05-08 -02-0050. The complexities of the Gradual Emancipation Act of 1780 are unpacked in Nash, *Forging Freedom*, 60–65, 71, 91–95, and Dunbar, *Never Caught*, 62–64.

22. George Washington to Tobias Lear, 22 November 1790, *Founders Online*, National Archives, https://founders.archives.gov/documents/Washington /05-06-02-0331.

23. See Lawler, "The President's House Revisited," 371–410.

24. "Washington's Household Account Book, 1793–1797 (continued)," *Pennsylvania Magazine of History and Biography* 31, no. 2 (1907): 177.

25. See Richard S. Newman, *Freedom's Prophet: Bishop Richard Allen, the AME Church, and the Black Founding Fathers* (New York: New York University Press, 2009), 73–75; Nash, *Forging Freedom*.

26. On servants in Federal Philadelphia, see Karie Diethorn, *Domestic Servants in Philadelphia, 1780–1830* (Philadelphia: Independence National Historical Park, 1986). I diverge from Ona Judge's biographers in my assumption that enslaved workers would have been constrained or confined from interacting with the community around them during this period. Gerson equates Martha Washington's careful oversight of her grandchildren as covering Ona and Moll too, but this seems unlikely due to the mistress's general beliefs about African Americans. Mrs. Washington likely saw the convenience of sending her trusted maid out to run errands and perform other tasks, and hours when she was involved in socialization with either her family or guests likely allowed the enslaved women hours to get exercise, fresh air, and see the city's sights. Likewise, Dunbar's belief that the Washingtons kept a constant watch on their enslaved people is challenged by accounts of giving them money for entertainment or shopping, and—I surmise—attributes more power for the presidential couple than really existed. Numerous accounts of city life in early Philadelphia note enslaved women moving about the city for work or other affairs.

27. Robert F. Dalzell Jr. and Lee Baldwin Dalzell, *George Washington's Mount Vernon: At Home in Revolutionary America* (New York: Oxford University Press, 1998), 174–75; on Virginia landscapes and buildings, see Isaac, *The Transformation of Virginia;* on the lives of Black workers in Virginia, see Mechal Sobel, *The World They Made Together: Black and White Values in Eighteenth-Century Virginia* (Princeton: Princeton University Press, 1987).

28. Billy G. Smith inspires this imagined historical walk, and many others, as a way of understanding the lives of people who lived long ago in a space that is familiar today. See Smith, *The "Lower Sort": Philadelphia's Laboring People, 1750–1800* (Ithaca: Cornell University Press, 1990), chap. 1.

29. The Philadelphia City Directories of 1795 and 1796 offer invaluable information for recreating Ona Judge's walk. See Edmund Hogan, *The Prospect of Philadelphia and Check on the Next Directory, Part I* (Philadelphia: Francis

& Robert Bailey, 1795); 1790 United States Federal Census, found online through www.ancestry.com.

30. S. Robert Teitelman, *Birch's Views of Philadelphia* (Philadelphia: University of Pennsylvania Press, 1983), plate 15, and William Breton, "London Coffee House," print department, Library Company of Philadelphia. Breton was likely portraying events prior to the 1780s, when the gradual abolition would have stopped public slave auctions.

31. Jean Soderlund, *Quakers and Slavery: A Divided Spirit* (Princeton: Princeton University Press, 1985); Gary B. Nash, *Race, Class, and Politics: Essays on American Colonial and Revolutionary Society* (Urbana: University of Illinois Press, 1986), 91–118.

32. Marcus Rediker, *The Fearless Benjamin Lay: The Quaker Dwarf Who Became the First Revolutionary Abolitionist* (Boston: Beacon Press, 2017).

33. My thanks to Susan Klepp, who shared her research on Alice with me during the time I was writing *Independence*. See chapter 3 for more information. For more on Alice, see Gary B. Nash, *Forging Freedom*.

34. Both of Ona Judge Stains's published narratives of the 1840s reveal the centrality of Christianity to her by that time and note that she had received no religious instruction while enslaved by the Washingtons. On the rise of African American churches, see Nathan O. Hatch, *The Democratization of American Christianity* (New Haven: Yale University Press, 1991), 107–9; Stephens' Philadelphia Directory 1796, 65. On Jones's work to free his wife and child from slavery, see the marriage notice from St. Peter's Episcopal Church found at https://www.pbs.org/wgbh/aia/part3/3h93.html.

35. Teitelman, *Birch's Views of Philadelphia*, plates four and five.

36. Charles Lee to General Horatio Gates, 4 April 1779, Philadelphia, Amer. 1779, II, p 140–1/2, Bancroft Collection, MSS, New York Public Library. Transcription in the archives of Independence National Historical Park, "Phila. City of Manners and Morals" file. See Clare A. Lyons, *Sex among the Rabble: An Intimate History of Gender and Power in the Age of Revolution, 1730–1830* (Chapel Hill: University of North Carolina Press, 2006).

37. Médéric Louis Elie Moreau de Saint-Méry, *Moreau de St. Mery's American Journey, 1793–1798* (New York: Doubleday, 1947), 311.

38. Papers of the Pennsylvania Abolition Society (PAS) (microfilm), Manumissions, Indentures, and other Legal Papers (Reel 23), Certificates of freedom, 1770–1826, Historical Society of Pennsylvania. Testimony dated Philad 19. 10 mon, 1787; Thomas Stapler, scribe.

39. See Boudreau, *Independence*, chap. 11; Rebecca Yamin, *Digging in the City of Brotherly Love: Stories from Philadelphia Archaeology* (New Haven: Yale University Press, 2013), chap. 6.

40. John F. Watson, *Annals of Philadelphia and Pennsylvania, in the Olden Time Being a Collection of Memoirs, Anecdotes, and Incidents of the City and Its Inhabitants, and of the Earliest Settlements of the Inland Part of Pennsylvania from the Days of the Founders* (Philadelphia, 1844).
41. See Dunbar, *Never Caught,* especially chaps. 8–11; Gerson, "Thirst for Complete Freedom," chap. 5.

INVALID JUGGERNAUT

Ann Pamela Cunningham and Her Quest to
Save George Washington's Mount Vernon

ANN BAY GODDIN

During the tumultuous decade of the 1850s leading up to the Civil War, an unlikely heroine by the name of Ann Pamela Cunningham rose from an invalid's sick bed to take on the challenge of saving George Washington's dilapidated plantation from the ravages of age and disrepair. A shrewd, determined, and emotionally charged planter-class woman armed with southern charm and a talent for high drama, she would, in saving Mount Vernon, set in motion America's historic preservation movement. She was brilliant, eccentric, and highly complicated. Moreover, and most significantly for the point of this essay, she was, as she often reminded everyone within her orbit, a "suffering invalid." As an unmarried, well-educated, and highly ambitious woman of the Old South, she suffered from a debilitating "nervous disease" not uncommon among elite nineteenth-century women. Set within the timeframe of the antebellum era, this essay will examine the causes of her invalidism and explore ways in which she used it as a powerful tool during the first seven years of her campaign to rescue Washington's home and final resting place as a gift to the nation.

Although the documented facts about her childhood are few, it is known that she was born on August 15, 1816, and that the birth likely took place in a hot and stuffy upstairs bedroom in her family's plantation house overlooking the Saluda River in upstate South Carolina. Tiny and frail right from the start, she was the second child born to Robert and Louisa Cunningham. Their first, a boy, had died a year earlier at the age of seven months. By 1822, her mother would give birth to two more sons, John and Benjamin, although only John would live to adulthood. There would be no other girls in the family to compete with Ann Pamela for attention. The family's cotton plantation, Rosemont, comprising more than 10,000 acres and supported by the labor of eighty-four enslaved workers, was one of the largest in the upstate region, and her father was one of the area's wealthiest landowners.[1]

When Ann Pamela was about six years old, Robert commissioned a large, formal portrait of his wife and their three children. Against the painting's classical backdrop, a plump, rosy-cheeked Benjamin, then about two years old, is seated on the floor, reaching for a rose his mother is extending to him from a bouquet on her lap. Ann Pamela, seated next to Louisa, is looking up intently from a piece of lace she has been tatting on a small, ivory shuttle. Her four-year-old brother John stands beside her, whittling a stick. The little girl's resemblance to her mother is striking: the same long, thin nose, slightly pointed chin, grey eyes, direct gaze, high forehead, and prominent cheekbones.[2]

Louisa, in a regal velvet gown, is portrayed as queen of the family, reflecting her stature and role in real life. She was widely considered among her upstate peers to be a charming hostess and a woman of beauty and superior taste who fulfilled the demanding role of plantation mistress with competence and grace. However, her personality was far from that of the modest self-effacing southern lady idealized at the time from the pulpit and in the popular press. Having been raised as a girl of impressive pedigree within a tumultuous no-holds-barred household of ten children on the central Georgia frontier, she brought to adulthood a sense of social superiority along with a quickness to take umbrage and a tendency to hold a grudge. Unlike most women of her time, place, and class, she seldom hesitated to speak her mind, even when it meant disagreeing with her husband.[3] The degree to which Louisa's strong personality impacted her young daughter's early development is a matter for conjecture. However, it may be assumed that like most little girls growing up on southern plantations, Ann Pamela was very close to her mother and that Louisa—never a force to be ignored or trifled with—was for her only daughter a powerful first role model.[4]

Even as a very little girl, Ann Pamela was a serious, bookish, and independent-minded child with a passionate interest in history, and her

Ann Pamela Cunningham at around the age of six with her mother, Louisa, and her two younger brothers, John (*standing*) and Benjamin (*seated*). Oil on canvas, ca. 1856, artist unknown. (Courtesy of Historic Waco Foundation)

biggest hero was George Washington. Although practically all nineteenth-century Americans loved and revered Washington, Ann Pamela's attachment to him seems to have been markedly above the ordinary for a young child.[5] Doubtless her feelings stemmed partly from knowing that for more than twenty-five years her maternal great-grandfather, John Dalton of Alexandria, Virginia, had been Washington's friend, fox-hunting companion, business associate, and fellow patriot—and that her maternal grandmother, Catherine Dalton Bird, had been, as a child, a household guest of the Washingtons. Moreover, every summer within her memory, a colorful display of perennials from Mount Vernon had been blooming in her mother's gardens at Rosemont, a gift sent from George Washington's nephew, Bushrod Washington, to Louisa after she had visited the plantation when Ann Pamela was a toddler. As long as the little girl could remember, her love for George Washington and the place where he had lived, died, and was buried had seemed very tangible and real.[6]

When Ann Pamela was just five years old her parents sent her off to boarding school, and she would stay away at one school or another until she was eighteen, coming home only for winter and summer breaks. Although the historical record is a bit sketchy regarding her schooling, it seems she attended three different schools in all, and the last of the three, known as the South Carolina Female Collegiate Institute, was located two miles outside of Columbia, at a place called Barhamville. It seems she enrolled there at the age of fourteen.[7]

The school was rather like a convent. Young men were barred from campus except on very rare occasions and other visitors were allowed only on weekends. Practically nothing ever happened there to distract an adolescent girl from her studies, which was just as the founding director, Dr. Elias Marks, intended. Although he had been trained as a physician, Dr. Marks found his true passion in preparing young ladies for the important role they were "destined to perform" as wives and mothers in what he liked to call "the great theater of human existence." His school was among the first in the South to offer the equivalent of a four-year, college-level, liberal arts education for women. The demanding curriculum, based on that of the ground-breaking Troy Female Academy in Upstate New York, eschewed rote learning (the pedagogy employed in most American schools and colleges at that time) in favor of engendering deep understanding through exploration, experimentation, and spirited but polite discussion.[8]

As an intellectually gifted girl, Ann Pamela thrived at Barhamville. She learned how to think and write clearly and how to craft an argument, abilities that would serve her well in later life. Moreover, she greatly benefitted from the diligent and unremitting habits of perseverance being urged upon the students. "Let it be impressed upon the minds of youth," Dr. Marks exhorted, "that patient and systematic perseverance is *essential* to success. . . . Superior intellectual capacity can do *nothing* without it . . . [and] all that charms by its excellence . . . has been the result of ceaselessly progressive action." Throughout her life, perseverance would be for her a deeply ingrained and highly productive habit, and one that would eventually come to serve her well in her efforts on behalf of Mount Vernon.[9]

Although Dr. Marks was the titular head of the school, everyone knew that his wife and codirector, Julia Pierpont Marks, was really the person in charge. An astute, charming, and professionally accomplished New Englander, she was much admired by both the students and their parents, who used terms like "gracious," "self-assured," and "queenly" yet "properly modest" to describe her.[10] In later correspondence Ann Pamela would refer to Marks as a "second mother," the "hand that bent the twig," and "the woman to whom I owe almost everything." Throughout her life, in times of duress, she would gather strength by recalling the lessons that Julia Marks had taught her. And it was under her tutelage that the young girl learned the all-important skill of gracefully finessing power in a world dominated by men. Julia Marks was, in fact, by far the most significant role model of Ann Pamela's youth.[11]

Upon leaving school in 1834, Ann Pamela returned home to live. As she approached her eighteenth birthday, she was at the point in a southern girl's life when her one and only assigned purpose was to attract a suitable mate, and her parents had spared little expense in preparing her for marital success. In their estimation, her first-rate education had been an investment in her future by distinguishing her as a young lady of purity and grace, deserving of a worthy husband.[12] It was perhaps with that in mind that they extended an invitation to a twenty-eight-year-old lawyer, journalist, and rising politician by the name of Benjamin Franklin Perry to join the family for the Christmas holidays that year. Perry had first met the Cunninghams two years earlier, when Ann Pamela, then sixteen, had caught his eye; and he had noted in his diary that she was "handsome—and a very interesting little girl."[13] He had not seen her again until that holiday visit to Rosemont, when it seems they spent a lot of time together under the watchful eyes of family members. As befitting the early stages of a southern courtship, they rode to church seated side by side in the family carriage, played a two-person game called "chips," and went "riding out" on horseback. Perhaps she entertained him on the piano, which she had learned to play extremely well during her years at school. It is likely they flirted, and maybe he even kissed her hand at the end of his visit. A week or so later, back at his lodgings in Greenville, South Carolina, he wrote in his diary: "I returned some days since from a Christmas visit to Captain Robert Cunningham's, where I spent five or six days remarkably well. . . . The daughter is quite pretty, very intelligent, and exceedingly graceful and dignified in her manners . . . a most bewitching creature!"[14] From that description it seems evident that Ann Pamela would have been considered a very good catch. Her parents must have been confident she would soon marry, if not Ben Perry, then someone else of suitable background and promise.

However, for one reason or another, Ann Pamela never did marry. The romance with Perry fizzled, and although she had other suitors, she seems to have refused them all. It appears that, like a growing number of other educated young women of the Old South, she was reluctant to submit to what was sometimes referred to as the "matrimonial noose." Perhaps she feared childbirth or signing away her legal rights in a culture where men had almost complete control over their wives' finances and lives. Maybe she was reluctant to trade the pleasures of female friendships and intellectual pursuits she had come to know in boarding school for the drudgery that would surely be involved in running a large antebellum household, as her mother's experience had shown her.[15] But whatever her reasons, it is fortunate that even though she did not marry Ben Perry, the two of them remained close friends, and when he married Elizabeth McCall of Charleston in 1838, she became close friends with her as well.

Ann Pamela's frank and revealing letters to Benjamin and Elizabeth Perry have been preserved among their papers residing in the Alabama Department of History and Archives in Montgomery, and in the South Caroliniana Library in Columbia. From her "unmercifully long" missives to them, written mostly in the 1840s when she was in her mid-to-late twenties, often between bouts of illness over the course of several days or even weeks, we can begin to understand why she later would, seemingly out of the blue in the 1850s, take on the challenge of saving Mount Vernon. We encounter a deadly serious and highly ambitious young woman, who felt compelled to achieve something of high importance, even though she did not yet know what that thing would be. She described herself as reading and translating from the French a "deep work on the southern literature of Europe by the deservedly great Sismondi." While admitting it a "laborious undertaking," she thought it would help her memory and "be always valuable besides." Writing further of her reading habits, she claimed the likes of Euclid, Dante, Byron, and Tasso as particular favorites, declining to waste her time on the escapist novels that had captured the attention of most elite women of her day. She was determined to live out her life in real time on a far grander scale than society would sanction, and she was not inclined to give up on her intentions. Moreover, she confessed to a "deep vein of patriotic enthusiasm" running through her character—a resistless strength that "women's occupation" could never satisfy. She spoke passionately of her early and continuing love of country and of how, from her childhood, John Paul Jones had been "a spark to set her all ablaze" and George Washington had been her "Bible." Now she was determined to serve her country and to do her heroes justice, if only she could figure out how—given the constraints of being a woman.[16] She wrote to Ben that if she were a man she would gladly risk her life as "a sentinel upon the watch tower" of the nation, adding that she was "not a little inclined" to envy his "lordly sex" the privilege of going wherever he wanted without a chaperone, while she was stuck at Rosemont, suffering from profound "ennui" resulting from enforced "idleness."[17]

Believing her life had no meaning, Ann Pamela became deeply depressed. And in her desolation, her already-delicate health began a steady decline. By the time she reached her mid-twenties, she regarded herself, as did others close to her, as a chronic invalid. From then on, in hundreds of letters written to friends, colleagues, and family over the next thirty-one years until her death in 1875, she would speak repeatedly and dramatically of the precarious state of her health. Her invalidism— or "nervous disease" as she called it—would soon become a defining part of who she was. And in years to come, while it often held her back, she also would use it to stunningly dramatic effect in her efforts for her Mount Vernon "cause."

Moreover, she was not by any means alone in her suffering; among educated elite women of the nineteenth century, an epidemic of female invalidism was sweeping the western world. While Emily Dickenson, Alice James, Louisa May Alcott, Harriet Martineau, and Elizabeth Barrett Browning were among the better-known examples of the so-afflicted, there were also countless other sufferers whose names are less familiar. An invalid's recurring symptoms ranged from head to toe and could be experienced singly or in combination with one another. Violent headaches, dizziness, muscle pain, inflammation of the eyes and gums, trouble breathing, dramatic weight loss, tremors, heart palpitations, numbness and weakness in the legs and feet, convulsions, and episodes of temporary paralysis were among the most common complaints.[18] Ann Pamela suffered from all of those things at one time or another, and an important question to our understanding of her is, "why?"

Among the several factors at play, the first was social conditioning. She grew up at a time when young women were thought to be especially vulnerable to sickness and early death, and the dying maiden was considered nothing short of a saint. Since invalids were thought to be more sensitive and intelligent than ordinary mortals, they were deemed worthy of special attention, and their families were admired for the sacrifices they made in assuming the burden of their care. Having an invalid in the family was in its way a status symbol.[19] Moreover, by retreating to her sick room, a woman could avoid the life-threatening risks of pregnancy and the relentless hard work of running a plantation household—and she even could, if so inclined, use her invalidism to escape from marriage altogether. Thus, it seems possible that Ann Pamela, as a young woman given to patriotic, romantic fantasies and dreams of personal achievement but having no way to realize her worldly ambitions, was drawn into invalidism as a way of gaining some of the acknowledgment and prestige she craved. And at the same time, her condition may have offered her a way—subconsciously at least—not only to *escape* from marriage but also to *retreat* from a world in which, as an unmarried woman, she felt she had no legitimate place or role.[20]

Her suffering, though, was not just "in her head." Her congenitally frail constitution was further weakened by the treatments she received at the hands of local doctors. Country physicians visited her at Rosemont often, prescribing along with bed rest and "tonics," a dangerous mercury compound called calomel. For years, calomel had been used as a purgative for treating practically everything from malaria and yellow fever to head colds and sore throats. Doctors thought that by causing diarrhea and vomiting, it would purge the body of whatever was making it sick. Not only did they seem not to notice it did not work, they failed to recognize its immediate side effects of anxiety, insomnia, weight loss, and depression—all things from which Ann Pamela suffered greatly. And even though the drug had been around for centuries, many doctors seem to have been unaware of the devastating effects of its prolonged use, which included arm and facial tremors, memory loss, and difficulty in walking and performing tasks involving fine motor skills. Eventually Ann Pamela would exhibit all of those symptoms, which suggests that mercury poisoning owing to her habitual use of calomel was very likely an important cause of her invalidism and certainly not the cure intended.[21]

And then there was laudanum, which after her late thirties would become her other main drug of choice. Although she does not mention it in earlier correspondence, she probably, like most people of her day, occasionally took laudanum's main ingredient, opium, even as a child, as it was a common ingredient in patent medicines. In an era when non-addictive pain killers like aspirin were as yet unavailable, laudanum had a place in nearly every home medicine chest. It was also highly addictive, as Ann Pamela would later find out as her adult use of it increased to the point of becoming an all-too-frequent habit.[22]

Moreover, her health was likely further weakened by the clothes she wore. From the onset of puberty, antebellum ladies routinely squeezed themselves into tightly laced corsets designed to cinch in their waists to circumferences of twenty inches or less. And to complete their desired "hourglass" look, they wore voluminous skirts supported by layers of petticoats weighing between fifteen and twenty pounds. While their corsets restricted their breathing, irritated their skin, and caused their back muscles to atrophy from lack of use, their heavy skirts kept them from engaging in few forms of exercise more vigorous than a stately stroll around the garden, a game of shuffleboard, or a sedate horseback ride by side saddle. Although by mid-century some health experts were beginning to caution that even more serious health problems might result from pursuit of the hourglass look, most women, including, it seems, Ann Pamela, chose to ignore such warnings. Her earliest extant photograph shows her wide skirts descending from an impossibly tiny waist, her hourglass figure clearly the product of heavy petticoats and tightlacing.[23]

By 1846, as she approached her thirtieth birthday, she and her parents began seeking cures that went beyond the usual bed rest and calomel regimen. For several months, a "Dr. Baker" came to treat her with

Studio portrait of Ann Pamela Cunningham, photographed by Broadbent & Co., Philadelphia, ca. 1859, not long after the Ladies purchased Mount Vernon from John Augustine Washington III. (Courtesy of the Mount Vernon Ladies' Association)

a device called an Electro Magnetic Machine, which was applied to her spine and forehead to help relieve her headaches, anxiety, and insomnia. And then, after Baker left the area, a mesmerist by the name of Dr. Kernuckles was called in, whose method of treatment was hypnosis at a time when mesmerism as a means of relieving physical suffering was highly regarded in America. For slightly more than a year, Kernuckles came to Rosemont daily to send her into a deep trance lasting for several hours each time. Under his care, her health seemed to improve, perhaps mainly because he required that she substitute "mesmerized water" for all of the medications she had previously been taking, including calomel.[24] But then he too left the area, and she once again began relying on local doctors and resuming the use of calomel. Over the next three years, her health declined precipitously, until finally, in October 1849, her parents took her to Philadelphia for a consultation with one of America's foremost physicians, Dr. Hugh Lenox Hodge, whose specialty was "diseases of females." By then she was thirty-three.[25]

At the time, Hodge was at the height of his career, and invalids from throughout the country were flocking to him for treatment. He diagnosed Ann Pamela's condition as "decidedly nervous" and placed her under his daily care through that first winter and into the spring.[26] After finding lodging for her in a very private boarding house located in a fashionable neighborhood near Hodge's offices on Walnut Street, her parents returned to South Carolina.

Hodge believed, as explained in a textbook he would later write, entitled *On Diseases Peculiar to Women, Including Displacements of the Uterus,* that it was because of their "irritable uteruses" that women were likely to fall victim to nervous disease. Once a woman's uterus became irritable, it would throw her entire system into freefall, causing "pains, twitching, cramps, spasms, convulsions" and "an infinite variety of morbid sensations," even giving rise in some cases to "delirium, insanity, and . . . various perversions of the intellectual and moral powers." His treatments, therefore, sought to calm a woman's uterus by removing the cause of its irritability. In Ann Pamela's case, he identified the cause as excessive "excitement of the mind," owing to "over-stimulation of the mental faculties," resulting from the superior education she had received. Pronouncing her as among the "frailest of specimens of delicate humanity" he had ever seen, "kept down entirely" by her nerves, he forbade her during those first several months in his care to indulge in any mental activity whatsoever—including reading, writing, or serious thinking. He insisted that until her health was completely restored, she must remain in an intellectually "vegetative state."[27]

Moreover, on daily visits to her bedside, he urged her to purge herself of any worldly ambitions that might be lurking in the deep recesses of her soul. Like other leading doctors of his time, he believed that a woman's only rightful place was in the home and that his sole purpose in restoring health to an independent-minded and intellectually inclined invalid like Ann Pamela was to bring her to the point where she would cheerfully embrace the singular, God-given domestic role for which her life had been intended. To keep her uterus free from irritation, not only must she not think too much, she must not harbor even an inkling of desire for personal achievement beyond the domestic sphere. Otherwise, she could never be happy, and her life would be wasted. He did not understand those women of Ann Pamela's generation who were desperately "seeking something as yet unknown" to give their lives "meaning and direction" in a "society not yet ready to absorb" their talents.[28] Instead, he saw her as a tragic example of an overly educated female. And therein lay the source of an unspoken tension between the two of them. While she wanted him to cure her of her physical infirmities, she had no desire to let him "cure" her mind or to erase the underlying proclivities of her passionate nature, which so desperately needed an outlet. And so, while appearing to heed his advice, she quietly waited for an acceptable means of escape from the constraints his ministrations were imposing upon her.

In the meantime, however, she found certain aspects of his treatment to be quite to her liking. Her health improved as a result of the wholesome meals, light exercise, fresh air, and frequent baths that he prescribed. Moreover, her spirits seem to have been lifted by being in Philadelphia and by such cheerful diversions as carriage rides through the city's busy cobblestone streets and upbeat conversations with the several new friends who would drop by her rooms to visit. Although Hodge occasionally administered tonics, he was opposed to powerful emetics like calomel. As a last resort for relieving her nervous distress, he sometimes prescribed laudanum, but it seems to have been only in carefully controlled amounts. Although he had not cured her invalidism by the time she left Philadelphia in the spring of 1851, his treatment had proven beneficial enough to warrant her return in the fall.[29]

Throughout the 1850s, Ann Pamela would spend at least several months of every year in Philadelphia under Hodge's care, and the year 1853 would be no different. That fall as usual, Louisa had accompanied her daughter to the city, and once Ann Pamela was settled in her rooms, began the long journey back to Rosemont Plantation, stopping along the way in Alexandria, Virginia. From Alexandria her course was to take her by steamboat down the Potomac River to the Chesapeake Bay and on to Norfolk, where she would board a seagoing vessel to Charleston. And, therefore, it happened that on a brightly moonlit November night after her river steamboat had departed from Alexandria, Louisa had stayed on deck to enjoy the view, when presently the ship's bell tolled and the captain announced they were passing Mount Vernon, the home of George Washington. Looking up, she had caught a glimpse of the property situated high on its hill overlooking the river, and even from her vantage point, the dilapidated state of the mansion and grounds had been woefully apparent, with the moonlight casting a ghostly pall over everything. Once back home, she had written to Ann Pamela that she had been "painfully distressed at the ruin and desolation of the home of Washington" and wondered if the women of America should not try to keep the place in repair since the men had failed to do so.[30]

From the moment she received her mother's letter, Ann Pamela could think and talk of nothing else but Mount Vernon. She would save it! She knew that she could do it and was determined to persevere until the job was done. However, because of the precarious state of her health, her friends and family did not at first take her newfound passion seriously. How could a "suffering, spent" invalid possibly engage in such a momentous undertaking?[31] Nonetheless, it soon became clear to them that her resolve was not to be shaken, for in truth, she needed Mount Vernon as much as it needed her. Its rescue was the very kind of worthy project she had been so desperately looking for to bring meaning and purpose to her empty life. But she first must gain the approval of her parents, upon whose financial support she depended, and of Dr. Hodge, under whose restrictive care she had been placed.[32]

In making her case to the three of them, she had a store of popular sentiment to draw upon, for in antebellum America nearly everyone dearly loved George Washington. No matter what a person's age, social station, or gender, no matter where they lived or how they leaned politically, all agreed that the Father of His Country was as close to a divine being as any living person could ever hope to be. And intrinsically tied to that universal love for the great man was a reverence for the sacred spot where he had once dwelt and now was buried. Especially during that decade before the Civil War, as Americans became increasingly aware of the estate's deplorable condition, some saw it as yet another sign of national fracture, disorder, and decline, suggesting that along with the home of its revered founder, the young republic itself might soon crumble and fall apart. Hence there was widespread sentiment, strongly held, that something must be done to save Mount Vernon.[33]

Moreover, Louisa Cunningham's suggestion that women could rise to such an important challenge was not as far-fetched as one might think. Most Americans supported the notion that it was the "special destination" of women, as an appropriate part of their socially sanctioned "domestic sphere," to rescue the nation from the male materialism and greed commonly associated with changes brought about by the Industrial Revolution. This way of thinking was known as the "feminine benevolence" doctrine. It held that although women were mentally and physically unsuited for engaging in the rough-and-tumble worlds of commerce, war, or politics, their inherent *moral* superiority made them uniquely qualified to serve as agents of spiritual uplift and social improvement. In addition, because of their highly tuned sensibilities and the selfless purity of their patriotism, they were particularly suited to guarding and preserving the nation's patrimony and historic symbols. So, by the time Ann Pamela received her mother's letter, the precedent for ladies to venture out into the world and engage in volunteer efforts of patriotic benevolence had been fully established. The groundwork had been laid. And thus she was able to convince both her parents and Dr. Hodge that saving Mount Vernon was an endeavor in which even she, as a "suffering invalid," could rightly engage.[34]

Ann Pamela started her campaign in early December 1853 by writing a fundraising letter to the "Ladies of the South," asking them to exert their "combined efforts in village, town, and city" so that the means could be raised from the "mites of thousands of gentle hearts" to purchase and save the home and grave of Washington. Because it would have been highly improper for her to use her real name on correspondence that would appear in public, she signed her letter, "A Southern Matron." It was promptly published in a South Carolina newspaper, the *Charleston Mercury*, and evoked an enthusiastic response from readers wanting to donate money and learn more about the campaign.[35] After that her invalid's sick room became her "Mount Vernon Headquarters," from which, with the help of friends and a Philadelphia cousin, Becky Mitchell, she acknowledged donations, answered inquiries, and wrote letter after letter to people she knew throughout the South, as well as to men of influence she knew in name only, asking for their help in promoting the campaign. Although the movement was initially confined to the South, by 1855 women of the North and West were starting to join in.

From the very beginning of her campaign, Ann Pamela demonstrated an astonishing ability to run a complex enterprise from her sick bed at a time when handwritten letters and the telegraph were the only means of long-distance communication. As she garnered the support of other patriotic women willing to take the lead in raising money within their individual states, she delegated them with the authority to operate as they thought best under local conditions, so long as they reported back to her regularly. Soon the states were in competition with one another as to who could raise the most money, with results being published in two of the nation's leading magazines, *Godey's Ladies Book* and *Southern Literary Messenger*. In 1856, the state of Virginia approved a charter for the organization, and then in 1858 the charter was revised, establishing the "Mount Vernon Ladies Association of the Union." Shortly thereafter the Ladies inaugurated their own publication, the *Mount Vernon Record*, which would prove to be an effective fundraising tool by acknowledging the names of donors and stimulating further competition among the states.[36] As the Association's director, Ann Pamela assumed the title of Regent, and appointed one well-connected Vice Regent to represent each state belonging to the national Mount Vernon network.[37]

And all the while, Ann Pamela was using her invalidism—and the fact that she was a shy and pure maiden lady, trembling with patriotism, "not of this world," as she put it—to evoke sympathy and admiration, which translated into widespread support for the cause.[38] In following a cardinal rule of the feminine benevolence doctrine, that a lady must never call attention to *herself* but only to the *cause* she was promoting, she seldom appeared in public and never spoke publicly in those years before the Civil War. Instead she mostly stayed in her Philadelphia "headquarters," where wrapped in shawls and propped up daintily by a mound of sofa cushions, she received an ever-increasing stream of visitors coming to pay their respects to the little southern matron with the soft voice and big grey eyes and to learn more about the patriotic cause she had so bravely undertaken. In her letters to potential supporters, she often spoke dramatically of her fragile health in a bid to make them want to come to her aid. For example, in writing for the first time, and successfully it turned out, to seek the help of the renowned author and actress, Anna Cora Mowatt Ritchie, she presented herself as a "tortured, worn-out frame & badly enfeebled mind . . . sustained only by a stern sense of duty."[39] In numerous letters to others, who were already her friends and supporters, she was forever describing her condition in equally woeful terms; and oddly enough, no one ever accused her of whining. Instead waves of sympathy and admiration flowed her way. Moreover, regardless of whether they had met her in person, the vice regents all adored her, most likely because she had given them soul-satisfying work to do, at a time when she was certainly not the only intelligent American woman craving a legitimate reason to stretch the boundaries of the domestic sphere. With her publicly expressed determination to overcome her weak body, and even risk death, in the interests of patriotic duty, she was for them— and likely for many other women who knew of her work—a compelling inspiration and role model.[40]

Moreover, in 1856, moved almost to tears by her fragile-but-determined patriotic persona, the great Edward Everett of Massachusetts, who eventually would come to refer to her as "my dear little daughter" and "an empress in her own right," volunteered to come to the aid of her cause.[41] In his sixties at the time and retired from a distinguished career as a statesman, classical scholar, and president of Harvard University, he was also a famous orator. In an era when audiences enjoyed sitting through long-winded speeches, people flocked and paid handsomely to hear his two-hour dramatic oration on the "greatness of George Washington." He traveled the country at his own expense, repeating the speech a total of 129 times and donating all of the proceeds, as well as money earned from a weekly column in the *New York Ledger*, to the Mount Vernon cause. In the end, his contribution totaled nearly $70,000, which was more than one-third of what the Ladies would need to purchase Mount Vernon for its owner's asking price of $200,000.[42]

However, despite all of the encouragement and support she received from Everett and others, Ann Pamela encountered right from the beginning one enormous obstacle to her crusade: John Augustine Washington III. Washington, by now the owner of the estate, did not want to accept money from a group of women, even though the Ladies' initial plan was to turn over the funds to the state of Virginia, which would then make the actual purchase. It was a matter of pride, he insisted. As a great-grandnephew of George Washington, he had inherited the property from his father, John Augustine Washington II, and was now living there with his wife, Eleanor, and their soon-to-be seven children. But despite his best efforts, the place was steadily falling apart because he lacked the resources to keep it up, especially at a time when the economy of the entire Chesapeake region, of which Mount Vernon was a part, also was failing.[43]

The mansion's roof was leaking, its timbers were rotting, and the columns supporting the roof of its once grand piazza were slowly being replaced by discarded ships masts. Out on the grounds, trees were fall-ing, mosquitoes were breeding, and weeds were overtaking the gardens. And, as the sightseers coming to the plantation in droves to pay homage to their nation's Father became increasingly critical of the state in which they found it, their criticism—and that of a negative press—stung John Augustine's sensitive pride. By now, he had reached the point where he desperately wanted to sell Mount Vernon but not without a guarantee it would be well taken care of, forever. He had approached both the fed-eral government and the Commonwealth of Virginia, but, preoccupied with other concerns in those years leading up to the Civil War, both had turned him down. Nonetheless, on the grounds that it would only serve to "commemorate the degeneracy" of his sex, he let it be firmly known there was no way he could ever bring himself to accept the "patriotic offerings" of a group of women.[44]

However, Ann Pamela did not give up on him. Persevering as always—even when she was too weak to sit up in bed, could barely lift an arm, or a pepper plaster covered her throbbing head—she wrote him letter, after letter, after letter for nearly four-and-a-half years. And his answer was always, politely, no! She also wrote to Eleanor, begging her to lobby him on her behalf, but to no avail. Finally, on a hot June day in 1856, she left Philadelphia, against doctor's orders, and in the company of her maid Grace and her cousin, Becky Mitchell, travelled all the way to Mount Vernon via canal boat, railroad, and river steamer to try to convince him in person. After the steamboat had landed at his crumbling wharf, she, in a near state of collapse, had been carried in a chair up the steep hill from the river to the mansion. Although she was cordially received by John Augustine and his wife, nothing she could say would change the man's mind. But, fortunately that afternoon her little party accidentally missed their return boat to Alexandria and had to spend the night at Mount Vernon, which gave Ann Pamela that entire evening and all of the next morning to make her case. Although she did not convince John Augustine before leaving with friendly feelings all around the next day, she gained new insight into the reasons behind his reluctance to sell Mount Vernon according to the plan she had laid out. While gazing deeply into his eyes, she came to understand how much he had been hurt by the way the press and the state of Virginia had been treating him, and she saw that he had assumed she felt the same way they did about his failure to keep Mount Vernon in repair. Once she had reassured him that she did not in the least share their opinion, he began to trust and understand her motives. Many years later she would write of that moment: "I held out my hand, he put his in mine. Then with quivering lips, moist eyes, and a heart too full for him to speak, our compact was closed in silence."[45]

After that turning point in their relationship, she eventually wore him down and convinced him to sell directly to the Ladies. By then they had become good friends. On a glorious and solemn occasion taking place in Richmond, Virginia, on April 6, 1858, they signed a final contract turning over Mount Vernon to the Mount Vernon Ladies Association of the Union. And in the course of those proceedings, Ann Pamela once again used her invalidism to dramatic effect. In later describing the circumstances surrounding the event, she reported that she had been extremely ill during the train ride to Richmond from Charleston, South Carolina (where she had been spending the Christmas holidays with her family), necessitating her traveling companions to hold her up to an open window for much of the way so that she could breathe. After her arrival in Richmond, there had been a doctor at her bedside almost continuously for a period of several months, fearing that at any moment she might die. When the day finally came for the contract to be signed, she had been so weak, having passed through a series of convulsions immediately beforehand, that her "lifeless fingers" barely could hold the pen. But she had persevered, and "all was got through." It was vintage Ann Pamela Cunningham.[46]

In 1860, John Augustine and his family moved out of the mansion, and Ann Pamela and her Ladies took full charge of the estate. Their purchase included the mansion, George and Martha Washington's tomb, most of the original outbuildings, and a two-hundred-acre parcel of land. The entirety of George Washington's original plantation of eight thousand acres had been divided among various heirs during the years following his death.[47] Only the most urgently needed repairs and improvements had been made to the property when the Civil War broke out in 1861.

Once the war was finally over and she could travel, Ann Pamela returned to Mount Vernon from Rosemont, where she had been stranded with her mother, and seized the reins from her secretary, Sarah Tracey, who had lived there throughout the war along with the estate's resident superintendent, Upton Herbert, a young lady "chaperone" by the name of Mary McMakin, and a small crew of free Black workers.[48] Ann Pamela's tenure as Mount Vernon's founding regent ended in 1873, when owing to her declining health and increasing dependence on laudanum to ease her many aches and pains, she resigned her position and returned to South Carolina. In a photograph taken near the end of her reign, she is seated front and right of center among her fellow board members, gazing upon the bust by Jean-Antoine Houdon of the man she had admired above all others practically all her life.

Less than two years after her retirement, on May1, 1875, she died at the age of fifty-eight, satisfied that she had managed to save the precious home and grave of George Washington as a gift to the nation. What she could not fully realize at that time, however, was that in saving Mount Vernon she had broken new ground. By creating a viable model for others to follow, she had launched the historic preservation movement in the United States. Moreover, her Mount Vernon Ladies Association of

Ann Pamela Cunningham seated in a ladderback chair, third from right among her fellow board members, gazing upon Mount Vernon's much prized Houdon bust of George Washington. Photograph likely taken by Alexander Gardner, 1870–1873. (Courtesy of the Mount Vernon Ladies' Association)

the Union had proven to a skeptical world that women were capable of achieving success at the very highest levels outside the home.[49]

Her favorite nephew, Clarence Cunningham, was with her when she died, and after seeing to her burial in the graveyard of the First Presbyterian Church in Columbia, South Carolina, he had a monument erected there in her memory. On the face of the granite is carved the following quote from her final words to Clarence: *"It is good for me that I have been afflicted."*[50] For her entire adult life, her very identity had been tied up in her invalidism. Although one may credibly suspect that she had suffered to a significant degree from hypochondria, it is clear from hundreds of extant letters describing her condition that she more often than not had been genuinely ill. What mattered in the end, however, was that she had managed to turn her condition on its head and use it to garner sympathy and support for the one thing that had given her life meaning and purpose. Without her beloved George Washington and his Mount Vernon, she probably would have died long before she did. And who knows what fate might then have befallen Mount Vernon?

Notes

I am grateful to the following institutions for making this essay possible: the Fred W. Smith National Library for the Study of George Washington at Mount Vernon; the South Caroliniana Library at the University of South Carolina in Columbia; the Wilson Library at the University of North Carolina in Chapel Hill, and the Rosemont Preservation Society in Laurens, South Carolina. I also wish to thank the Historic Waco Foundation of Waco, Texas, for waiving the publication fee on the Cunningham family portrait appearing in this essay.

1. Christy Snipes, *Rosemont Plantation, Laurens County, South Carolina: A History of the Cunningham Family and Its Life on the Land*, 2nd ed. (Laurens, SC: Rosemont Preservation Society, 2010), 27–33; Michael Trinkley, Natalie Adams, and Debi Hatcher, "Plantation Life in the Piedmont: A Preliminary Examination of Rosemont Plantation, Laurens, South Carolina," Research Series 29 (Columbia: Chicora Foundation, 1992), 16.

2. Unknown Artist, *The Cunningham Family*, c. 1822, oil on canvas (Waco, TX: Historic Waco Foundation).

3. Benjamin Franklin Perry, "Mrs. Louisa Cunningham," in *Reminiscences of Public Men with Speeches and Addresses*, 2nd series (Greenville, SC: Shannon & Co., 1889, Biblio-Bazaar reprint), 53–57.

4. On the influential role of plantation mothers in their daughters' early development, see Elizabeth Fox-Genovese, *Within the Plantation Household: Black and White Women of the Old South* (Chapel Hill: University of North Carolina Press, 1988), 110–11; Thavolia Glymph, *Out of the House of Bondage: The Transformation of the Plantation* (New York: Cambridge University Press, 2012), 32–62; Stephanie E. Jones-Rogers, *They Were Her Property: White Women as Slave Owners in the American South* (New Haven: Yale University Press, 2019), 1–24; Ann Firor Scott, *The Southern Lady: From Pedestal to Politics: 1830–1930* (Charlottesville: University Press of Virginia, 1970), 4–7.

5. Ann Pamela Cunningham to Benjamin Franklin Perry, 25 March 1843, Benjamin Franklin Perry Papers, South Caroliniana Library, University of South Carolina (hereafter SCL); Ann Pamela Cunningham to Hugh Lenox Hodge, 13 November 1865, Early Records, Mount Vernon Ladies Association, Fred W. Smith Library for the Study of George Washington (hereafter MVLA).

6. Perry, *Reminiscences of Public Men*, 55.

7. The first two schools Ann Pamela attended were the Academy at Powellton and the Sparta Female Academy, both located near her maternal grandmother's house on the Shoals of the Ogeechee River in central Georgia. At both institutions she was taught by Julia Pierpont Warne, who would later marry Elias Marks and become Julia Pierpont Marks.

8. Elias Marks, "Hints on Female Education with an Outline of an Institution for the Education of Females, Termed the South Carolina Female Collegiate Institute" (Columbia: David W. Sims, State Printer at the Telescope Office, 1826), 21–22.

9. Christie Ann Farnham, *The Education of the Southern Belle: Higher Education and Student Socialization in the Antebellum South* (New York: New York University Press, 1994), 3, 13, 111, 126, 171; Henning Cohen, ed., *A Barhamville Miscellany: Notes and Documents Concerning the South Carolina Female Collegiate Institute 1826–1865: Chiefly the Collection of the Late Henry Campbell Davis* (Columbia: The University of South Carolina Press, 1956); Mary Kelley, *Learning to Stand and Speak: Women, Education, and Public Life in America's Republic* (Chapel Hill: University of North Carolina Press, 2006), 91–102; Sally G. McMillen, *Southern Women Black and White in the Old South*, 2nd ed. (Wheeling, IL: Harlan Davidson, Inc. 2002), 96.

10. Isabelle Margaret Blandin, *History of Higher Education in the South Prior to 1860* (New York: Neale Publishing Company, 1909), 130; Farnham, *Education of the Southern Belle*, 62; Mrs. J. D. Gaillard, "Barhamville Pen Pictures

Number Two," 1–16, South Carolina Female Institute Collection, SCL; Kelley, *Learning to Stand and Speak*, 73, 87–90; Scott, *Southern Lady*, 62–75; Ann Firor Scott, "The Ever Widening Circle: The Diffusion of Feminist Values from the Troy Female Seminary, 1822–1872," in *History of Education Quarterly* 19, no.1 (spring 1979): 3–25.

11. A. P. Cunningham to Margaret Ann Comegys, 25/26 January 1861, Early Records, MVLA; A. P. Cunningham to B. F. Perry, 14 December 1846, Perry Papers, SCL.

12. Anya Jabour, *Scarlett's Sisters: Young Women in the Old South* (Chapel Hill: University of North Carolina Press, 2007), 81.

13. Benjamin Perry Diary, 21 December 1832, Volume 1, Series 2, Southern History Collection, Wilson Library, University of North Carolina (hereafter SHC).

14. Perry Diary, 6 January 1835, SHC; Candace Bailey, *Music and the Southern Belle: From Accomplished Lady to Confederate Composer* (Carbondale, IL: Southern Illinois University Press, 2010), 15; Lilian Adele Kibler, *Benjamin Perry: South Carolina Unionist* (Durham: Duke University Press, 1946), 177, 470.

15. On the reluctance of educated young antebellum women to marry, see Farnham, *Education of the Southern Belle*, 3–4; Jabour, *Scarlett's Sisters*, 85–86, 89–97, 136–38; Craig Thompson Friend and Anya Jabour, eds., *Family Values in the Old South* (Gainesville: University Press of Florida, 2010), 91–94.

16. A. P. Cunningham to B. F. Perry, 25 March 1843, Perry Papers, SCL.

17. A. P. Cunningham to B. F. Perry, n.d., 1846, Perry Papers, SCL; A. P. Cunningham, diary entries referenced by Snipes, *Rosemont Plantation,* 52–53. On loneliness, boredom, thwarted ambition, and depression among young graduates of southern female academies, see Jabour, *Scarlett's Sisters,* 99–111.

18. Catherine Clinton, *The Plantation Mistress: Women's World in the Old South* (New York: Pantheon Books, 1982), 21; Carroll Smith-Rosenberg, "The Hysterical Woman: Sex Roles and Conflict in Nineteenth-Century America," in *Disorderly Conduct: Visions of Gender in Victorian America* (New York: Oxford University Press, 1986), 200–209; Hugh Lenox Hodge, *Diseases Peculiar to Women, Including Displacements of the Uterus* (Lexington: ULAN Press, reprint; Blanchard and Lea, Philadelphia, 1860), 93–101; Barbara Welter, *Dimity Convictions: The American Woman in the Nineteenth Century* (Athens: Ohio University Press, 1976), 66.

19. Welter, *Dimity Convictions,* 10–12.

20. Clinton, *Plantation Mistress,* 143; Lorna Duffin, "The Conspicuous Consumptive: Woman as an Invalid," in *The Nineteenth-Century Woman: Her Cultural and Physical World,* ed. Sara Delamont and Lorna Duffin (New York: Barnes & Noble Books, 1978), 26–56; Hodge, *Diseases Peculiar to Women,* 21–22; David B. Morris, "Hysteria, Pain, and Gender," in *The Culture of Pain* (Berkeley: University of California Press, 1991), 197–216; Smith-Rosenberg, *Disorderly Conduct,* 203–5; Welter, *Dimity Convictions,* 66, 71–72.

21. Larry E. Davis, "Unregulated Potions Still Cause Mercury Poisoning," *Western Journal of Medicine* (July 2000). Time and again in correspondence throughout her life, Ann Pamela mentioned dosing herself on calomel. And Benjamin Perry in a letter to his wife Elizabeth on 10 October 1843 expressed the hope that "Miss Pamela" had forgotten there was "any such thing as a nervous disease . . . or such medicine as calomel" (Benjamin Franklin Perry to Elizabeth Perry, 10 October 1843, in *Letters of Benjamin Franklin Perry to His Wife* [Nabu Public Domain Reprint], 22).

22. Clinton, *Plantation Mistress,* 145; Hodge, *Diseases Peculiar to Women,* 184; Barbara Hodgson, *In the Arms of Morpheus: The Tragic History of Laudanum, Morphine, and Patent Medicines* (Buffalo, NY: Firefly Books, 2001), 2, 62–67, 102–11.

23. Clinton, *Plantation Mistress,* 100; Duffin, "Conspicuous Consumptive," 30, 39; Jabour, *Scarlett's Sisters,* 34; Susan Pryor, "On Taking Great Pains with Fashion," Colonial Williamsburg Foundation Research Report, Series-324 (Williamsburg, VA: Colonial Williamsburg Digital Library, 1990).

24. A. P. Cunningham to Elizabeth Perry, 11 January 1845, Perry Papers, SCL; A. P. Cunningham to B. F. Perry, 21 September 1846, Perry Papers, SCL; Jeffrey R. Basford, "A Historical Perspective on the Popular Use of Electric and Magnetic Therapy," *Archives of Physical Medicine and Rehabilitation* 82, no. 9 (2001): 1261–69; Robin Waterfield, *Hidden Depths: The Story of Hypnosis* (London: Pan Macmillan, 2004), xxxiii, 132–33, 168.

25. Snipes, *Rosemont Plantation,* 87–88; A. P. Cunningham to Sarah Yancey, October 1850, Benjamin Cudsworth Yancey Papers, SHC.

26. Louisa Cunningham to Sarah Yancey, n.d. 1849, quoted in Snipes, *Rosemont Plantation,* 87.

27. A. P. Cunningham to Sarah Yancey, October 1850, Benjamin Cudsworth Yancey Papers, SHC; Hodge, *Diseases Peculiar to Women,* 179.

28. Catherine Clinton and Christine Lunardini, *Columbia Guide to American Women in the Nineteenth Century* (New York: Columbia University Press, 2005), 99.

29. Hodge, *Diseases Peculiar to Women*, 19–22, 200–206; "Hugh L. (Hugh Lenox) Hodge (1796–1893)," Penn University Archives and Records Center; R. A. F. Penrose, M.D., *A Discourse Commemorative of the Life and Character of Hugh Lenox Hodge, M.D., LL.D., Late Emeritus Professor of Obstetrics and Diseases of Women and Children, Delivered October 6th 1873 before the Trustees, Professors, and Students of the University of Pennsylvania* (Philadelphia: Collins Printer, 1873), 5–30.

30. Edward Alexander, *Museum Masters: Their Museums and Their Influence* (Nashville: American Association of State and Local History, 1983), 179.

31. Grace King, *Mount Vernon on the Potomac* (New York: Macmillan, 1929), 22–23.

32. King, *Mount Vernon on the Potomac*, 13–14; Mary V. Thompson, "The Early Years of the Mount Vernon Ladies' Association: 'A Mite from Their Hard Earnings Cheerfully Given,'" in *Mount Vernon Ladies' Association: 150 Years of Restoring George Washington's Home*, ed. Stephen A. McLeod (Mount Vernon, VA: Mount Vernon Ladies' Association, 2010), 118–24.

33. Lydia Brandt, *First in the Homes of His Countrymen: George Washington's Mount Vernon in the American Imagination* (Charlottesville: University of Virginia Press, 2016), 25, 41; Jean B. Lee, ed., *Experiencing Mount Vernon: Eyewitness Accounts, 1784–1865* (Charlottesville: University of Virginia Press, 2006), 207; King, *Mount Vernon on the Potomac*, 10–12; Patricia West, *Domesticating History: The Political Origins of America's House Museums* (Washington, DC: The Smithsonian Institution Press, 1999), 3.

34. Brandt, *First in the Homes*, 43–45; Christine Carter, *Southern Single Blessedness: Unmarried Women in the Urban South, 1800–1865* (Urbana: University of Illinois Press, 2006), 118–22, 141; Lori D. Ginzberg, *Women and the Work of Benevolence: Morality, Politics, and Class in the Nineteenth-Century United States* (New Haven: Yale University Press, 1990), 5, 11–35; Elizabeth R. Varon, *We Mean to Be Counted: White Women and Politics in Antebellum Virginia* (Chapel Hill: University of North Carolina Press, 1998), 10–40.

35. Alexander, *Museum Masters*, 180; King, *Mount Vernon on the Potomac*, 19–21; Lee, *Experiencing Mount Vernon*, 197–98; Virginia Watson Campbell, "Reminiscences of Miss Cunningham," n.d., Early Records, MVLA.

36. Brandt, *First in the Homes*, 44–47; King, *Mount Vernon on the Potomac*, 50–54, 83–85.

37. King, *Mount Vernon on the Potomac*, 52–53; West, *Domesticating History*, 12–15; Thompson, "The Early Years," 119–20.

38. Alexander, *Museum Masters,* 180–82; Brandt, *First in the Homes,* 44–50; King, *Mount Vernon on the Potomac,* 19–22; Varon, *We Mean to Be Counted,* 124–25; West, *Domesticating History,* 7–10.

39. A. P. Cunningham to A. C. Ritchie, 4 January 1855, Early Records, MVLA.

40. See letters from Ritchie, Walton, Dickenson, Fogg, Comegys, Mitchell, Hamilton, Goodrich et al, 1856–1860, Early Records, MVLA.

41. Edward Everett to A. P. Cunningham, 14 March and 25 June 1859, Early Records, MVLA; Edward Everett to A. C. Ritchie, 7 January 1858, Early Records, MVLA.

42. Linda Ayres, "Their Unfailing Friend: Edward Everett and the Mount Vernon Ladies Association" (Power Point presentation, George Washington Symposium, Mount Vernon Ladies' Association, Mount Vernon, VA, November 8, 2003); Castle Freeman Jr., "Vita: Edward Everett, Brief Life of a Statesman Orator: 1794–1865" in *Harvard Magazine* (November–December 2013): 1–3; King, *Mount Vernon on the Potomac,* 36–41; Ronald F. Reid, *Edward Everett: Unionist Orator* (New York: Greenwood Press, 1990), 1–8, 147–74.

43. Thompson, "The Early Years," 119; Dennis Pogue, email message to author, 11 November 2019.

44. Alexander, *Museum Masters,* 181; Brandt, *First in the Homes,* 41; Scott E. Casper, *Sarah Johnson's Mount Vernon: The Forgotten History of an American Shrine* (New York: Hill and Wang, 2008), 44–46, 67–70; King, *Mount Vernon on the Potomac,* 8–12; Mount Vernon Ladies' Association, "The Last Private Owner," *Yesterday, Today, and Tomorrow* (fall 2011): 12–13; Varon, *We Mean To Be Counted,* 126; West, *Domesticating History,* 8–9, 13–14.

45. A. P. Cunningham, "A Letter from the Founder and First Regent of the Mount Vernon Association by Miss A. P. Cunningham of S. Carolina," 26 May 1866, Early Records, MVLA.

46. Cunningham, "A Letter from the Founder and First Regent," Early Records, MVLA.

47. Alexander, *Museum Masters,* 183–88; West, *Domesticating History,* 25.

48. For an account of how Mount Vernon survived the Civil War, see Dorothy Troth Muir, *Mount Vernon: The Civil War Years* (Mount Vernon, VA: Mount Vernon Ladies' Association, 1993).

49. Alexander, *Museum Masters,* 194–200; West, *Domesticating History,* 36–37.

50. King, *Mount Vernon on the* Potomac, 198; Snipes, *Rosemont Plantation,* 161.

CONTRIBUTORS

JAMES G. BASKER is the Richard Gilder Professor in Literary History at Barnard College, Columbia University. He is also the president of the Gilder Lehrman Institute of American History, founder of the Oxbridge Academic Programs, a fellow of the Society of American Historians, and a member of the American Antiquarian Society. Basker's scholarly work focuses on eighteenth-century literature, specifically the life and writings of Samuel Johnson and the history of slavery and abolition. Among his books are *Amazing Grace: An Anthology of Poems about Slavery, Early American Abolitionists,* and *American Antislavery Writings: Colonial Beginnings to Emancipation.*

GEORGE W. BOUDREAU is Senior Research Associate at the McNeil Center for Early American Studies at the University of Pennsylvania. He is a cultural historian of eighteenth-century Anglo-America, specializing in the history of Philadelphia, the work of Benjamin Franklin, and public history. Boudreau was the founding editor of the journal *Early American Studies.* He has published extensively, and his book *Independence: A Guide to Historic Philadelphia* explores the sites related to the nation's founding and the diverse people who lived within them.

CHARLENE M. BOYER LEWIS is Professor of History and Director of American Studies at Kalamazoo College. She specializes in women's history and American cultural and social history in the eighteenth and nineteenth centuries. She is the author of *Ladies and Gentlemen on Display: Planter Society at the Virginia Springs, 1790–1860* and, most recently, *Elizabeth Patterson Bonaparte: An American Aristocrat in the Early Republic.* Her next project is an examination of Margaret Shippen Arnold, the wife of Benedict Arnold, and American culture in the revolutionary era.

SARA GEORGINI is series editor for *The Papers of John Adams* at the Adams Papers editorial project at the Massachusetts Historical Society. She is the author of *Household Gods: The Religious Lives of the Adams Family,* and she frequently writes about early American history, thought, and culture for *Smithsonian.*

ANN BAY GODDIN has worked at the Smithsonian Institution as both a writer and administrator, including as Executive Director of what was then the Institution's Center for Education and Museum Studies, and she has served as Mount Vernon's first Vice-President for Education, a position she held until her retirement at the end of 2010. She is currently writing a biography of Ann Pamela Cunningham.

KATE HAULMAN is Associate Professor of History at American University and the author of *The Politics of Fashion in Eighteenth Century America,* and coeditor of *Making Women's Histories: Beyond National Perspectives.* She co-curated the exhibit *All Work, No Pay: A History of Women's Invisible Labor* at the Smithsonian's National Museum of American History, and is working on a book about gender, race, and commemoration through the lens of Mary Ball Washington.

CYNTHIA A. KIERNER is Professor of History at George Mason University and author of many books, including *Scandal at Bizarre: Rumor and Reputation in Jefferson's America* and *Martha Jefferson Randolph, Daughter of Monticello: Her Life and Times.* Her current projects include two biographies: one of an outspoken Whig woman in revolutionary North Carolina and the other of Joan Whitney Payson, philanthropist and founding owner of the New York Mets.

LYNN PRICE ROBBINS regularly serves as a scholar for the George Washington Teacher Institute at Mount Vernon, lecturing on Martha Washington, women in the late-eighteenth century, and politics. She has also worked with George Washington's Mount Vernon on Washington's financial ledgers, agricultural reports, and the Bibliography Project. Robbins coedited two documentary volumes, *George Washington's Barbados Diary, 1751–52* and *The Papers of Martha Washington,* while serving as Associate Editor of the Washington Family Papers at the University of Virginia.

SAMANTHA SNYDER is the Reference Librarian at George Washington's Mount Vernon. She holds a master's degree in history from George Mason University. Her specializations include women's history and genteel societies of the early republic. She also has a master's in Library and Information Studies from University of Wisconsin-Madison. She is the coauthor of *Warriors Saints and Scoundrels: Brief Portraits of Real People Who Shaped Wisconsin.* Her current project is a biography of Elizabeth Willing Powel, an influential Philadelphian who was invaluable in the founding of the republic.

MARY V. THOMPSON currently serves as the Research Historian at George Washington's Mount Vernon. Before joining the Mount Vernon staff in 1980, she worked as a volunteer at two United States Army museums and as a field researcher on a grant project, sponsored by the National Endowment for the Humanities, to identify practitioners of traditional folk crafts in central Alabama. She is the author of: *"In the Hands of a Good Providence": Religion in the Life of George Washington; A Short Biography of Martha Washington;* and *"The Only Unavoidable Subject of Regret": George Washington, Slavery, and the Enslaved Community at Mount Vernon.*

INDEX

Page numbers in italics refer to illustrations.